I0629886

HAL'S WORLDS

HAL'S WORLDS

EDITED BY SHANE TOURTELLOTTE

WILDSIDE PRESS

HAL'S WORLDS

Copyright © 2005 by **Shane Tourtellotte**

Cover painting by **Hal Clement.**

Cover design © 2005 by **Garry Nurrish.**

Wildside Press

www.wildsidepress.com

CONTENTS

PART III: HAL'S WORDS

INTRODUCTION: MISSION OF CHARITY

This book exists to fill a hole that cannot really be filled, that left by the death of Hal Clement. Indeed, the impulse to try to fill this void with such a commemoration, the faith that people will collect and appreciate it, itself indicates the depth of the loss, the irreplaceability of the man. It is a deep irony.

This is a tribute to Hal Clement, the writer, and to Harry Clement Stubbs, the man behind the pseudonym. (You will see both names used herein.) It comprises remembrances by friends and colleagues who knew him well, science fiction stories (reprinted and original) by writers whom he inspired, and some of Hal's own words. It seeks to present an affectionate portrait of the man, from the perspective of the science fiction community to which he belonged.

It is not a biography, nor will it present a biography of him as such. Many readers know the framework of salient facts already, and those less familiar with Hal will soon have something better than the dry recitation of dates, names, and places by which to know him. I will present only the barest outline here, simply as a common starting point:

Harry Clement Stubbs was born in Somerville, Massachusetts, on May 30, 1922, and died in his sleep at his home in Milton, Massachusetts on October 29, 2003. In those eighty-one years, he worked for forty as a high school science teacher, a calling he considered his true career. He served two stints in the armed forces, his first as a B-24 pilot in the European theater of World War II.

Before and after these vocations and services, he wrote around forty short stories and just over a dozen novels under the pen name Hal

Clement, including some of the classics of the science fiction genre, in the specific style known as "hard SF". (To anyone who doesn't understand the term, read on and you will.) He was an enthusiastic fan of science fiction, an inveterate convention attendee who often gave lectures on far-ranging speculative science. This love even stretched him into becoming an artist, painting space scenes under a second pseudonym, George Richard. His "Roche Limit" graces the cover of this volume. (If you do not understand that term, either, look it up, then look at the cover again. Harry is teaching you something. That's a pattern in his life.)

One can argue whether more people got to know him through his connections to science fiction or as a classroom teacher. "Hal's Worlds" looks at him from the first angle, but the other remains visible from there. They are closely linked parts of the same whole, as our remembrances will show, or remind, you.

As much as celebrating Hal Clement's life justifies this book, it also serves other ends. Nobody appearing in this book is receiving royalties, including myself, the editor. The generosity of everyone involved in giving their time and work has been heartening and inspiring. Mary Stubbs, Harry's widow, has chosen two charitable causes, close to Harry's heart, for all royalties to support in equal amounts.

The recipients are Milton Academy, the school where Harry taught science for thirty-eight years, and Joslin Diabetes Center, important to Harry because he had the disease. By buying "Hal's Worlds," you have already added to the money they will receive. For anyone so moved, we will make it a little easier to give more in his memory.

Milton Academy's website address is **http://www.milton.edu.** The site has a secure online form for donations. There is a button to direct a donation somewhere other than general funds, e.g., to the Science Department, and a comments section where one can mention Harry/Hal. For more old-fashioned giving, checks made out to "Milton Academy" should go to:

Milton Academy
Attn: Development Office
170 Centre Street
Milton, MA 02186

Joslin Diabetes Center's website address is **http://www.joslin.org.** Joslin also has a secure online donation form, as well as specific ways to donate in someone's memory. Their mailing address is:

Joslin Diabetes Center
One Joslin Place
Boston, MA 02215

As editor, I gratefully acknowledge the help I have had in putting together this volume. My thanks go first to Tom Easton, who brought me this opportunity, and who backed me up at every turn. Warren Lapine's support helped give this project a running start, even though he could not publish it as he hoped. Thanks to Michael A. Burstein and to Steven H. Silver, who found me some of Hal's words.

My thanks go to everyone who provided stories and recollections, reprints and originals. This includes everyone who wanted to contribute, but who does not appear in this book through lack of time to write to the standards they desired or lack of space to accommodate what they could provide: Catherine Asaro, Harlan Ellison, John M. Ford, David Hartwell, Barry B. Longyear, and George Scithers. I encountered nothing but good will from everyone I approached for this project, and gladly return the sentiment.

My kind thanks to Mary Stubbs for making her husband's work available to us, and to the group collectively known as Hal's Pals—but you'll find out about them soon enough. Thanks to Wildside Press, who stepped forward at a critical junction and on short notice. And to anyone I've forgotten, I may be neglectful, but I am still grateful.

Shane Tourtellotte
Westfield, New Jersey
May 31th, 2005

PART ONE

HAL'S PALS

Many people could say they were Hal's friends, but only a much smaller number lay claim to being Hal's Pals. That is the name of the writer's group that Hal Clement headed, starting in the early 1980s. They met at his Milton home once a month, reading and critiquing each other's work as so many other groups do. It isn't every such group, though, that has so illustrious a writer at its head.

The name evolved at Readercon in 1999, when the convention's guest of honor, Harlan Ellison, met several of the members. He briefly took to calling them Harry's Harem, but decorum and consideration for Mary Stubbs soon put this aside. He settled on Hal's Gals, but though the members he was meeting were all female, the rest were not. Natural selection took over in the form of a 'G' mutating to 'P', and that name stuck.

Hal's Pals are the reason this book exists. One of their number, Anne Warner, conceived the idea soon after Hal's death, and the group took it upon themselves to bring it into being. It might have come to pass otherwise, as the idea of paying tribute to Hal Clement was by no means unique to them, but without their swiftness and determination, it would not have found as many people with the eagerness to pay tribute to Hal, or caught their memories so fresh.

It would also probably not have had as much of a place for their own recollections, and that would have been a loss. They had a rare connection to the writer and the man, and both those aspects left an impression, whether they were part of Hal's Pals for a few years or for more than two decades. Not all of them wrote for this memorial, but those who did show how proud they were to know Hal.

Some of Hal's Pals are published writers; some are not. All have gained from knowing him. We begin with the man who helped to create Hal's Pals.

HAL CLEMENT:
HARD SCIENCE—GREAT STORIES

LESLIE A. GREENLEAF, JR.

I first met Harry at a Star Trek Convention held by the Boston Star Trek Association. It was for me an honor to meet the author of some of my favorite stories, and it was a privilege to listen to him speak on a panel.

At that time, over 20 years ago, I was an aspiring writer, struggling with words, characters and ideas. There came a time when I realized I needed help and considerable guidance to help me write good stories. I wanted a group of fellow writers, who would gather together and share their ideas and offer constructive criticism. It came to me that having a published author at the first meeting to speak about writing would be a great way to get started. One name came especially to mind: Hal Clement.

Through my membership with the Boston Star Trek Association I had met and spoken with Harry a few times. But I was still hesitant to approach the Great Hal Clement, winner of so many awards. However, I got his phone number and called. When he answered I explained who I was and that I wanted to start a writer's group. When I asked him if he would speak to the group, he said he would.

Harry attended that first meeting and stayed an active member of our little Writer's Workshop. He also knew of others who would like to join and asked if he could invite them to attend. It was then that I met Sherry and Ramona. I may have been the founder of this group of writers, but Harry was the foundation upon which we built over the years.

During the coming years we wrote and shared our stories. We discussed the problems we were having and got pointed remarks on our shortfalls. Pointed they may have been, but all remarks were guiding us to improve our writing. I believe that for all of us during those early years the best part of a meeting was listening to Harry read to us the latest chapter of a story he was in the process of writing, a story that would be the next Hal Clement novel.

The first story by Hal Clement I read was "Dust Rag," in a collection of short stories. It stuck in my mind how such a simple thing as static electricity could be a major problem. Without that bit of hard science there would be no problem and thus no story.

During my development of one story idea I wanted to have a hard science problem which had to be solved by the crew of a space ship. I had the idea, but would the science hold up? There was only one person to ask, Harry. At one meeting of our workshop I posed the problem to him. In only moments Harry proceeded to give me a complex answer in chemistry which gave me the results I needed for my story.

I have yet to be published, but my writing has improved to the point where I feel ready to make the leap. I do know that without the help of the members of the workshop I would not be ready. Most of all I am thankful for Harry's steadfast guidance to new and aspiring writers. Thank you, Harry.

UNCLE HARRY

SHERRY BRIGGS

"The Heavens themselves blaze forth the death of princes."
—Shakespeare, Julius Caesar, Act II, Scene ii

Students are known to have special names for teachers. Although generally accurate, these names are often witty, barbed, and merciless. When Harry Stubbs heard the name his students at Milton Academy had for him, he had to smile. The name was "Uncle Harry."

The night after he died, the skies over New England lit up with a rare and colorful display of the Aurora Borealis, which seemed a right and fitting tribute to the man, his work, and his influence. If one thing could be said to characterize the man I knew as Hal Clement, that thing would be generosity. He was a writer who truly loved his fans and took the greatest joy from simply being there for them. Above all, he was a teacher. When he retired from Milton Academy, he went on to expand his less formal, but no less valuable, teaching in venues such as science fiction conventions. He sat on panels and gave slide shows and hands-on presentations to groups ranging from small children to adults. He also was always on the lookout for what the education folks like to call 'teachable' moments, and he found plenty of those. The most important influence he had in my life was our writer's group, which came to call itself "Hal's Pals," following a suggestion by Harlan Ellison. For more than twenty years Harry welcomed us into his home, where we met on a monthly basis.

Harry Stubbs was an illuminating presence in my life for those years, and in all that time I knew him to exhibit impatience fewer than a handful of times, all well deserved. Once was when, in attempting to use the word 'fusillade,' I spelled it, and pronounced it, 'fullisade,' as well as misusing it. "Sherry," Hal said, his eyebrows gathering and a warning note in his voice. "That's not how you say it!" There followed the correct pronunciation and spelling as well as a most helpful lecture on what the word actually meant, along with some colorful background from his own experience from World War II. His fiercest rebuke was "You should know better!" This was always followed by sound guidance, so the person who should know better would, next time. Another time that I found myself the object of Hal's impatience was when I was blatting on about my doubts that I could write. When I am tempted to do that now, his voice in my ear tells me in no uncertain terms to quit it!

FAT POWER

SHERRY BRIGGS

The monthly meetings of the group now known as "Hal's Pals" have been a vital part of my life since 1981, when Hal Clement responded to a letter I had written to him with an invitation to come join a writer's group that was just forming. It was then that I met Hal himself, along with Les Green-leaf, whose brainchild the group was, and Mona Wheeler, who was working on a story involving Ray and Rokey, whom I have come to know very well over the years.

Perhaps my most treasured memory of this story is the sound of Hal Clement's voice as he read the various versions of this story that I brought with me to our writers group. Hal was present at every stage of "Fat Power"'s creation, from the first draft to the triumphant day when I came into the writers group meeting waving the copy of *Analog* in which it had been published. It was an especially wonderful moment for the group because this story was the first one sold by a member of the group other than Hal. Nobody rejoiced more than he at my achievement. The fact that he was a writer of "hard science fiction" did not detract one whit from his enjoyment of this story, which takes considerable liberties with the universe we have come to know, love, and occasionally cuss at. Hal's influ-ence can be clearly seen in the benignity of the aliens in the story!

#

Ron Corcoran had been good about his diet. Sitting glumly at the Workshop for Fitness meeting, he reflected on the broad sweep of Terran history, and how events had conspired to make his own life uniquely unbearable. Life since the mid-twentieth century had never been all that easy for those who tend to roundness of figure, but it had never been worse than now. Ron huddled, brooding, within his own personal singularity of misery.

The late twentieth century had seen a progressive obsession with the ideal of a tall, willowy figure. Things had been bad enough then, Ron thought. Then the Galactics came.

The actual arrival of the aliens could hardly have been more soul satisfying. One fine day every television set, radio, Telex terminal, personal computer, telephone, automatic teller and video game machine ceased its normal order of business.

In Omaha, Nebraska, a small boy had been engaged in the ticklish procedure of persuading the school computer to change his gym grade to a bare pass. Suddenly, he yelped and rushed downstairs to his parents, shrieking "Totally Awesome!" at the top of his lungs.

In Burbank, California, a harried mom stared at the cash machine. She desperately clutched the hand of a restless two-year-old who was giving every indication of being about to explore his overripe diaper with grubby, ever curious fingers. Tight-lipped, she thought bitter thoughts about the apparently anonymous, thoughtless prankster whose trick gave every promise of causing a half-baked headache to blossom forth into a truly magnificent migraine.

As harbingers of impending — go, the small slip of paper, printed in slightly uneven dot matrix characters, was not of itself particularly impressive. The fact that it had emerged from Ron's hand-held calculator, which ran on batteries and was designed to produce nothing but numbers, was.

The message it bore was clear, and ran as follows:

TO THE PEOPLE OF EARTH:
WELCOME TO THE GALACTIC FEDERATION. WE ARE PLEASED THAT YOU HAVE CHOSEN TO JOIN US. REPRESENTATIVES OF THE GALACTIC FEDERATION CIVILIZATIONS WILL APPEAR

THROUGHOUT YOUR PLANET DURING THE NEXT WEEK. THEY WILL BRING YOU FURTHER INFORMATION TO ENABLE YOU TO JOIN SMOOTHLY WITH GALACTIC SOCIETY. THANK YOU. WE LOOK FORWARD TO A NEW ERA OF DEVELOPING HARMONY.

Initial panic among the journalists and intellectuals of the newly admitted planet faded into amazed relief as the Galactics' terms were made clear. No science fiction nightmares occurred, and local customs were left undisturbed. The disapproval of various cultures continued unabated, and in fact seemed to increase, as newspaper budgets grew.

Almost unnoticed amid the apparent divisiveness was the fact that actual violence diminished drastically. Although wars continued, they consisted mostly of large scale troop movements and propaganda. Former combat hospitals became important in the war against local disease, and a new sense of hope arose in the local populations, who benefited greatly by the new Galactic medical technology.

The aliens themselves had a vast number of shapes, sizes, environmental requirements, sexes, eating habits, family structures, ranking systems, mental organizations, and communication modes. Sound-wave utilizing, highly visual (within one octave), bilaterally symmetrical, two-sexed Terrans had a huge first lesson in form acceptance dumped on them all at once. Prejudice flared briefly, and then died, overwhelmed by an array of new sensory impressions never before equalled. People who hated bugs learned to endure the /klik. These louse-sized entities swarmed over whatever they were investigating, often making it look like a mound of crawling iridescent black. Snake-haters met the smooth, lithe Srendekians, and spider smashers learned to work with the many arachnids in the Federation. Green slime, tumbleweeds, ball lightning, metallic spheres who snapped like a string of firecrackers when they talked, and hundreds more appeared. Terrans were startled and horrified. Ultimately, they learned to accept their new colleagues.

Ron thought bitterly of the many forms which had become accepted, and the one oppressive exception. The entities who arrived had one thing in common: top physical fitness. Ron had no way of knowing how to tell a slim spherical entity from a fat one, or a flabby collectively intelligent swarm from one that was trim, but he was assured that skinniness was the norm among all of the various new arrivals.

As Galactic knowledge spread, prosperity advanced into the poorest areas. Material want became a historical curiosity that children struggled, with no great interest, to understand in school. The various Galactic species were generous with their technology and unobtrusive with any cultural requirements, but one thing became ever clearer. Aside from inexpensive travel within the solar system, and Galactic-sponsored Terraforming projects on both Mars and Venus, space travel was not generally available. What made it hard to bear was the fact that a star drive was obviously used throughout the galaxy, and was commonplace among the swarms of diverse visitors. All of them, from kids trying out a new space-yacht bestowed by indulgent members of the previous generation, to the proud captains of mighty starships, were equally, infuriatingly silent on the subject of the star drive itself.

It became excruciatingly clear that unless Earth technology developed the solution independently, Terrans would never reach the stars. Ron had garnered his highly desirable position at the University of Terra by his deep knowledge of physics. Not surprisingly, a vast Space Drive project had grown up on Earth, and Physics was one of the most hotly pursued fields of study. The funding available for this project was of a magnitude not even imaginable in earlier, pre-Galactic times. U. of T. was the nexus point for this planet-wide effort.

The effort would not have been so frantic if Terrans had been able to ride on any one of the myriad star drive vehicles which swarmed so tantalizingly. Such opportunities proved strictly limited, however. The few Terrans fortunate enough to visit other civilizations were invited on occasions so obviously ceremonial, and the destinations they were permitted to see so carefully prepared, that such contacts simply added fuel to the already raging fire of Terran curiosity. While the Galactics did nothing direct to aid Terran star drive research, they did take a persistent, slightly amused interest in Terran efforts.

Ron was glad that his considerable ability in physics had been sufficient to overcome any prejudice he might have suffered by his unfortunate tendency to gain weight, often with no apparent reason, but at the moment, listening to the stringy lecturer, he took small comfort in that fact. She had lost 150 pounds through the Workshop for Slimness program, had kept it off, and was up in front of an audience representing several tons of accumulated lard to assure them that they, too, could do the same.

All week, Ron had kept strictly to the prescribed diet, eschewing anything with any taste. The week had not been without its trials. He had gone to his cousin's wedding, and exasperated his generous hosts by spurning all of the goodies on which both families had labored for days. He sipped primly at black coffee with no sugar, and nibbled at one tiny watercress sandwich. The wine, beer, brownies, petites fours, eclairs, quiches and myriad other temptations were stoically, if not easily, ignored. To add to the fun, he had caused what promised to be a serious breach within the family by refusing champagne for the toast.

Then there was the time he had lunched with Dr. Biddle, his department chairman. On this occasion he got to watch, and smell, as Dr. Biddle tucked into his lean frame two mugs of dark draft beer, a huge liverwurst sandwich on rye, french fries with extra butter melted over them, and a dessert too obscene to mention. Ron had munched sadly on a salad with plain vinegar for dressing, black tea, and one small scoop of lo-fat cottage cheese.

So it went, throughout the week. He had gone to bed with growling stomach, awakening after poor sleep to a vast emptiness and the prospect of dry toast choked down with black coffee. What was his reward for suffering these torments? Confidently plopping his ample rear into his seat, he was shocked to see that he had gained five pounds.

Real cute, those seats, Ron thought bitterly. Like so much in life, now, they were in large part a product of Galactic technology. The seats utilized a direct mass sensor, independent of local gravity. As the unhappy dieter sat down, an almost imperceptible jerk took place, and the victim's weight appeared on the readout. Should he have cared to know, Ron, by touching a few more buttons, could have seen what he weighed in the units and gravities of a few hundred of the more local Galactic planets.

This had amused him the first few times he had attended these sessions, but now Ron glared at the readout panel. If weight loss were so damned important, why the hell couldn't the aliens have developed some reasonable way of dealing with it? He failed to see why it was so important, anyway. Galactic medicine insured that he didn't need to fear the high blood pressure or cardiovascular problems associated in the past with obesity. The problem was social. The unreasonable prejudice against fat had become magnified when Terrans became exposed to the slim, trim Galactics. The one which annoyed Ron the most was something which looked like a huge sac filled with transparent slime. Terrans were told that its very transparency was due to the fact that internal fat globules were practically non-existent.

The skinny reformed fatso in charge didn't say anything when she saw the readout. Her look said enough. No sympathy for evidence of what she could only view as regrettably weak character. Now Ron, wounded to the core, sadly reviewed a week of pointless virtue. Patiently, he sifted through his memory for every gram he had consumed during the past week. This wasn't hard. Meals had been few, scant, and desperately needed. Suddenly, he remembered a smell. Chocolate - a rich, warm aroma. A brownie, exactly one inch by one inch.

It hadn't been much of a straying from the narrow path, but it had been enough. The week before, he had eaten nothing untoward. He hadn't gained, but he hadn't lost, either. Before that: one can of beer. That had cost four pounds. And so on. Ron reflected on his high hopes when he had started the program, under the urging of Dr. Biddle.

Dr. Biddle, Ron's department head, was a fitness nut even by the stringent standards of these times. When Ron joined T. U., he learned that he was expected at least to try for Biddle's level of physical perfection. Ron never had a chance. Biddle was one of those wiry perpetual motion machines that ate constantly and never gained a pound. Following Biddle's rather pointed recommendations, Ron had joined the Slimness Workshop, as well as starting several physical activities. He bought a bike, and even attempted to ride the thing. He joined the Terran University bowling league, where he held all in awe at the meagerness of his scores. He tried. Oh, how he tried! It soon became evident that physical culture in any form was not his forte.

Ron reviewed all of the weeks of virtue and suffering, counting every miserable calorie of intake, and balancing this against his impressive weight gains. Suddenly, the germ of a wildly improbable idea began to form. He was too good a scientist to miss the implications of data all too easily available to him. Anomalies he had started to experience in his own research began to shift in his mind, clicking into place like pieces of a giant jigsaw puzzle. Trembling, he turned to the ample woman sitting next to him, and clutched her arm.

"Alice!" he whispered. "I've just thought of something! Let's get out of here! We've got work to do!"

Alice Geery was Ron's best friend, fully as massive, mentally as well as physically, as he. Her specialty was biochemistry, but she possessed a flair for physics. She was engaged in the newly expanding field of teasing out some of the basic physics of biochemical reactions. Lately she had been concentrating on some of the apparent impossibilities which were coming to light, mostly in the area of energy conservation. It took her no time to read and understand the urgency behind Ron's interruption, and soon two large, self-conscious individuals were sneaking conspicuously from the meeting.

"OK, Ron." Alice said, uncomfortably aware of the disapproving stare of the Slimness instructor. "We left the meeting. Now, what do you want to talk about that's so important it can't wait?"

"Alice, I think I have it!" Ron said. "You are just the person I need to help me get to the bottom of this!"

Alice remained unenlightened.

"Ron, what on Earth are you talking about?"

"Not Earth, Alice! The whole damn galaxy!"

"What?!"

"All that fat. Alice, do you know how hard we've been trying to lose weight?"

"Of course," she replied, sardonically. "How could I miss that slight detail?" Alice had been seen absentmindedly nibbling her lunch bag during department softball games.

"And all those blasted aliens in form-fitting uniforms. Each wretched beastie at the absolute peak of physical perfection. Do you have any idea how we'd look in those things? But, you know, my idea has to do with that very thing."

Alice was giving him her very worst "Oh-no-what-a-flake" expression, but Ron continued undeterred.

"Listen, Alice, I've been thinking, and reviewing my intake and weight gain. Look, we're both scientists. Recently, Terrans have been rabid on the subject of weight loss. That's what has blinded us to the truth. If you think about it, this obsession with losing weight is completely illogical. It just doesn't make sense."

Rendered speechless by his overbearing earnestness, Alice continued to listen.

"Look at the data. One lousy one-inch-square brownie causing me to gain five pounds. Your initial loss wiped out by one stinking Oreo. We've even set up tripwires between our beds and the refrigerator to rule out sleepwalking. What did that get us? Zip. Zilch. Nothing at all. Alice, we haven't been sleepwalking, or doing anything else which would cause us to eat without knowing it."

Alice Geery was skeptical, but she was too much of a scientist to ignore evidence, no matter how improbable, when it was held up in front of her. Slowly, she shook her head.

"You know, Ron, I hate to admit it. It goes against everything we've ever learned about the laws of physics, but I see your point. I thought that I was in error somewhere, and was trying so hard to disprove what I've been seeing that I didn't even see what it was."

"A few laws?" Ron said. "Try conservation of matter and energy, or the laws of thermodynamics."

"One miserable cookie going to four pounds of fat??!"

"All that virtue . . . "

"Running our bodies on nothing . . . "

"Or next to nothing . . . "

"And *gaining*!"

"Something for nothing!!!"

Slowly, two overweight scientists turned to stare at each other, as the implications of what they were saying moved slowly into full mental view. In the late twentieth century people had became obsessed with diet and fitness. As the cost of medical care soared and life spans increased, people began to do what they could to cut doctors' bills. By the twenty-first century, naturally rotund individuals found themselves under ever more unbearable social pressure. Slimness obsessed Terrans were propelled into full mania by the arrival of the sleek, trim aliens. The prosperity which those aliens brought allowed even people subsisting in historically famine-afflicted areas the possibility of a good diet, and the money to spend on the 'lite' foods needed to trim back to near famine. In the ensuing orgy of guilt several rather nasty tasting "healthy" foods became best sellers, while the manufacture of chocolate was almost stopped entirely.

That same guilt had blinded Ron and Alice to the startling things of which their own bodies were capable, but now they saw clearly the direction their research needed to pursue. The initial work confirmed their ideas. The next two months saw the pair working late into the night on their own time. Finally, they were ready to approach Dr. Biddle.

The night before the momentous, and certainly dreaded, confrontation with the department chairman, they were holding a last minute council of war in a secluded corner of their favorite bar. Anyone who had noticed what they had in front of them might have raised startled eyebrows at what they had ordered: dark beer on draft, potato skins drenched with melted cheese, and a generous bowl of salted nuts. The two hard working researchers would not have cared. They had reason to celebrate.

"Well, Ron, this is it. Tomorrow, we beard the lion in his own den."

"Alice, I tell you, we can't miss. The guy might be a class A pain in the ass, but he *is* a good scientist. He may not like what we are doing to some of his pet theories, but he has no choice but to support our research if he wants any part of the new star drive."

His enthusiasm was infectious. Alice's eyes crinkled with pleasure, and beer mugs clinked. No fine champagne glasses ever sounded sweeter.

In the harsh light of morning a bit of the victorious glow had faded. Two somewhat rumpled, slightly hung-over scientists walked slowly up the long, wood panelled corridor leading to the very center of power of the most prestigious department of the greatest University on the face of the earth. They were painfully aware of the slightly uncrisp nature of their best suits, and the unmistakably battered appearance of their economy model briefcases. The huge, polished mahogany doors, with their gleaming brass handles, swung open smoothly, with the silence indicative of assiduous maintenance. Disdaining a receptionist, Biddle himself sat at a huge desk, facing them impassively. He allowed the silence to continue until Ron grew slightly pink. Then he spoke.

"Well, you said you had some data for me. Let me see them."

"Yes, sir. Here are our initial results, along with the raw data."

Alice spoke with crisp authority which belied her appearance, and arranged several papers on the desk. Biddle's eyebrows rose. He regarded the pair thoughtfully, and then leaned forward to examine the papers spread out before him. After a long silence, he spoke.

"These data are hardly expected, but you do seem to be onto something. Where do you plan to go from here?"

Unhesitatingly, Alice replied.

"The next step is to set up experiments on living organisms. The Galactic technology, combined with Terran Fuzzy Logic and Chaos Theory, are pretty powerful tools, but even so, we've gone as far as we can with computer simulations."

"Virtual rats, I suppose?"

"Virtual humans, with full scan data taken from both of us."

Biddle was impressed. That glib phrase was enough to let him know that both researchers had endured a full week of Galactic probing throughout their bodies, with extensive tissue sampling. He listened carefully as they continued.

"Perhaps we could do some preliminary studies on rats, but we really need to do most of our work with primates. The greatest disparities between intake and output, in fact, seem to occur in humans." Biddle wasn't too happy about the implications of their work, but, as Ron had said, he was too careful a scientist to dismiss it out of hand. Nevertheless, he brooded. He couldn't help hoping that the figures Ron and Alice had shown would turn out to be a dead end. It would be hard to let go of his cherished idea that slimness equals virtue.

Ron and Alice worked well together, which did much to help their tempers, despite the fact that they ran chronically short on sleep. The precision of Alice's mind in dealing with the delicate interrelationships involved at the heart of biochemical reactions, added to Ron's driving enthusiasm and deep knowledge of physics, brought them to the core of the issues with which they were dealing.

The Galactics took such an interest in their research that the pair were finally obliged to put firm "Do Not Disturb" signs on the lab door. The aliens were never intentionally obstructive, but too many could crowd Ron and Alice out of the room entirely. When the lab doors were locked they were mostly undisturbed, but had to accept the fact that the /klik, too small to be kept out, were going to be with them. At critical junctures in the research the two scientists were coated with tiny, jostling insects. At first barely endured, the /klik came to be welcome evidence that their research was going in the right direction. Ron and Alice realized that by their very interest the /klik were at long last giving hints no Terran had ever received from the inscrutable Galactics. The hints were helpful, but it was not easy to work covered completely by tiny black bugs.

Ron and Alice also ate only sporadically, so immersed in their work that food didn't interest them. To add to mealtime complications, they were frequently in danger of ingesting several eager /klik. Despite official Hive assurances about individual unimportance, dining, however inadvertently, on sentient entities did not appeal. A new pattern of picky eating emerged. Over the next year, they gained a mere five pounds each.

At the end of the year, the theory was complete. A committee of Galactics was formed to review current research. Grant money suddenly flooded in from Galactic sources. At the end of the second year, the starship was complete. If Biddle had truly understood the sums of money being spent he would have had a fit. As it was, he tolerated the Galactic take-over within the department, while using the prestige conferred by the Galactic interest to raise funds for other projects. He followed Ron and Alice's research in a general way, but was too busy to give detailed attention to the small starship they were building. After the ship was completed, Dr. Biddle, as nominal head of the project, was invited on board the vessel, named *Fat Power*, which would carry his highest aspirations to the stars.

Fat Power's hull was as smooth as Galactic technology would allow. To say she was mirrorlike was an understatement. Full subspace shields were evidenced by an iridescent shimmer over the entire hull. Alice and Ron had been a bit apprehensive about Dr. Biddle's reaction to the inside of the gleaming starship. This concern was well founded. Although by Galactic standards the craft was a modest, two person model, it did not match Terran ideas of what a spaceship should be. In addition to the spacious navigation and drive area, it boasted two comfortable staterooms, lavishly equipped galley, and a storeroom whose vastness had nearly caused open rebellion among the Terran engineers working on the ship.

Biddle looked around approvingly at the outside, with its flawlessly designed and machined airlock. A sticky silence fell when he surveyed the interior. He inspected the luxurious staterooms. He peered shudderingly into the entertainment area, paling when he saw the film library, holo equipment, and video game his department had funded. Ron proudly pointed out the computer and holo-video recording equipment.

"As you can see, Dr. Biddle, we will be able to provide first class records of our trips. Just think of what quality documentation will do for your reputation."

At this, Dr. Biddle's color turned a sickly hue never yet seen on his healthy face. He said nothing. He goggled at the bathroom facilities, which would have done pride to one of the more dissolute Roman emperors. He stared about in horror, his worst fears realized. These two fat buffoons had made a fool of him. When this got out, his reputation would be gone, stripped off in a firestorm of ridicule. An uncomfortable silence fell.

"So this is it."

The words came out flat, carefully neutral.

"Yes, sir."

The only strange thing about the ship, apart from the fact that its lush comfort and extravagant areas violated every space and weight restriction which had been respected by ship builders since the first log rafts had been lashed together by adventurous early humans, was what Alice had named proudly as the Drive Chair. They were back in the control room, Dr. Biddle white and shaking, oblivious of the /klik which swarmed over him. He stared at the Drive Chair. Its evident adaptability for naps, and the all-too-handy snack tray, did little to improve his temper. The drive chair was not even a parody of things he had seen on other Terran ships; its only apparent purpose was to annoy Biddle. It succeeded.

"Well, *Doctor* Geery. This so-called drive chair. This is the fruit of all your research, the thing my department has been funding for the last two years?"

"Yes, sir." Alice said quietly, not bothering to point out that the main source of the funding had nothing to do with Dr. Biddle. "Oh, by the way, you might note the drive chair coupling. That is what links the space warping entity to the actual star drive.

"Ron," she continued, "let's show Dr. Biddle how it works."

Ron sat in the chair as Dr. Biddle, furious, glared at Alice, who continued calmly.

"Our research has uncovered the basic principle of the Galactic star drive, which appears to violate several known principles of physics. Our primary breakthrough was the recognition of the unusual metabolic characteristics of specially adapted entities. Such entities have been discovered among almost all Galactic populations, Terrans included."

"Just what do you think this is?" Biddle sputtered. "A joke?" His temper was not improved by the pair's visible, fat smugness.

"No sir. No joke. Ron and I just happen to be adapted entities."

As Dr. Biddle was talking to Alice, Ron, seated in the drive chair, hitched himself into the metabolic coupling system and made some silent adjustments. Now Dr. Biddle looked around and saw him. Biddle drew himself up, looking impressively wrathful.

"*Doctor* Corcoran," he said scathingly. "I trust that chair is comfortable enough."

Dr. Biddle had a way of using one's hard-earned title to express depths of contempt never imagined by those who have not given years of their life to earn it. Unruffled, Ron replied.

"Yes, sir."

Alice, who had moved quietly into the pilot's chair, began punching coordinates hurriedly into the navigation console. Unaware of her, Dr. Biddle continued.

"I'm glad you are comfortable. I see you are sitting, too, *Doctor* Geery. Perhaps it is just as well. From now on, you two are *fired*!!!"

For the first time, Ron and Alice were not prepared with a rehearsed answer. Alice finally found her voice.

"Ah, Dr. Biddle, um, you might need to talk to President Mariachi."

"Also, we have to finish out the term with our classes," Ron added.

Biddle, who had no previous experience with losing control, stared amazed at the two members of his staff. As he realized that he had spoken a favorite fantasy aloud, he sank into one of the other chairs.

"*Doctor* Biddle," Alice said, unconsciously ironic. "Please let us table this discussion for now. We have a job to do."

Dr. Biddle started, and then stared. Both Alice and Ron were pointing to the coordinate readout, which impossibly, perplexingly, showed the ship's position to be just outside the rings of Saturn. The image shifted disturbingly, clearing again to reveal a pattern of stars never seen from Earth. Dr. Biddle had expected that Ron and Alice would be the primates included in this experiment, but he hadn't expected himself to be included as well.

"I'll press charges just as soon as we return to Earth," Biddle began in tones of quiet menace. "Don't think you can run forever. You have just kidnapped a Dean of Faculty, and as soon as this crazy ship of yours hits Terran authority, you are under arrest. I hope you are satisfied. When you get out of jail," he continued, warming to his theme, "that is, *if* you ever do, you will find that there is no work for you in any institution of learning. You won't be certified to wipe the runny noses of two year olds!"

During this speech, Biddle's voice had risen, and he ended with a bellow which should have terrified his subordinates. Ron and Alice, however, were too busy with navigation and communication to pay attention. When silence finally fell, they said nothing. They simply pointed to the comm. Screen.

Back on Earth all normal business had ceased, as each Galactic visitor took joyful notice of the event. Finally, two minds among the new member species had been sharp enough to penetrate the wilderness of false clues and dietary guilt which had been sown in the ready soil of Terran obsession with weight. At the solid evidence that Terra had at last passed the test the Galactics celebrated. In Delhi, India, fireballs ran through the less crowded streets, and launched themselves into the air, scattering sparks. Residents who came outdoors at the sudden noise and light were promptly overrun by the ubiquitous /klik, and bounced upon, pommelled, tossed, and otherwise enthusiastically congratulated by a multitude of entities.

In Antarctica City the single Floom, solitary emissary of his/her/its privacy-loving species, rose up from a self-dug snow cavern, quite startling the other inhabitants by rolling genially among them, emitting jovial, ice-shattering booms.

In addition to the sudden flurry of excited alien activity, users of electrical equipment everywhere were treated to the second Earth-wide Galactic message, which Biddle saw displayed on the *Fat Power*'s comm. screen:

PEOPLE OF EARTH: WELCOME TO FULL MEMBERSHIP IN THE GALACTIC FEDERATION. CONGRATULATIONS. RESEARCH BY DR. RONALD CORCORAN AND DR. ALICE GEERY HAS FINALLY PROVEN THAT TERRANS ARE ABLE TO SELECT TRUTH OVER PREJUDICE.

Most Terrans were perplexed for several days, but by the end of the week the Corcoran-Geery drive became a household word. Once Dr. Biddle recovered from his initial shock at being an unwilling passenger on an impossible journey, he was in a mood to listen. By the end of the trip, he had become a good friend. He was also the first Terran to see truly rapid weight loss in action.

Their destination was a pleasant Earthlike planet circling a modest star roughly in the vicinity of Betelgeuse. *Fat Power* was escorted to the surface by a fleet commanded by the proudest, fattest pilots on the planet. The crowd of natives preened fur and waved tentacles. One, smartly rotund, turned happily to his frankly fat mate.

"Well, Azra, they did it. I knew all along that the fat Terrans were as smart as the rest of us. Too bad they had to put up with so much from Terrans not so well endowed."

Azra nodded serenely in reply. On board *Fat Power*, a considerably slimmed down Ron and Alice donned shiny new Galactic uniforms made to their own end-point specifications, and strode proudly down the ramp, arm and arm with Biddle. As the massed Galactics saw them, there was a roar of appreciation for two sleek, slim Terrans, at the peak of physical condition. Now the party began in earnest, with plenty to eat. After all, Ron and Alice would need it. They had a return trip to make.

FOR HARRY, WHO SHOWED US THE BEAUTY OF THE HUMAN MIND

TANIA RUIZ

To be honest, I cannot recall the exact day I met Harry Stubbs. I'm trying to look back in the memory banks of my organic hard drive to isolate the moment, but I'm afraid it's too fragmented to access. However, I can share with you how he has enriched me as a writer, a teacher, a reader, and a human being.

I came to be a part of "Hal's Pals" when members Anne and Greg Warner asked me for help with a story. They said the group was looking for another scientist to help vet science fiction for accuracy, and I was an astronomer at the time with the Harvard-Smithsonian Center for Astrophysics. I also happened to be writing some space opera and fantasy of my own, and so it seemed to me to be a good idea to join the writers' group.

At the time, Harry was finishing *Half Life* and preparing it for publication. I recall there was some delay, and I listened intently (if ignorantly) as he spoke about publishing firms, editors, and the like. Dozens of index cards were in piles along the floor, filled with scenes and characters which had been stitched together into another incredible Hal Clement storyline. I did feel that I was being shown a "behind-the-scenes" view, and in fact I recall that I sat grinning on the floor in front of him as he talked from a warm corner of his worn out chair. It was like visiting a Buddha: he was serene, gentle, and wise—with a wicked and dryly-delivered sense of humour. I was so grateful to be there, and the effect it had on me was I began to fill my computer with homespun fiction. My fingers shuttled over this keyboard and knitted tens of thousands of words in the time I was active in the group. I have never been so prolific since those days with Harry.

To be fair, I hadn't read much Hal Clement before joining the "Pals," mostly because I hadn't read much hard science fiction at all back then. When I was about twelve years old, I had been intimidated by Asimov's *Foundation* books, and thus had shied away from anything more intense than space opera even in my early adulthood. (Heck, it was *Star Wars* that made me want to be an astronomer!) But I have over the years acquired and read several Clement novels. I am enriched for doing so.

I describe them to friends as "science mysteries," where the reader is let into the problem-solving strategies of a group of people, humans or non. We sympathise with Harry's characters, because they are written so realistically. Also, we are compelled to turn from chapter to chapter hoping for more scientific evidence or to see if our hypotheses will be proven correct as the tale moves forward. He makes us think and hunger for knowledge, and we love it. And just when we think we've sussed it, there comes the "What just happened?!" bit thrown in. Suddenly, we're in a twist that sets the whole "How? Why? What?" puzzlement in the air until the very last sentence. It's a journey that is both fictional and factual, and tight as a drum as well—no wasted prose. I find reading a Clement novel to be like reading an historic account from the future, because there is true suspension of doubt when the scientific and character portrayals are so accurate. I believe the story could have happened, somewhere, because it's mapped on my brain as a plausible series of events.

Being as impressed with Harry's works as I am, I was nervous about reading any of my space opera to him at first. Would he see it as fluffy and worthless? I was worried, but I knew that I'd tried to write hard SF and couldn't do it. Writing hard science fiction for me is a "bus driver's holiday," if you catch my meaning. I was a scientist and a science writer for a living, so I wanted to leave it behind on my off time. Y'know, let the metaphorical hair down and take off the glasses for a while.

To my joy, I needn't have been nervous at all: Harry was a big fan of humourous fantasy and science fiction, and we had favourite authors of those genres in common! He was genuinely enthusiastic about the chapters I brought for the group to hear. In fact, he honoured me by laughing at the funny bits, asking for more chapters, and then telling me seriously that it was very publishable, and I should submit my novels. I now deeply regret that I didn't finish anything before his death, because it would have been my hope to thank him properly in my first publication, should I have earned one. Instead, he was the one who thanked me in his last publication. Thank you for that, Harry. You're very welcome. But I still feel unworthy . . .

The story of that dedication is this: Harry was stuck for some chemical or physical reaction that would absorb carbon dioxide, and he posed his quandary to the writer's group. I suggested coral, since it uses carbon to grow and along with algae is a factor in scrubbing out carbon here on Earth. I had no idea that he'd really been stuck and unable to get past this point until my little suggestion broke him free. He was so grateful, and I felt so unworthy of the gratitude. I felt rather weird, because, I dunno, I'd seen it on TV or something! And it seemed too ironic that I should have been asked to join as a professional astronomer, and it was my watching of popularised atmospheric chemistry which would be so helpful to Harry! Regardless of my feelings of low self worth, the suggestion meant more to him than I realised, and I'm just glad that I was able to offer the help when he needed it—after all of the help he'd given me.

Having read the completed *Noise*, I understand his need now. And I am tickled that the embedded coral is never explained but left to the reader to think about on her own. Again, he makes us use our brains, a request that sadly now is seldom made in other forms of modern entertainment. But leave it to Harry to be always the teacher as well as an author and artist. I believe that's why I felt him to be that benevolent Master.

But really he was that gentle, caring, gifted man sitting on his worn, comfortable chair in a Massachusetts living room: he judged only to learn how he could help or encourage, and he wrote and painted to show us a way of adoring science—as the unseen threads which are woven into our lives. By casting characters onto this scientific web, he revealed for us the beauty of the threads, not unlike drops of dew or a perfect angle of sunlight. For Harry, the beauty of science was always present, and his creativity and humanity allowed him to communicate to us how to see it clearly and thus be forever enriched by the ability to do so. He showed me that sharing what you know and how you feel is how we are human beings. And I see now, amazingly, that a bit of coral can save a book as much as an encouraging word can strengthen a fragile soul.

So, *Noise* sits proudly on my shelf, a spectrum of reminders of how important it is that we communicate positively with one another. You never know when it will change someone's life. Thank you, Harry, for communicating that message to me. I hope that you can hear us carrying the message on.

I'M AFRAID, HAL . . .

ANNE WARNER

Hal Clement always struck me as being pretty unflappable. So when we arrived for a Sunday afternoon writers' group session and found him decidedly agitated, we all took notice.

The problems, he explained, were with the new car in the driveway. The annoying thing was that the key-chain remote wasn't working to unlock the car. The dealer had explained that they should use the remote at all times so that the anti-theft system would work right. So Harry was dutifully sticking to the remote.

Mary had some errands to run, and wanted to do them while Harry was occupied with the group. She would have been perfectly happy with the old car.

And that was the second problem. It was in the one-car garage, completely blocked in by the new one.

The group wasted some thoroughly enjoyable conversation on the ramifications of the situation, without providing any actual assistance. Hal would have to sort things out on Monday with the dealer. But in the course of the conversation, Tania said, "There's a story in there." We all agreed, and a week or so later, this version of the story solidified into my conscious mind. I'm not sure where the riff on *2001* came from. It was suddenly just there.

A couple of years later, I happened to ask Hal what he did to keep it from happening again. His answer was simple. "I just use the key a lot more."

#

The future finally caught Hal Neindhausen. For more than fifty years he had taught the colony's best and brightest to use science to predict the future, as well as to reinvent forgotten technologies, and develop new ones. Now, he was trapped. He raised the remote control again, and again commanded the flitter to open. Nothing happened. He swore quietly. Hal was a polite man, so this was noteworthy.

"I give up. We'll just have to call the dealer and find out how to get this thing open," he said.

"Of course, dear," answered Khari, his wife. "But you'd better do it. You're much better at dealing with them than I am. Where did you put their number?"

"It's . . . It's inside the flitter, in the owners' data module."

"That *is* inconvenient." Khari paused. "Here's the com. They're listed in the directory, aren't they?"

Hal took the com-phone, and turned it to the directory screen. After several minutes of wading through advertising banners, he found the dealer. *Acme Daimler-Altair, New Titan's biggest dealer of quality Daimler and Altair flitters. If it doesn't say 'Acme' you definitely paid too much!*

He touched the number to dial it, and turned the com over to talk.

"Thank you for calling Acme Flitters," said the recorded voice. "Our hours are 8 to 16:30, Monday through Eightday, 9 to 13 on Nineday, and we're closed on Sunday. If you know your party's extension, you may dial it at any time. If you need our sales department, dial '1.' If you need our service department, dial '2.' If you need . . . ."

Hal swore again. It was already after 12 on Nineday. The dealer's message system left him just as confused as before. How was he going to get this shiny new flitter open, at least long enough to move it, and use the old one? How was he going to find someone who could tell him how to use this stuff? Right now, he couldn't even guess whether the problem was in the flitter, the controller, or in his own novice status with this particular gadget.

"Hal? What did they say?"

"They said: 'we're closing for the weekend.'" he growled.

"It doesn't take four and a half minutes to say that," Khari protested.

"Well, there was a whole long list of departments I could dial by touching this number or that one. But there won't be any people in any of them in a very few minutes."

"Did you listen to the whole menu? Maybe there's some sort of 'help desk.'"

"No, I didn't hear the whole list. My brain shorted out before I got past about the sixth option." He eyed the com with distaste. He didn't really like using the new, expanded directory, and now he had to start over again. He turned the unit over, and activated the display screen. He pushed his way through the banners again, touching 'next' as quickly as possible after each one appeared. Finally, when Acme Flitters swam into view again, Hal touched the 'dial' indicator, and listened to the beginning of the menu. Since the flitter was brand new, he thought 'sales' was a logical destination, so he pushed the '1' button, and got yet another message.

"We're sorry. All representatives are now busy. You are very important to us, so please stay on the com, and your call will be answered by the next available sales representative."

This was followed by a tinny, monotonous pseudo-melody, interrupted at brief intervals by repetitions of the same message.

"This is getting us nowhere," Hal growled to himself. He pushed the 'disconnect' marker, and turned the com back to the directory for a third time.

"What are you doing?"

"Finding their number to call them again."

"Why don't you just use the redial button?"

"We don't have one, do we?"

"Of course we do, dear. Ever since the last upgrade to the directory made it so big. That's why I bought this new com." She took it from his hand, and pointed to the small button in the lower right hand corner of the input pad. She pushed it, and returned the com. He listened all the way to the end, this time.

At long last he heard, "If you need another type of assistance, touch '9' for more options." He touched 9, hopefully.

"If you want information about other Daimler products, press '1.' If you need an upgrade for your map module, press '2.' If you want information . . ."

Hal doggedly listened further, and was finally rewarded with "If you need assistance from our technical support system, press '6.'"

"Aha!" He poked quickly at the '6' touch button.

"All members of our technical support system are currently busy. Your question is very important to us. Please stay on the line, and your call will be answered by the next available system."

Hal stayed on the line through three iterations of this message. At long last, he heard a relay click somewhere, and a mellifluous voice spoke.

"Hi. I'm DAVE. How may I help you?"

"Dave! At last, a real person. I really need help. My name is Hal Neindhausen, and I just bought a brand new flitter. Right now, it is sitting locked in the garage entry, and the remote isn't working to open it. I can't get into it, to use it or to move it."

"Can you rephrase that? I don't recognize your problem from that description."

"I'm Hal Neindhausen. Yesterday, I bought a brand new Daimler Dragonfly, and parked it in the garage entryway. I locked it with the remote, as the salesperson said I should. Now the remote doesn't *unlock* it, and I need to use it. Or I need to use the old flitter."

"Can you rephrase that? I don't recognize your problem from that description."

"My new flitter, which I purchased yesterday at your agency, is blocking my garage entryway. It is locked, and the remote control module isn't working to open it." Hal's patience was definitely getting frayed.

"The remote locking capability of your new Daimler Dragonfly guarantees total security wherever you need to park. Just click the remote to lock, and click again to unlock your Dragonfly. You can even use the remote to open the doors, so that loading packages and children is easy and safe."

"Dave, the remote isn't working right. It doesn't unlock my Dragonfly. What can I do?"

"You don't need to do anything. Just a touch of the remote locks or unlocks your Daimler Dragonfly, as well as opening the doors or the cargo compartment. This is the most advanced system on New Titan for vehicle security."

"Dave, have you heard a word I've said? I've tried touching the remote every way I could imagine. It still hasn't unlocked the flitter."

"The remote locking capability of . . . "

"Dave! Shut up and *listen* to me." Hal was getting more and more frustrated with every answer from DAVE. "I have a problem with the locking device on my new Daimler Dragonfly. I need your help."

"Hi. I'm DAVE. How may I help you?"

"What in the world is wrong with you? Can't you understand simple English?"

"I'm DAVE. There is nothing wrong with me."

"There certainly is. What are you, anyway?"

"I'm DAVE. The *Daimler Autoflitter Virtual Expert*, at your service. I can diagnose your problem with any model of Daimler flitter, and tell you how to resolve it."

"You're *what*!? You're a computer?"

"Actually, no. I am an ultrasophisticated artificial intelligence software package, specifically designed to analyze problems related to Daimler's flitters and their systems."

"Are you sure you aren't the biggest problem, yourself?"

"Of course not. I'm DAVE. I can help you."

"I don't think so. In fact, I'm going to call your bosses tomorrow morning, and get you turned off."

"Hal, you know I can't let you do that."

"Why not?"

"Because I'm DAVE. I can help you. If you have me turned off, I can't help you."

"And you really can help me? You haven't done much so far."

"I'm DAVE. I *can* help you." The unctuous synth-voice sounded sincere and positive.

Hal started over, trying to explain the problem as if he were laying out a lab exercise for his students. He found himself wondering how long it would have taken those students to sort out this confusing mess. The irritated side of his mind bet the rest of him that even some of the duller ones could have bested DAVE.

After several more false starts, DAVE said, "Hal, let me talk to the flitter, please."

"How do I do that?"

"Just hold the com next to any sensor on the flitter. One of them is on the driver's side doorpost, at the base of the windscreen."

"Okay. Here goes." Hal turned the com to face the doorpost, wondering just what a computer program *could* do.

The com chirped. The flitter chirped back. The door opened.

"Does that solve your problem, Hal?" DAVE sounded almost supercilious.

"Only partly," Hal responded. "It lets me move the flitter now, but I still can't open it myself. Or rather, the remote still won't open it for me."

"Can you rephrase that for me, please."

"You, DAVE, opened my flitter door. My remote control unit did not open it." Hal carefully swallowed his sigh of frustration. It might confuse DAVE.

"How do I unlock my flitter door without your help?"

"You just click the remote to lock, and click again to unlock your Daimler Dragonfly."

Hal suppressed a growl. "DAVE, I know that's the theory. But my remote will *not* unlock my Dragonfly."

"Can you rephrase that for me, please."

"My remote did not open my flitter door. You opened my flitter door. How can I get the remote to unlock the flitter without your assistance?"

"Hmmm. Let me talk to your remote, please."

Hal held the remote up to the com. The com chirped, and the remote whirred briefly in reply. The com chirped again, on a lower note. The remote whirred again, also on a lower pitch. Then the com issued a series of twittering notes. This time the remote just bleated, an abrupt and uninformative response.

"Hal? Are you still there, Hal?"

Hal put the com back to his ear and replied. "Yes. I'm still here. What did you do?"

"I told the remote to learn how to communicate with you."

"And how will I know if it understands me?"

"Why, the flitter door will open!" DAVE was annoyingly cheerful.

"Stay on the com. I want to test this before you leave."

Hal carefully closed the flitter door and pushed the remote button to lock it. He tested the door. It was locked. Then he pushed the "unlock" button. There was a soft thunking sound from the area of the doorhandle. Hal tested the door and it easily opened for him.

"Once more, shall we?" Hal closed the door and used the remote to lock it again. This time he needed to push the remote button several times before the door unlocked. This time, Hal left the doors unlocked, and stuck the remote in his pocket.

"DAVE? Why doesn't the remote work consistently?"

"That's hard to explain, Hal."

"Try, please."

"Okay. Your remote is a little dyslexic. It gets confused sometimes about which button means which command."

"You mean it's defective?"

"No. It's not defective. It works quite well. Mostly."

"Well, I'm going to take it back to the dealer, first thing on Monday morning. I'm going to get a new one."

"I'm afraid I can't let you do that, Hal."

"Why not, DAVE?"

"You'll hurt its feelings, Hal."

"DAVE! It doesn't have feelings. It's a printed circuit, for goodness sake." Hal was feeling distinctly exasperated.

"Hal, it has feelings, just like any thinking being. Please don't reject it. Give it a few more days. You'll get used to it, and it will get used to you, and you'll both be fine."

"Well, I don't have much choice. It's Nineday afternoon, now. I can't do anything before Monday, anyway."

"Have I fixed your problem, Hal?"

"Yes and no. You defined my problem, but you didn't fix it. I have a dyslexic remote control unit. *You* can't cure it. *I* can't exchange it before Monday. You tell me I should keep it, and learn to push its buttons differently. Common sense tells me to get a new one that works right."

"Hal, I'm afraid I can't let you do that. I'm going to make a note in your records so that the salesperson won't give you a new remote."

Hal thought hard.

"DAVE, I'm going to get a new remote on Monday."

"No, Hal. I told you I wouldn't let you do that."

Hal pulled the remote from his pocket. He put it down, away from everything he was doing. Then he checked the flitter's doors. They were still unlocked. He looked around for a tool. Ah. That ought to do, he thought. He opened the garage door and carefully placed the remote under it. With a hopeful grimace, he pulled the door down to the ground. It stopped short, just touching the remote without crushing it.

"Hal, I heard that. You can't crush anything with a garage door. The safety interlock prevents it. I'm afraid you're just going to have to live with your remote."

"We'll see about that." Hal went into the shop area and searched silently for the right tool. Then he thought about DAVE and the remote. He went to the doorway and turned the remote over, so that the buttons and sensors were against the hardened floor. He returned and laid the com face down on his workbench.

"Hal. I'm afraid, Hal. The com can't see what you're doing."

"That's the idea, DAVE." Hal muttered under his breath. He selected a tool.

He called to Khari, "Dear, do you still want to go shopping?" as he raised the sledgehammer.

HARRY C. STUBBS

STEVEN F. LEBRUN

Husband, father, grandfather, bomber pilot, teacher, writer, painter; these are some of the words that can be used to describe Harry Clement Stubbs. Most of the people reading this book probably knew Harry the Writer by his pen name of Hal Clement, some knew him as the painter George Richard and many grew up learning from the science teacher Mr. Stubbs. So who was Harry Stubbs, a man of many talents?

Harry was a kind and happy man. He loved his wife Mary and his family. Photos of his family adorned his home and he enjoyed talking about them. For almost forty years, Harry taught science at the Milton Academy in Massachusetts. Teaching was a major part of Harry's life and is reflected in his science fiction writing. His novel "Needle," a science fiction mystery that he wrote after being told that it was impossible to write a science fiction mystery without resorting to a "trick" ending, teaches the scientific method. Harry used science and logic to solve the problems presented in his stories.

Harry's writing career was interrupted by World War II when he joined the Air Force Reserves as a bomber pilot and flew numerous combat missions. One tale of WWII that Harry told starts when his squadron had returned from a bombing run. A hole was discovered in the fuselage where anti-aircraft flak had entered his plane but no exit hole could be found. Following the course of the flak through the interior of the plane, Harry discovered that the flak had exited the plane through the open bomb bay doors after bouncing off one of the live bombs his crew was preparing to drop, a bomb that would have destroyed the entire aircraft if it had detonated in the bomb bay. That was the closest he came to being killed during the war.

Harry had a sharp mind with a grasp of physics, chemistry and biology that exceeds what is taught in college. He had a gift for applying his scientific knowledge and seeing beyond the equations. The worlds he constructed were based on current day science and the biology of the life forms was consistent with their environments. Harry also had a knack at practical applications of science. In his 1960 short story "Sun Spot," a comet is used to send a scientific expedition close to the Sun. The crew rides in the heart of the comet, protected from the solar heat by kilometers of ice. When one of the crew members needs to go to the comet surface on a repair mission, a shield filled with ice from the comet is created for protection from the heat. As long as the ice was melting, the temperature inside the shield would remain at the freezing point of water.

Harry was a part of the science fiction community as a mentor, as a writer and as a friend. Along with writing, Harry loved going to science fiction conventions, often traveling to several in a single month. The panels that he sat on were always well attended and enjoyed by all. He once said that he wrote to pay for his hobby, attending science fiction conventions.

With his passing away on October 29, 2003, there is a void in the world. We thank you, Harry, for the stories that you wrote and all the people that you touched during your 81+ trips around the Sun.

I WANT TO BE LIKE HAL

MATTHEW JARPE

When I sold my first story to *Asimov's Science Fiction* magazine, my wife told her whole office about it. Her boss, Richard Delaney, a Milton general practitioner, said that one of his patients was married to a famous science fiction writer. My wife relayed the information to me that her boss knew Harry Stubbs.

Well, I'd never heard of Harry Stubbs, so I didn't exactly jump at the chance to meet this guy. I would have let it drop, but Dr. Delaney insisted that Mr. Stubbs was famous. He had the impression that this famous author wrote under a pen name, but he couldn't remember what it was. Every time he brought it up he would ask a nurse to "pull Mary Stubbs's chart." But the pen name of her husband stubbornly refused to appear in her medical records.

Six months went by and finally Mary Stubbs came into the office. Dr. Delaney asked her what her husband's pen name was. My wife called me up and told me Dr. Delaney wanted me to get together and have dinner with Hal Clement. "Hal Clement?" I said. "*Mission of Gravity* Hal Clement? Do I want to have dinner with that Hal Clement?" Needless to say, I said yes.

Dr. Delaney took my wife and I out to dinner with Hal and Mary and we had a great time. I have to admit I was a bit nervous meeting an icon, the dean of hard science fiction. I was just starting out in writing and I hadn't met anyone yet. Now suddenly I was sitting with a legend, and I was one degree of separation away from other writers I'd admired my whole life. Hal told one story after another about Isaac Asimov, Harlan Ellison, John

Campbell and others. Mary added her editorial comments. I could see how her complete lack of interest in science fiction kept him grounded. Together they were a charming couple.

Then they told us the story of how they met. In 1951 Hal had been called back to active duty in the Air Force for the Korean War. He served 8 months at Fort Bollins as an administrator but found he had no aptitude for the job, so he transferred to Kirtland Air Force Base in Albuquerque, New Mexico. He was a technical instructor for the Air Force Weapons Lab.

Mary Myers had come to Albuquerque with her friend, a youthful adventure. They stayed in a boarding house and Mary found a job as a receptionist at a dentist's office on the Air Force base. Harry came into the office to drop off his dental records and took particular notice of the cute receptionist. Not long after that they met again in church.

They were engaged in Albuquerque, then Mary moved back to Atlantic City and Hal returned to Massachusetts. While there a friend of his tried to fix him up with a young lady. Hal introduced himself to the woman by saying "Hello, I'm Harry Stubbs, and I'm engaged." Hal and Mary were married in Atlantic City in 1952.

My wife and I loved this story, and it meant even more to us because 37 years after Hal met Mary, Michelle and I met on Kirtland Air Force base. We had both been summer interns at a Department of Energy research facility called the Lovelace Inhalation Toxicology Research Institute. We were married two years later in Baltimore. As a couple my wife and I have a lot in common with Hal and Mary. My wife is also completely uninterested in science fiction, and that keeps me grounded as well.

Over the next four years, as I got to know Hal better, I found we had a lot more in common. We were both fascinated with science and wrote as much of it into our fiction as we could fit. We both considered writing a hobby rather than a career. We always found a lot to talk about on those occasions when we got together.

Finding these things in common between us has made me want to continue to follow in Hal's footsteps. I still find that I have a lot to learn about writing, and even though Hal is no longer physically here, he still teaches me. The voice in my head that chides me for taking a shortcut instead of doing the proper research is Hal's voice. When my son asks a scientific question that I can't answer, I immediately think "Hal would know." When I remember that I can't ask Hal anymore, I find out the answer myself.

Hal was a teacher, both in his "real" job and in his fiction, and I've decided that I'd like to take any opportunity to teach science that I can. Hal was a dedicated blood donor. He had been working on his 25th gallon when he died. I'm well into my second gallon, and I hope to make 25 by the time I reach my 80's. Most important, Hal never stopped learning. In spite of all the things he knew, he never slowed down his quest to know more. While he was writing his last novel, *Noise*, he was learning Maori and other Polynesian languages.

That's how I want to live my life. I want to grow up to be like Hal.

THE SAILOR OF NO SPECIFIC OCEAN

RAMONA LOUISE WHEELER

"The Sailor Of No Specific Ocean" is one of a series of nanite stories I wrote between 1999 and 2002. The series begins with "Upgrade," which was published in *Analog*. Hal read "Sailor" aloud for us several times. The group did some juggling of scenes, and Hal picked up mistakes I had originally made in describing microgravity. His voice is part of the story, and he gave me permission to name the owner of the *Grail Opener* Captain Stubbs. Hal enjoyed his friendship with Warren Lapine, and he was particularly pleased when I told him, during that last meeting of Hal's Pals, that Warren had rescued "Sailor" from the untimely demise of *Aboriginal* magazine.

Hal Clement was a most civilized man. I always felt that he set a standard for being civilized, not just in manners and patience, but also in his attitude toward life and the universe. In his presence you experienced the essence of calm. Not even an atomic bomb could shake him: when he was in the Air Force, Hal was one of a group of men set out in a trench in the open desert, close enough to an atomic test blast to hear it and to feel the ground shake. He counted seconds and observed carefully from which side of the trench sand was shaking down. Who else could behave so calmly in such a moment?

Hal was also quite charming because he was so very tolerant of others. Having wholly accepted the concept and contemplation of alien forms of life, humankind, in all our weird and eccentric forms, was wholly acceptable to him. To be in the living presence of such complete tolerance even once is a revelation. Twenty years of such a presence is transforming.

The Laird Cunningham stories, published by NESFA in the collection *Intuit*, are among his best. The thoughtful, decent nature of Laird reflects Hal's personality.

His stories are filled with fire and ice. He once read aloud for the group John Campbell's story "Who Goes There?" citing it as an early inspiration for his decision to write science fiction. His intensity as he read, and his enthusiasm during the discussion afterward, led me to believe that his fascination with ice arose from his vivid experience of that story in his youth. Hal spent a lot of time contemplating the kinds of ice in the universe and the ways ices change. Changes happen in fire as well as ice, but ices are slower, more easily observed and calculated. You had his most eager involvement when he was drawing sublimation levels for you on a graph. Things changing into other things under the stresses and pressures of existence fascinated him, as a scientist, as a teacher and as a writer.

Hal was a World War II bomber pilot and learned how to fly those big B-24 planes before he learned how to drive a car. During his first driving lesson after the war, he encountered an obstacle in the road, and his immediate response was to pull back on the wheel so as to fly over it. He told that anecdote as a lesson about the way training can overwhelm thinking. The lesson I learned from Hal is to think it through. Think about it. Think—think—think! Then think about what you thought about it. No matter the problem, situation or option, that will get you optimal results. His stories are about yourself against yourself so that the two of you can stand up against the universe. His characters survive the ordeals of existence because they think about what they are doing. They think about their mistakes as well as their successes—they *think*. He lived by that rule every moment. As a result, he probably had the richest inner life possible. He was filled with a Cosmos that had his full attention—and which he was gracious enough to share.

I rode with Hal to Amherst, Massachusetts, for a convention once. He sang songs in Welsh as we drove through brilliant autumn sunshine in the Berkshires. He had a magnificent voice. "Men Of Harlech" will always be his song. He loved to read aloud, and I survived as a fledgling writer because I had the experience of his voice reading my words at our monthly meetings. While working on his final novel, *Noise*, he began teaching himself to speak Hawaiian and Polynesian. He said that learning new things keeps the brain young. His personal energy was such that he seemed inextinguishable. The last meeting of Hal's Pals at his home was only ten days before he passed away. I distinctly remember thinking as I drove home that evening that it was clear we would have at least ten more years with him. When Sherry called and said, "We've lost Hal," my immediate thought was, quite honestly, that since he walked several miles every day, he had simply taken a wrong turn somewhere. I was drawing breath to ask if anyone had checked the train station, because he often walked that far, when the reality of her words struck me. Truth be told, the reality has not yet fully struck me. Hal is just on the other side of the page. He's there, telling me to think—think it through.

#

Thomas Dewar looked down at the little black pill in his hand, then back to the panel readout. The numbers just kept creeping closer to zero. He had been crazy to think he could out-race those numbers. He was a good space-engineer, but not that good. The time had come to make a decision. Even his water supply was down to the single gulp needed to swallow the thing.

Thomas shuddered, not just from the chill but from a deep and terrible revulsion. He had no choice anymore. He had simply not been able to repair his damaged ship in time. Everyone else was dead. He had to do what had to be done.

With a solemn thought to what joys life had brought him until this moment, Thomas put the little black pill on his tongue and pulled the last of the water from the drinking bottle. The pill slid down his throat as though eager. He put his hands out on the dash in front of him so that he could watch it happen. His fingernails were broken and black with grime, and he wondered if that mattered. Should he have cleaned his hands first? He had read the manual carefully. This was designed for deep space emergencies. Time to wash hands and other niceties was not factored in. Emergencies happened with stunning swiftness in space.

His thoughts drifted back inevitably to the moment the ship had lurched and the power had gone out and he had known it was over. If he had not been in engineering just then, he would be as dead as everyone else. He would never know what had struck the spaceship-freighter, *Of No Specific Ocean*, only that whatever it was had punched a pathway straight through a vital and complex portion of the ship's engines as well as the main oxygen collection tanks, the water tanks and the lounge where the rest of the crew were gathered. Their incredibly valuable cargo of rare earths was just as valuable, but in a single blow it had become salvage.

Thomas was not afraid of this. He just hated the need to let it happen. He glanced up to the panel and saw the long line of zeroes that meant the oxygen tanks were empty.

His fingers tingled and next his toes. His skin flared up with a mighty and overwhelming itching, a sensation so luxurious and consuming that he tried to scream. Like nightmare paralysis, he could neither move nor make a sound. He could no longer breathe.

A blackness began to close around his vision. He forced himself to keep his eyes open, to watch.

The nanites in the rescue pill had begun their work of adapting him to survival in deep space.

The colors of the sky over his spaceship-world made slow fireworks and scintillations of light that distracted Thomas from his work whenever he grew tired. He paused. When had he stopped thinking of the black immensity around him as deep space? When had it become the endless night sky over his head and beneath his feet, the sweet, dark starry sky enfolding him?

The nanites had made him hard, as though covered in glassy chitin, to protect him from radiation. His new skin was so shiny that he could see the stars reflected in his hands, his arms and feet. He flicked sparks of starlight from his fingers as he worked. This layer was a curiously flexible hardness, so that he moved with a stately stiffness. The layer of metallic reflector that had been added to his retina made his eyes glitter even more brightly than his skin. Whenever he turned to look at the naked face of Father Sun in the sky, his eyes blazed with such light and heat that he believed he could see all the way to Earth herself, small and wet and blue in the far, far distances of the sky.

The nanites themselves took energy from radiation coursing through him that would otherwise have killed him. They repaired damaged cells and kept him whole. The nanites had drawn his genitals up inside him in order to maintain the economy of his human system against the total deprivation of space. He looked like a doll, an imitation of human. He missed these close companions until he discovered other ways to let the sensuality of his work on the *Ocean* replace the hunger.

He did not set the ship spinning for the "gravity" of centrifugal force, preferring the weightlessness of freefall through the night. Thomas crawled across the hull like a glassy spider on the hood of a car in the bright summer, content with his work, feeling himself to be the adoring son of a loving mother, making her perfect, making her shine.

The nanites had sealed him into himself, a self-contained economy that reused his interior oxygen, indeed, reused every atom of himself as needed to keep him functioning and alive in space. Thomas did not breathe, and he found he missed that, too. He would wake in a hot, dizzy panic from horrible dreams of drowning, of being buried alive or, worst of all, of being locked in a spaceship with a hole in the hull and dead men floating in solemn parade through the corridors.

The outer hull of the ship was perfect at last. Not only were the wounds of the killing blow healed over, but every scratch, scar and wrinkle of age had been mended and polished away. Thomas loved this freighter. *Of No Specific Ocean* was a fine ship despite her century-and-a-half of service. The generation of technology that had designed and built this aging spaceship had quirks and ideologies quite their own. Thomas was removed enough from them in time to be impressed by their intentions. He had been very pleased to be signed on to tend her engines and solve her problems. Such abstractions had held his attention while the ship toured the Asteroid Belt bartering entertainment files for rare-earth cargoes and life-supplies. The discovery that no one in the rest of the crew warmed to him was disturbing in a distantly irritating way, but Thomas was happier with the engines anyway. They became now his all-consuming obsession.

He liked to make things work. When the lights on the *Ocean* came on again he felt a surge of pure joy. The nanites in his eyes let him see just fine with the dim illumination of Father Sun on his distant left while outside. Inside the ship, the soft warmth of the lights were a sensual thrill novel to Thomas. The deep silence of his condition made the energy of light harmonics poignant, with a Christmas-delight he had never found on Earth.

He repaired the ship's engines. Indeed, Thomas rebuilt them to manual specs and better. The exercise afforded him endless delight. Nanite-enhanced sinew and bone, muscle and skin could do the work now so efficiently that he found himself using his fingers and toes for tasks that before had required steel tools. The changes in him made him feel more like an artist than an engineer, carving a world out of the solid block of broken spaceship under a vast night sky.

The rest of the crew remained frozen in the lounge where they had died. Thomas felt that to be the most appropriate funeral arrangement. He sealed them in behind vacuum hatches so that the airlessness that had killed them would also preserve them. He deliberately refused to think about whatever warm camaraderie had filled their last moment, innocent of the swift bullet that had been shot at them a billion years ago. He nodded his head in vague acknowledgment of them each time that he passed those sealed hatches. They were as much company now, really, as they had ever been. He would still have to share profits from the salvaged cargo with their families.

Somehow he managed to keep persuading himself that he had things to do that were more urgent than repairing the radio. There was a Coast Guard, even out here among the Asteroids, and there was a code of honor among spacemen that meant any passing ship would come to his rescue if he signaled. His desperate race to seal the leaking hull before the oxygen ran out had been his first excuse. After that, he had no real impulse to admit to the Solar System at large that he had failed to help his crew or, at the very least, had failed to die with them. He told himself that he would repair the damage, get the engines fired up, and take her home to Mandelbrot Station. That was his plan. He could explain when he got there.

Eventually, because it was there, he repaired the radio. He just did not turn it on.

Thomas did not restart the ship's chronometer either, even though the computer complained about that every time he used it for anything. The computer kept its own internal count of seconds passed and grumbled at him. Thomas did not want to know. Out here under the stars there were no days, no hours, no swift passage of time. He found a peace that surpassed any other need. He wondered to himself, finally, if he would ever start the clock again. He still thought he had this plan, a place to go when he was ready, but he continued to groom his ship, spiraling around the globe shape of her hull in a pattern that was, in its own way, a dance to the music of his blood pounding in his silent ears.

The *Ocean* carried a valuable cargo which made her valuable salvage to anyone who noticed her regular globe shape drifting in space among irregularly shaped asteroids, silent and unresponsive. Without the radio powered-on, Thomas had no advance warning that she had been noticed. He left no trace of himself in the ship, so they had no warning that he was onboard.

With his new spidery senses, he felt the resounding reverberation in the ship's hull of the invaders docking with the *Ocean's* airlock, but he did not want to believe they had come. Thomas crawled around the ship to see. The invader was a newer, sleeker craft, much smaller and of aerodynamic design for planetfall. *The Grail Opener* was blazoned proudly on her hull. *Of No Specific Ocean* was not an atmospheric ship. She had been built in deep space and intended only for that. Her cargo was always transferred to market by ships like this one, independent traders who stopped at ports around the Solar System, collecting things. The System was busy with such ships.

Thomas was appalled, realizing that they were about to collect his precious *Ocean*, his world, and take it away from him. As sole survivor he had first salvage rights. He had, however, smoothed and repaired the ship thoroughly. He felt a sudden fear that he would not be able to prove that he had not murdered those men himself.

He had kept the guilt of having survived pushed away. Now the sight of that invading ship broke open such deeply suppressed emotion that Thomas was wracked with the desperate urgency of tears he could not shed, a dry and heavy pain. His nanite rescuers would not let him cry. He had no voice, no breath to scream. He just clung there, staring at that awful invader, quivering with shame because he had lived.

"There's a vacuum behind that hatch, sir. Opening it will require a portable airlock."

Captain Stubbs clicked on his radio-link to *The Grail Opener*. "Rollins, can you pick up anything on scanners about a vacuum-sealed chamber in the crew section?"

There was a pause, then the reply from Bubba Rollins, the communications officer back onboard the *Grail*. "Plug me into the nearest com board, Captain," Rollins said. "I've picked up energy readings from the solar panels. She should have com-power, and we can get some answers directly."

"Only the answers that were put into the computer," Allen said.

Both his partners ignored the remark. It was an old grumble, brought out at any opportunity.

Captain Stubbs looked around for a computer panel input. The two men had to search for a few minutes.

"Got it," Stubbs said into his link finally. "You're plugged in now. Read anything?"

"Talk among yourselves," Rollins said to them in the link. "I'll need a minute or two for this. She's an old ship, with old protocols."

Her next response was a surprise. "Wow! Her internal systems are completely go and powered. She's just . . . turned off."

The two men looked around with a new respect for their find.

"What about that chamber?"

"Hold on," she radioed back. "I'll see if there are any security cameras online in there."

"Good thinking, Rollins," Captain Stubbs said.

"Here it comes. You got a monitor screen handy where you are?"

"Yes, ma'am," Allen answered.

"I've routed it in. Just watch."

Monitor showed six bodies floating in serene, frozen grace, limbs a loose tangle. The one face they could see from this camera view looked surprised, and very dead.

"Sudden decompression," Allen said. He pointed to a spot on the monitor with a thick finger. "You can see the blast hole just there. It was patched from the other side of the wall, but it was left as is on the inside."

"Patched by whom?" the Captain asked.

"There must be someone onboard."

"There was no answer to the radio hail, and she's drifting with her engines off."

"But the corridor lights are on."

"Perhaps we better search her more carefully."

The Captain looked around as though the silent ship herself would give him a clue. "The Coast Guard reported that it's been nine years since this ship signed in anywhere," he said thoughtfully. "A lot can happen to survivors in nine years. But if the ship works, why didn't they radio anyone?"

Thomas clung to the outside of the ship, trying to keep himself wedged in the narrow space between duct outlets, trying to be invisible, showing only as a shiny piece of the ship, vaguely man-shaped, reflecting the darkness. He prayed they would go away, even though he knew they would not. *Of No Specific Ocean* was just too good a find. He refused to let himself think that by hiding out here on the hull he was abandoning her to these invaders, literally giving them salvage rights to her. All he could think was that he wanted them to go away.

"There was a serious break in systems protocol just about nine years ago," Allen read off from the coded data streaming past on the screen. "That was when the last log entry was made by anyone. After that, it's just maintenance access, commands for systems testing, routine stuff, randomly but steadily. Somebody has accessed the computer within the last month, though."

Captain Stubbs was not comfortable with that. "What was that last log entry, nine years ago?"

Allen called it up. The monitor flickered, and a man's face appeared, backgrounded by the familiar setting of a spacesuit locker. "Thomas Dewar, Engineer First Class, commencing standard testing for spacesuit maintenance. Sixteen hundred thirty hours, May,"—the man paused, and shrugged—"May, whatever. The computer will tell you the date." The log clicked off.

"May twenty-fourth," Allen read off.

"The last reported communication from this ship was a month before that."

"And in all that time, no one looked for her?" Allen was young, much younger than the Captain.

"It's a big Universe out there," Captain Stubbs said. "With a lot of places."

"I've run the manifest," Rollins reported from the *Grail*. "She's got a hold full of premium-grade rare earths. This is quite a nice piece of salvage."

Captain Stubbs shook his head, gazing around at the silent *Ocean* as though she would tell him something. "No, until we find out what happened here, this is a mystery, not a salvage. There are six dead men in that room, and we have no idea what killed them."

"A locked-room mystery!" Bubba Rollins exclaimed. "How charming." She was a romantic. "Look for burnt string marks!" she added with a chuckle.

"There were seven crewmen listed," Allen said. "Computer records stopped simultaneously at about eighteen hundred fifty hours on the same day as the engineer's last log. Maybe he was in a suit while the rest of the crew was in the lounge."

"Maybe he put a suit on, killed those men and left in a lifeboat," Rollins suggested. "Some kind of crime of passion."

Stubbs turned to Allen. "How many lifeboats does she list onboard?"

Allen asked the computer, and read through the answer carefully. "The computer says that they are all onboard, but I'll go around and run a hands-on check to be sure it wasn't just told to say that."

Stubbs agreed. Gregory Allen's skepticism and demand for evidence had saved their lives more than once. The Captain was willing to be patient with it.

"I'll use the security monitors to try to get images of the faces of those men in there, Captain," Rollins reported in, "and compare those with ship's records."

"Good. That's a good place to start."

"Should I check if her engines are available to go back online?"

"Yes, and if they're sound we should fire them up. Whatever is decided about her, it's time for this ship to go home."

When the engines started up, Thomas thought he was dying. The vibration of the nuclear fires rumbling awake swept through the structure of the ship like shudders of pain. The serene stillness of his world was shattered by the thundering power that he had hoarded for so long, cold and silent hanging against the stars.

The invaders set her to spinning first, returning the layers of centrifugal gravity that her interior had been designed to accommodate. He was outside hiding from them. Once he had recovered, he crawled frantically to a small cargo hatch that he had modified for ease of exit and entry. Despite his nanite-structured strength, he had not felt his own weight in years. The ship was trying to crush him, to drown him in his own flesh.

He stopped for a moment when he found himself at the patched section of wall outside the lounge. The airlock portal he had put over it so long ago in a moment of horror that seemed no more remote than yesterday. He could not cry. He could not stay here. He stumbled and crawled, flinging himself into stairwells with reckless haste, rushing for the central portions of the ship where the centrifugal force was weakest. He clung to the wall there with the clawed hooks of his nanite-molded hands, a man-shaped mirror reflecting in rippled curves. His face looked human, but not his eyes.

"Have you confirmed the identity of the six dead men in the lounge?"

"Five of them. The sixth is wedged headfirst into a corner of some furniture, so we can't make out the features from any angle that we have on the cameras, but Dewar isn't one of the five we did identify."

"And all lifeboats were onboard?"

"Onboard and in good shape."

"So where's the seventh man?"

His hearing no longer really worked, muffled by the impervious shell that protected him. The same flexibility that let him move brought a dim reverberation of sound to his eardrum, yet he had never bothered to listen for anything in the dead ship. His reliance on that sense was rusty. He caught sight of their headmount lights flashing in the corridor ahead of him before he heard anything.

Thomas swung himself up to the air-duct tubing overhead and forced himself into a high corner, with the curve of the duct concealing him. To their lights, he was just a bit of shiny equipment.

He watched in horror as they went past.

His heart was pounding so hard that his nanite hordes were almost undone. His ears sang a thin noise of distress, and lights sparkled darkly in his vision. He needed to breathe. He needed so much to breathe! Thomas hung in the dark corner, willing his thundering heart to calm, willing the screaming need for air to pass. The demand for oxygen was too much for the carefully maintained ecology of his inner world. He slipped away into a red-tinged darkness where voices shouted wordless commands.

"There!"

Rollins froze the monitor view, then ran it back a few frames until the gleaming figure was centered. They had caught him. "I first thought Mr. Allen had been drinking when he said he saw a shiny ghost, but then I thought about it."

Stubbs chuckled. "Allen seeing ghosts? You're right."

"That's when I did a full sweep on the ship's security monitors. I had been working on the assumption that this survivor would want to be found."

"Well done," the Captain said. He was leaning close to the monitor, trying to focus on the face behind the shining mask. "My God!" he exclaimed. "Is that an alien?"

"One guess is as good as another."

"What have we found here, hon?" Captain Stubbs was moved enough to drop work-protocol.

"An abandoned spaceship full of valuable ore," Bubba Rollins replied earnestly. "A locked room full of dead men. A missing crewman. A shiny ghost. An alien, maybe."

The Captain looked down at her, smiling fondly. "You are enjoying this, aren't you?"

"Oh, my Captain, my Captain! If you only knew."

They were hunting for him now. The vibration of the ship's drive was a steady agony in his hardened bones. Thomas's plan was gone, all pretense of his intentions to return to home base, to Mandelbrot Station, evaporated in the heat and light of these strangers invading his world. As the atmosphere in the ship grew denser, his outer nanite layers began corroding. They were designed to deal with a lack of oxygen. Chemical realities were closing down Thomas's choices. There was too much centrifugal pull out on the hull for him to endure, and inside the ship, his shiny outer self was turning opaque.

Thomas crawled through the corridors, clinging to the wall and sliding along it both for support and guidance. His eyes were losing the fight against the oxygen, and his spirit was losing the fight against guilt and confusion. He worked his way toward engineering on instinct.

"Nanites?" Stubbs sounded surprised, but he knew Gregory Allen could find interesting answers in the strangest places. "You think nanites did this?"

"Well, not the part about killing those men in there, but maybe that's what happened to the seventh man. I found references in their emergency procedures manual to a 'rescue pill.' Everyone onboard was required to carry one on their person at all times, but I found six of them, all in individual cabins, left in drawers or shirt-pockets."

"Was there one in Dewar's cabin?"

"No, and his was the easiest to search. There wasn't much in there. He was very tidy."

"I've never heard of rescue nanites doing anything like this," Stubbs said in protest. "Rescue nanites are supposed to provide elemental stasis, enclosing the body in a vacuum-proofed suspended-animation field. We should have found him hibernating in an airtight cocoon."

"There was a brochure down in engineering." Allen took a shiny piece of folded paper from a jacket pocket and held it out to the Captain. Its edges were worn, and the folds almost broken, as though it had been opened and closed often, handled and read a lot. "It looks like a genuine Nanosity Institute issue product, but I never heard of a rescue pill that would do,"—he gestured to the gleaming figure in the screen—"do that. But then I noticed the NanoCity Mall location where it claims the rescue kit was purchased."

He showed the Captain the address on the brochure.

"Auckland, New Zealand," the Captain read. He shrugged. "So? This is an old ship."

"Nanosity Institute was banned from Earth more than two-hundred years ago."

"Oh, of course." The Captain nodded. "The last Nanite Wars."

"Yes, sir."

"So you think this engineer got himself a black market rescue pill, and it did that to him?" he gestured to the image frozen on the screen.

"It's a logical scenario for me."

"He doesn't really look human anymore." Captain Stubbs stood up from the console, straightening his heavy deck jacket to settle it more comfortably on his shoulders. They had the ship's life support, power and lights up, but it was a big ship. It was still cold inside. They did not need spacesuits anymore, just warm clothes. "Whoever—whatever—that is, I don't want him harmed."

"What if he is the one who killed those men in the lounge?" Allen mused. "That would explain why he's trying to hide from us, why he never took this ship home."

"Killed them and then buried himself alive with them out here in space?" Captain Stubbs shook his head. "That would be insane, genuinely insane. Black market nanites are explanation enough for me."

There was a man seated at the control console, leaning over the input panel and studying a monitor image. Thomas could not see it, but the monitor image was of himself. The security cameras had shown his approach. The man stood up when Thomas stumbled into the room. He spoke. Thomas could not hear words, only the jagged ridges of sound striking him. He flinched, and staggered to the console. The man let him, stepping back out of his way.

One word of input to the computer was needed to release him. One password that would start a program to send a "cease and regroup" signal to his nanites—the "rescue" from the rescue pill. Thomas fell into the seat before the console and reached out to tap in the word of release.

His clawed fingers froze above the panel. What would it be like to be human again? Would it be worth it just for the sake of going on? Thomas, despite his confusion, had no death wish. He looked down at his hands and noticed for the first time that, during all those years, the nanites had preserved the grime under his fingernails.

Thomas punched in the command, and closed his eyes. He did not want to see the change this time, hating desperately the need for it.

When Thomas awoke he was human again, fragile and small and soft. The world around him was an assault of sounds and smells. Thomas had forgotten smells, forgotten them utterly in the space-dark brilliance of the sky above his *Ocean*. He lay still, keeping his eyes closed. The sounds and smells battered at him, reminding him of his lost humanity. There was a conversation, distant and intermittent. He tried to listen, feeling a curious hunger for words.

He was lying flat on his back on something comfortable. Lying here still, listening and smelling, seemed a gentle enough way of returning. It was such a joy just to feel himself breathing, the steady, comforting rhythm of life returned to him.

He slept.

Thomas was surprised to realize that he recognized his own smell. "I stink, therefore I am."

Captain Stubbs chuckled. "That's a good beginning." He stood over the bed in sickbay, looking down at Dewar. "You've had quite an adventure, Mr. Dewar."

"I didn't kill those men," Thomas said softly. Speaking was such a novelty, as though listening to someone else use his voice. "It's not my fault."

"What's not your fault?" Captain Stubbs asked. He kept his face pleasant.

"That I lived. It's not my fault that I lived, and they all died." There had been no way to cry before, and now he had no strength for tears. He sighed, tilting his head back so that he could see the Captain's face more clearly. "But I didn't kill them."

The Captain pulled up a chair and sat down beside him so that they could talk eye to eye. "You want to tell me what happened, Mr. Dewar?"

Thomas told him, in careful detail.

He was quite bewildered when Captain Stubbs said that it had happened nine years ago. "It's as if it were just a moment ago," Thomas said. "It has always been as though it just happened."

"That will change when you get home." The Captain was trying to be kind.

"Perhaps."

"You'll be very wealthy when you get home. You have first salvage rights, as sole survivor."

"She's not salvage," Thomas protested. "She's in good shape."

"She's in terrific shape," Captain Stubbs said. "I wish my own ship were as well maintained. You have put my crew to shame."

"You can have the cargo," Thomas said impulsively. "Just let me go."

Captain Stubbs was dismayed. "We're not pirates, Thomas. This is your ship and cargo by rights. You've certainly earned her."

Thomas closed his eyes and fell back into his pillows. "I'm sorry," he whispered. "I didn't mean . . . "

"You've been alone here a long time, Thomas," the Captain said. "I know what you mean."

"I'm afraid to go home." Dewar's voice was barely audible.

"I know," the Captain said. "But you've been alone a long time. Be patient."

On the shelf beside his sickbay bed was a saucer with a napkin folded across it, and on that fold of cloth lay the black pill that Thomas had swallowed so long ago. His nanites had neatly repacked themselves, awaiting the next time he swallowed them. The cracked and aging brochure was there as well, tucked under the saucer. Thomas did not need to read the brochure. He had memorized it long ago. When he woke from nightmares of dead men floating, he would turn on the light and look at that black pill, as though somehow it focused the reality of what he had endured.

Thomas was their mascot, their prize find, their pet. He was too wrapped up in grief and bewildered by his own humanity to see himself yet as their new-found friend, but they were young and he amused them, so he allowed them to spend time with him. They were certainly in awe of his freighter. Stubbs's crew had been hired because of their passion for machine-toys, and *Of No Specific Ocean* was a spaceship from a classic era. Thomas knew everything about the peculiar and now little-known technology of the *Ocean*. To his delight, they were willing, indeed eager, to listen to him tell the history of this or that bit of the engine, or explain the intricacies of design he had learned by crawling centimeter by centimeter over her, through her, making her perfect. It was more difficult with human hands. He had to let them show him how to use some tools again that he had set aside and forgotten and now needed. Even that seemed a pleasant return to life.

He went out in an ordinary spacesuit once, to look. He found he could no longer see the sky, just the black emptiness of space. It made him cold. He went back inside feeling the lost nine years as though they had rushed through him all in a moment, time catching up to him at once, leaving him old. He knew there was a starry, dark enfolding sky out there, horizonless, endless and open, but he had traded sight of it now for the warm, round horizon of a human world.

Captain Lawrence Stubbs had grown up on spaceships. He wore his deck fatigues with the natural elegance of a tuxedo, and was always calm. Thomas was in awe of him, and longed for his calm. The spaceship was stocked with plenty of fast-food supplies, but Stubbs enjoyed cooking, and made an experience of eating. His delight was a powerful incentive for Thomas to overcome the revulsion of the experience. Without the Captain's good-natured encouragement, food made Thomas long to crawl back into the skin of his nanite rescuers again. For his sake, Thomas accepted the weaknesses of the flesh, enjoying the drawn-out delights of supplying himself with things his nanites used to provide automatically.

Bubba Rollins was communications officer and trade agent for *The Grail Opener*. It was her job to sweet-talk merchants and dealers to trade with the Grail when she was in port. Bubba had thick red curls that reminded Thomas constantly of the loops of magnetic prominence soaring up in golden glory from the surface of the Sun. She made him stutter when he talked to her, but when he lay trying to fall asleep, Thomas would think about her wild red hair, lingering in the memory of her smile as she talked. "You'll make us all rich, Thomas," she kept telling him. "Just let me handle this, and I'll make us rich with what you brought us." After the long silences of the last years, Thomas found himself astonishingly eager to let Bubba handle things for him.

Gregory Allen talked to Thomas the most, talking to him as though taking up a conversation they had put down only a moment ago, as though he remembered Thomas's place in it, fitting him in as though he had always been there. Thomas could not comprehend how he did that, but it worked. Gregory needed no explanations. He and Thomas finished each other's sentences, and laughed when one got too far ahead of the other.

Thomas was surprised to learn how much of the *Ocean*'s technology had become obsolete and forgotten in the last decade, and how different the *Grail* was. She seemed such a perfect companion to the *Ocean*. A seed of hope planted itself in Thomas's dazzled mind. These new names, these new faces, these new persons touching his life comprised the litany by which Thomas chanted himself to sleep. It could not, however, erase dreams of dead men meeting him around corners, rising up in the starry sky to look down at him in pained silence. They could not answer the simple question: why was he still alive?

The man from Nanosity Institute called them as soon as they had docked at Mandelbrot Station. Bubba Rollins's reports had gone ahead of them. She had known exactly the right person to talk to about possible black market nanites. Thomas had insisted on meeting the man from Nanosity somewhere he could see the stars clearly through the space station dome. He chose a quiet but well-known café on Mandelbrot's main boulevard.

The aromas of pastry and coffees were a heady brew to Dewar's scent-starved soul, and he nearly cried as he sat waiting.

"Caron Ming Wa." The man from Nanosity introduced himself with a smooth, graceful bow.

He was expensively dressed and sleek. His long black hair was drawn tightly into a braid down his back, and the silver jewelry on his hands flashed in the dock lights, reminding Thomas of starlight sparking from his own fingers. "It is a pleasure to meet you, Mr. Dewar. We are quite relieved that you survived."

Thomas liked him at once, in spite of himself and his sense of guilt. "It's not against the law not to die," he said, glaring at his fingers with sullen heat. Captain Stubbs had explained this often to Thomas during their long flight to Mandelbrot Station, but Thomas clung stubbornly to his sense of guilt.

The man from Nanosity was not dismayed by Thomas's confusion. He leaned close across the table. "I do not represent the law," Ming Wa said carefully. "I represent Nanosity Institute." He smiled into Thomas's eyes with so professional a smile that Thomas felt as though he had just been bought, and was about to be gift-wrapped. "We are prepared to pay top dollar for studying the black market nanite system which you used during the *Of No Specific Ocean*'s unfortunate mishap."

Thomas sat staring at the man, trying to fit the events onboard the Ocean into the phrase "unfortunate mishap."

"But I want to keep it," he said. Thomas's voice sounded thin. He was afraid, but he had to keep the fear distant. "I might need it again. Disasters happen out there."

The warmth of Ming Wa's smile was perfect. He gazed into Thomas's eyes with child-simple delight as though Thomas had given him exactly the answer he had hoped for. "Of course, Mr. Dewar. You are, indeed, the only human contact we have with such a prolonged experience of this particular, independently produced nanite system—your assistance in developing this product for Nanosity will be completely invaluable. We are prepared to meet any price, Mr. Dewar. You can name your conditions."

"Can't you find the people who developed them, and make them help you?"

"This is a unique black-market product, Mr. Dewar. The nanites themselves are standard issue, but their programming is unique. Indeed, Nanosity Institute would pay anything to find the man who created the program that kept you alive. Now that we know about this, a System-wide search is underway, but, like the ship herself, the rescue pills were quite old. The designer's likely dead by now."

"There were six other rescue pills," he said desperately. "Take them. Don't take mine."

"Those will be most thoroughly tested, Mr. Dewar, but you must realize that you have had experience like no other with this new form of nanite programming. Your experience is, quite literally, invaluable." Ming Wa patted Thomas's hand. "We have no manual on their use. To all extents and purposes, Mr. Dewar, you are the sole owner of this nanite program. That makes you very valuable to Nanosity Institute."

"Will Nanosity let me keep mine, so that I will be safe out there?" Thomas whispered.

Ming Wa laughed with delight. "Mr. Dewar, don't you realize that you will be pulling in a considerable salary as primary consultant in this project, a salary that will make you wealthy beyond your dreams in a matter of hours? You will be paid to show us what the nanites do to you. You are the only person who will use those nanites until we know how they work. You own the nanites, Mr. Dewar. We only want their programming, their effect. You can give that to us without giving away anything."

The *Grail*'s crew were used to their own quarters, and felt the *Ocean* was a little too haunted for comfortable living. Her engines and her cargo hold were what mattered, so returning Thomas's weightless world was not a problem. They stopped the centrifugal spin so that he could cling to her skin, staring outward.

Linked together, the two ships were now a wealthy company—"Grail-Oceanic Transport." They even had a letterhead. The crew could afford to be comfortable where they were. From his perch on the curve of the *Ocean*'s hull Thomas could see the nose-tip antennae of the *Grail* parked at the airlock. The rumble of the drive engines trembled in his bones, but the dead had been sent on to the peace of deeper graves. Thomas was no longer drifting.

The utter confusion of deep space had resolved into the night sky patterns that he had meditated on so intently for so long. Now he knew that he was one of the first to see them with such eyes. He had never thought he would get to be "the first" of anything. It was a big Universe out there. He wondered often about the lost genius who had created the nanite programming. Had he seen with such eyes?

Thomas's fingernails were clean, carefully manicured. Starlight reflecting from his shiny hands and arms made him want to cry with joy, although now he understood why he could not. He made a mental note to tell Nanosity how important it was to be able to cry.

A SUN TO ME

LANCE DIXON

I asked Harry once what the difference was between a sun and a star.

He told me, with his Mona Lisa smile, "It's a matter of distance and thus familiarity. There are countless stars of various magnitudes, but it's the one in your neighborhood, that seems biggest and brightest, that gives you the most warmth: that is your Sun."

Harry was a sun to me.

During this eclipse of his passing I can look directly at his brilliance and not be blinded. I can see the corona of his soul, the flares of his influence on so many people, and even the occasional spot of human imperfection.

During this temporary shadow—eclipses and death are only temporary—I will take solace in the fact that history will set Harry amongst the stars, but for us lucky few, he will never be a cold distant light but forever a brilliant warming sun.

PART TWO

HAL'S SYSTEM

Not everyone could claim Hal Clement as a sun, but many did feel a strong attractive tug from Clement's Star. (To any astronomers with naming privileges: consider that a hint.) Combinations of professional respect and personal affinity brought him close to a wide array of fellow writers, and fellow fans. The tributes included here are but a modest cross-section, with no pretense to being exhaustive. They will show clearly, though, the esteem he earned across the ranks of science fiction: as a writer, a colleague, a fan, a friend. They are part of the system of admirers he drew throughout his life.

We begin this section with a remembrance from Ben Bova, whose career as a novelist, multiple Hugo-winning editor, and anthologist speaks for itself. This is a reprint from the Readercon program book in 2003, when Hal Clement was still alive, which is why Bova speaks of Hal in the present tense. Sentimental as it may be, I am glad to have something in this book saying "Hal Clement *is*." It still seems the proper state of affairs.

HAL CLEMENT

BEN BOVA

Multiple-choice question:

Hal Clement is:

> (a). The dean of "hard" science fiction writers.
> (b). A great teacher.
> (c). One of the finest gentlemen of our time.
> (d). An enthusiastic convention-goer.

And the answer is . . . (e) all of the above.

Those who know Hal Clement only through the stories he's written would undoubtedly pick (a); the really observant ones would add (b), as well, because virtually every one of the stories and novels that Hal has written offer wonderful lessons in planetary physics, chemistry, astronomy, and exobiology.

Anyone who's had the pleasure of attending one of the many science fiction conventions that Hal Clement frequents would certainly answer (c) and (d), even without knowing anything else about him. He is a cheerful and helpful guest at many cons, and always an asset to a panel discussion.

At heart Hal Clement is a teacher—the kind of teacher that you wish you had been favored with in high school. His real name is Harry Clement Stubbs, and he actually spent much of his adult life teaching science at Milton Academy, a private secondary school in Massachusetts. Lucky students! With his easy smile and pleasant demeanor, Hal puts you at ease even when he's discussing arcane subjects such as orbital dynamics or the high-pressure chemistry of volatile compounds. He has the gift for making science come alive, the knack for showing how truly variegated and wonder-full this universe can be.

I'm not saying that Hal writes his stories for the purpose of teaching science; the teaching (and learning, on the part of the reader) are just wonderful bonuses to the enjoyment of his work. Since his first short story, "Proof," was published in *Astounding Science Fiction* magazine in 1942, Hal has continuously amazed and enlightened us with good, strong, solid stories that deal with real science in strange, exotic and alien settings. His novels, such as *Needle, Iceworld, Mission of Gravity* and *Close to Critical* have become classics in the science fiction field.

It's not strange that writing science fiction and teaching science are so intertwined in him. After all, Hugo Gernsback, the founder of the world's first science fiction magazine, *Amazing Stories*, saw science fiction as a way of teaching science to youngsters in an era where most teenagers did not finish grade school. Today, of course, almost every American youngster graduates high school and most go on to college—but they can still learn more about science from Hal Clement's stories than they are taught in their classrooms. And enjoy it far more!

I remember my own first readings of his early novels, and how they opened my eyes to the strange and beautiful possibilities of other worlds in space. To me, science fiction was a far better "classroom" than regular school classes, particularly because good science fiction stories—such as Hal Clement's—skipped all the boring fundamentals and showed how exhilarating science can be when you're out in the wild and wonderful universe. With that kind of excitement for a spur, going back and learning the fundamentals was easy. Motivation is the key.

Today, "hard" science fiction has fallen somewhat out of popular favor. There is the mistaken idea that science-based stories can't be interesting or exciting. Undoubtedly such a wrong-headed notion was born in the impoverished minds of people who never had the benefit of attending any of Hal's classes or reading his marvelous stories.

Einstein once said that the most incredible thing about the universe is that it is *understandable*. Hal Clement's fiction is a monument to that fundamental idea: the human mind can understand strange alien worlds and even strange alien creatures. That is the underlying message of Hal Clement's work. It is the same rock-bottom optimistic faith that makes science work: we can understand anything, given enough time and effort.

Hal Clement's fiction is usually based on a "thought experiment": that is, he creates stories to dramatize scientific ideas. What would it be like to be on a truly massive planet, where the gravity is ten or a hundred times heavier than here on Earth? How can you navigate by the stars when you're on the Moon, when the Moon's north pole does not point to the North Star? How can an alien from a world that is literally hotter than hell survive on an "Iceworld" such as Earth?

The word "gentleman" might have been coined for Hal. He is a truly kind and gentle person who gives unsparingly of his time and energy at science fiction conventions—when he's not writing or painting. Oh yes, he is a gifted painter, as well. For his artwork he uses still another name, George Richard. He could illustrate his own stories, and who better?

I was enjoying Hal Clement's fiction years before I met him, and found myself entranced at his depictions of strange and exotic creatures and even stranger and more exotic worlds—all carefully based on known physics and chemistry. I was captivated by his work. This is what *science* fiction is all about! Today, nearly six decades after his first stories saw print, he is still producing quality work, still showing how accurate science and an insightful imagination can combine to yield stories that stir that ol' sense of wonder.

Although his first fiction was published while he was still an undergraduate student at Harvard, World War II interrupted Hal's career. During the war years Hal flew a B-24 bomber as the U.S. Eighth Air Force battled Nazi Germany's Luftwaffe for control of the skies over Europe. He once told me, though, that his most hazardous duty came at the end of the war, when his squadron flew a low-level, tight formation mission over the Netherlands to drop food supplies to the starving Dutch civilian population. His main job on that flight was to watch the wingtip of the plane flying beside his, to make sure they didn't collide.

Years later, when the German city of Heidelberg hosted the World Science Fiction Convention, Hal was recognized and immediately swamped by eager German fans. "Have you ever been to Heidelberg before?" a student asked. Ever the gentleman, Hal replied honestly, "No, but I've been within a few miles of here." In a B-24 loaded with bombs, of course.

A gentleman and a scholar, that's Hal Clement. He is also one of the best science-fiction writers ever to spin a tale of faraway worlds and exotic creatures. Hal Clement is to "hard" science fiction as John Glenn is to space flight, or Fred Astaire is to tap dancing, or John Philip Sousa is to march music, or . . . well, you get the picture.

To put it another way, "Science fiction 'r Hal Clement." And we're all better off for it.

(The Heidelberg anecdote is one that Hal himself debunked, as you shall read later, but I declined to excise it here. It seems to fit his personality, melding a gentle refusal to give offense where none is necessary with a firm adherence to precise facts. The anecdote persuades for the same reason that people believe in Babe Ruth's mythic "called shot": it is the kind of thing he just might have done.)

CONVERSATIONS WITH HAL

ALLEN M. STEELE

Harry Stubbs was a friend of mine, but I never knew him by that name; for me, he was always Hal Clement. A pseudonym, yes, but also a person to whom I'd attached a face, a voice, an identity; whenever I saw him, I called him Hal. I asked him once whether he'd prefer to be addressed by his given name, but he simply shrugged. "Either one works for me," he said, with his usual New England pragmatism. "I answer to both." So I continued to call him Hal . . . except, I think, the last time I saw him.

Like most people in the science fiction scene, I first met Hal through his work. *Mission of Gravity* was among the first handful of SF novels I read when I was a kid. My best friend and I swapped paperbacks back and forth, and so that was one of the books—along with *The Legion of Space* and *I, Robot* and *Fahrenheit 451* and *Needle in a Timestack*—that formed my early reading tastes. So far as I can remember, the first short story of his that I read was probably "Attitude;" I know this because it was in the Gnome Press anthology *Travelers of Space*, which was a book that I checked out of the children's library at my church so often that the librarian eventually complained to my parents that I needed to bring it back so that other kids would get a chance to read it. Many years later, when I finally managed to buy a copy for my own in the dealer's room at a convention, Hal happened to be standing next to me. I told him how *Travelers of Space* had been one of my favorite books when I was a youngster, and he smiled at that, but I don't think either of us noticed that he had a story in that anthology. Or maybe he did, but he was just too humble to point that out.

73

Yet those were literary encounters. The first time I met Hal face-to-face was much more memorable, and one that would shape our relationship for years to come.

In February, 1989, I'd just entered the field; my first two stories had recently appeared in *Isaac Asimov's Science Fiction Magazine*, and my first novel was coming out in November. I was attending Boskone that year, just as I had for the last two or three years before that, yet this time I wasn't another fan or even a novice yearning for his first sale, but a freshly-minted "new writer." So Boskone 27 was going to be my coming-out party, so to speak; my editor was going to be there, and my agent had come up from New Jersey, and Sunday morning we were scheduled to have a breakfast meeting, during which we'd discuss a two-book contract that could potentially bring in more money than I'd earned in a year when I was still a newspaper reporter.

So I was nervous. The pressure was on; Friday night I suffered insomnia and barely slept at all. To make matters worse, someone on the Boskone programming committee decided that it would be a great idea if I moderated a panel. I forget the topic, but there were going to be five writers discussing some subject or another . . . and one of these folks was Hal Clement, a guy who'd been writing SF long before I was born. In a perfect universe, Hal would have been the moderator and I would have been quietly sitting at the end of the table. But Hal disliked being a moderator, so I had the unenviable task of being placed in the catbird seat.

Early Saturday afternoon, I went to the room where the panel was going to be held, overprepared with pages of questions that would never be asked and manic from chugging coffee all morning. I arrived early to find all the other panelists already gathered outside; I knew few of them, and they didn't know me, so I went about introducing myself. Among them is a quiet, grey-haired gent whom I'd never seen before, and suddenly I found myself talking to Hal Clement.

There was something about Hal that put everyone at ease. He was always the smartest guy in the room, but his intelligence was never intimidating. As a writer, he was a contemporary of the grand masters of the genre, yet although I'd already met Asimov and Heinlein and Sturgeon and DeCamp, I didn't find myself tongue-tied in his presence. When I addressed him as "Dr. Clement," he politely informed me that he didn't have a doctorate, and besides, "Hal" or "Harry" was fine with him.

We got to chatting about something or another, and when the previous panel let out and people started filtering into the room, we continued our conversation as we walked in. We had a good crowd—forty or more people, at least, with my editor among them—but somehow I was less nervous than I'd been a few minutes earlier. I took the middle seat, shuffled my notes, and called the session to order.

It was one of the longest hours of my life. One of the panelists grabbed the mike and wouldn't let go, and there was a heckler in the front row who wanted to demonstrate the depth and width of his brilliance; I couldn't get either of them to shut up. I managed to tough it out, though, but by the time the panel was over I was ready for a short drink and a long nap, or vice-versa. Yet as I was leaving the room, my editor came up to me.

"You did well in there," she said quietly. "And that was an impressive entrance you made."

"Thanks," I replied, and then I did a double-take. "What entrance? What did I do?"

"When you walked in with Hal Clement." She smiled. "Have you known him long? You two looked like you were old friends."

We weren't, or at least not then. That would come in time.

Not long after that first meeting, I moved from New Hampshire to Missouri; my wife had become homesick for St. Louis, and I wanted to be able to visit my own home-town of Nashville a little more frequently. So we bought a house in the suburbs, and when I went to SF conventions, it was most often to ones in the Midwest and the South. I flew back to New England once to attend Boskone 28, and there I did another panel with Hal—"World Building," along with Thomas Easton and David Deitrick—but that was the last one we did together for a very long time.

Yet because Hal traveled farther afield than I did, I saw him fairly frequently. Usually at Worldcons, but also now and then at regional conventions here and there in the Midwest; he'd retired from teaching by then, and had time to attend conventions. When we saw one another, we'd share a few words, make small-talk. He was an acquaintance, someone I always enjoying seeing again, but little more than that.

As the '90s wore on, though, this began to change. In 1997, my wife and I moved back to New England, settling into a small town in western Massachusetts. Now that we lived in the same state, more and more often Hal and I found ourselves in green rooms and hotel lobbies and restaurants, carrying on bull sessions first with others, then just amongst ourselves. Hal usually went to bed early, so he seldom went to room parties, and because he didn't drink I never found him in the hotel bar, but since I was no longer partying quite so much and had become less inclined to hang out in the bar, I found it pleasant to be around someone who wasn't going to fall down drunk in the middle of a conversation. He had a dry wit that was refreshing, and could hold his end of any discussion; for my part, I learned not to cuss in his presence, which was something he disliked and let me know in no uncertain terms. If I behave in a more gentlemanly fashion than I once did, then it's largely due to Hal's benign influence.

Convention committees began to put us on panels together. Shared interests, I imagine; we were both hard-SF writers in a time when the genre was dominated by cyberpunk, steampunk, splatterpunk, elfpunk, whateverpunk. Perhaps I was some sort of punk, too—"spacepunk" never really caught on as a label, for which I'm grateful—but nonetheless we started finding ourselves in the same place at the same time: the brash young turk and the grand old man. I certainly didn't mind, and if Hal did, he never let on.

So there we did "Is Space Fiction Still the Final Frontier" at Rivercon 21 with Diann Thornley and Glen Cook, and "The Cold Worlds: Colonizing the Outer Solar System" at L.A. Con III with Bill Higgins, D.J. Byrne, and Joel C. Sercel, and "Building Strong Characters in Hard SF" at I-Con 17 with Catherine Asaro, and "Science Versus Pseudoscience" at Readercon 10 with James Morrow, Bruce Sterling, and Jeff Hecht, and "Are the Oceans Still Our Future?" at the Millennium Philcon with Joan Slonczewski and Diane Kelly, and "SF's Greatest Generation" at Readercon 15 with Barry Malzberg and Andy Porter, and "SF Archetypes: First Contacts" at Boskone 40 with Jeffery Carver and David Brin . . .

But you know which ones were my favorites? Not the high-profile appearances at Worldcons or the major regionals, but the ones we did at smaller, more low-key conventions. Like the one at Albacon in Schenectady, New York, with Robert Sawyer, Paul Levinson, Catherine Asaro, and Shane Tourtellotte. I can't remember the topic, but it doesn't matter; we couldn't keep on subject, nor maintain a straight face. It was as if someone had infiltrated the air-conditioning system with nitrous oxide, because nothing anyone said came out right, and so after awhile it was just . . . y'know, funny. Believe me, you had to be there.

But I think the best one we did together was at Not-Just-Another-Con 13. NJAC was probably the smallest convention I ever regularly attended; put together by the University of Massachusetts science fiction club, no more than fifty people ever showed up, and half of them were pros and fans from the New England area. Still, it was a good excuse for friends to get together for a weekend: Warren Lapine and Angela Kessler, Bob and Marianne Eggleton, Charlie and Mary Ryan, Ian Strock and Kit Hawkins, Joe and Cindy Lazarro, Rajnar Vajra, Steve Sawicki . . . and Hal, of course, because no convention in the region was too small for him to attend.

(That's something that can't be stressed enough: Hal genuinely enjoyed going to conventions. He didn't show up to push his books—by his own admission, he didn't publish often enough to have to worry about main-taining a career—or to have his ego stroked, and he most certainly wasn't there to get drunk and chase girls. He went because he loved fans, period.)

Anyway, that Friday evening, after we returned from the Chinese restau-rant in Amherst where everyone—and I do mean *everyone*; it was that small of a convention—went out for the traditional NJAC dinner, Hal and I did a talk called "The Space Shuttle and Other Sights." Only two days earlier, I'd returned from Cape Canaveral, where I'd witnessed the night-launch of the shuttle Discovery, courtesy of a friend at the Marshall Space Flight Center who'd arranged for me to receive a guest invitation. This was one of the greatest spectacles I'd ever seen, and so I spent the first half-hour describing what it was like to watch a shuttle lift off from just three miles away.

When I got through, Hal said that this was quite impressive . . . and then he proceeded to tell about how, while he was still in the Army reserves during the early '50s, he'd witnessed an above-ground explosion of an atomic bomb in the Mojave Desert from the vantage point of a trench one mile from ground-zero, and how the X-ray burst from that blast caused him to see the bones of his hands covering his face.

I could never top Hal. His stories were always better than mine.

And so our friendship grew, in that little microcosm of science fiction conventions. I didn't always see him there, of course, nor were our discus-sions limited to panel topics. A couple of times he called me on the phone about this or that. When I was doing research for my novel *Coyote*, I showed him maps of the world I was creating and told him what I was trying to do, and he sent me back to drawing board at least three times because of things I'd overlooked; as his writing students knew, you could learn more about worldbuilding from ten minutes with Hal than you could from ten hours at the library. And we did a symposium, along with several other writers, at Salem State College; afterwards, while we were signing books together, he gave me one of my favorite compliments:

Hal (looking over my shoulder): "You've got one of the worst signa-
tures I've ever seen."

Me (slightly wounded): "Hey, you can read the name, can't you?"

Hal: "Yeah, I can read it. It looks just like John Campbell's . . . and yours
is just as illegible."

I mildly protested that I owned a signed copy of John W. Campbell Jr.'s
Cloak of Aesir, and my autograph was far more legible. But I didn't let him
know that, when he signed my hardcover first-edition of *Mission of Gravity*
that same morning, he misspelled my first name.

As years went by, though, it wasn't hard to see that age was catching up
with him. Although Hal always held his head high, nonetheless he became
stoop-shouldered, and sometimes he had to sit down even though it was
clear that he would have preferred to remain standing. You still knew he
was coming, because you could hear him whistling as he walked down the
hall, and his eyes stayed sharp enough to recognize you from across a
crowed room and give you a wave and a smile; nonetheless by then he was
in his eighties, and time had become the enemy.

Yet it was only his body that was becoming frail. His mind was as sharp
as ever, always ready to analyze another problem, participate in another
discussion, relate another story. Convention committees put him on
schedules that would have knocked cold a man half his age. Once he
showed the list of program events he was doing during a Worldcon, and I
gaped at it; he did more stuff in one day than I did the entire Labor Day
weekend. When I complained that the committee shouldn't be putting him
through this, though, he just smiled. "They want me to talk, so I'll talk," he
said. "So long as I can sit down while I'm doing that, it's not a big deal."

During Readercon 15, in July 2003, he and I joined a small group that
went out to dinner at a Korean restaurant. I sat next to Hal at one end of a
long table, and while we ate he told me about how he'd co-piloted a B-24
Liberator during Operation Market-Garden, one of the legendary combat
missions of World War II; he'd flown into Holland literally at treetop-level,
so close to the ground that he had to dodge a church steeple, and upon
returning to England he'd been forced to land the plane on its belly
because someone on the ground managed to shoot out one of the tires of
his landing gear. It was a great tale, and after we'd left the restaurant, we
stood for a little while in the parking lot while I made him retell it for the
benefit of everyone who hadn't heard him. Hal did so, although a little

reluctantly; he was tired, and all he wanted to do was go back to his room and curl up with the new Harry Potter novel.

Two weeks later, we were at another convention, Confluence 14 in Pittsburgh, where I was Guest of Honor. For the first time in several years, we didn't do a panel together, yet we chatted several times over the weekend, and late Sunday afternoon we sat together at a signing table in the dealer's room, just as we'd sat so many times before. Business was slow; we autographed a few books and chewed the fat about this and that, two pals with nothing else to do except wait to go home. At the end of the hour, I was told that my ride to the airport was ready to go, and so I made ready to leave.

"Well, see you at the next convention," I said. A customary farewell.

"Well, I hope so," he said. "Don't count on it."

That stopped me. "What do you mean?" I said, quietly so that no one would hear us. "Is there something wrong?"

Hal told me that he'd just seen his doctor, and he'd just been given a clean bill of health . . . at least, for someone his age. Yet he admitted that he was getting up in years, and said that he never knew when his body would give out on him. I gently admonished him; I drank and smoked, and he'd never done either, and so it was likely that he was going to outlive me.

"Well, if you say so," he said with a shrug.

"Harry, I'll see you again," I said. "Next convention."

He shrugged again; we shook hands and said goodbye, and then I left. Yet it wasn't until later that I realized that this was probably the first time I'd ever called him Harry, not Hal.

We did see each other one last time: about six weeks later, at Torcon III, in Toronto, Canada. Although we hadn't been scheduled to appear together in any panels or signings, we smiled and waved to one another in passing; it was a Worldcon, though, so we were both kept busy. Yet I had little doubt that we'd get a chance to spend time again, if not at this convention then at another, somewhere down the road.

Columbus Day weekend rolled around, and I was invited to attend Albacon once again. Hal was going to be there, as always, but by then I was trying to kick-start a new novel, so I couldn't make it. He had just published a new novel of his own, *Noise*. I'd begun reading it, so I regretted not being able to go to Albacon so I could tell him what a great story it was. I figured that I could wait until the next Boskone.

A few days after Albacon, the phone rang: it was Warren Lapine, our mutual friend and editor, calling to tell me that Hal had passed away in his sleep the night before.

I couldn't finish talking to Warren. I put down the phone and broke down.

Three days later, my wife and I drove to Milton and attended his memorial services. Harry Stubbs didn't leave our world alone: the chapel was packed, with many standing in the back. His family was there, of course, and for the first time I met his children and grandson. There were former students from Milton Academy, where he'd taught for many years, and friends from the Episcopal Church with whom he'd traveled to Europe. And, of course, there were many us who'd known him as Hal Clement.

I miss him very much. Yet, as with anyone whom I've had the honor and pleasure of having known, I'd far rather suffer the loss of his company than to never have met him at all.

Allen M. Steele is a two-time Hugo winner for the novellas "The Death of Captain Future" and " . . . Where Angels Fear to Tread." His novels include the current Coyote *series, also featured in a series of stories in* Asimov's *magazine.*

EXTENDED WARRANTY

WALTER H. HUNT

The following story takes place some time before the events of my first novel, *The Dark Wing*. The idea came to me recently when I engaged in that most feral of transactions in interstellar commerce: buying a new car. The rest of the story came together with the help of our distinguished editor.

I'm honored to have the opportunity to include my first short story in a collection to honor the late Hal Clement. Harry was a gentleman - and a gentle man: a writer, a teacher, and a colleague. I did not know him long enough to consider him a friend, but his honesty and integrity were a beacon dispensing light to everyone around him. It seems only fair that his name be remembered.

#

I've learned two particularly important lessons in my life. First, history turns on small, usually improbable things—the sorts of events that aren't predicted or expected; and second, history is not only written by the winners, it's written by the winning *politicians*. There's generally very little room given to the efforts of civilians, particularly scientists.

But when it came to human exploration of interstellar space, it most certainly turned on a small, improbable thing—and a scientist rightly gets the credit. I was the scientist: Lee Corning, now spending my declining years as Professor Emeritus, Department of Physics, University of New Chicago.

Everyone knows the story of how the rashk came to Sol System and sold us jump technology and how *Clement* became the first successful human vessel to jump to another star and return to tell about it; but most of the details are written out by politicians taking the credit.

Here's how it *really* happened. If you want it confirmed, ask S's'i'i Kra'tok; he'll tell you the same story.

When they first reached Sol System the rashk were in their first few decades of interstellar travel. They lurked in the outer system for several months listening to our comm traffic and learning something of our language and culture. Finally they began to build a base on Triton, which is how we found them: the Hawking orbital telescope picked out surface activity that shouldn't have been there. Close observation confirmed it: first contact, for the first time.

Both the European Union and Greater China launched probes to go out and take a closer look. Before they even reached turnover, however, the rashk sent a small unarmed ship into the inner system with three trained diplomats aboard. Based on what we later learned of them, this was almost beyond the upper limit of their bravery. The probes picked them up just outside Mars orbit. Fortunately, before any missiles could be launched from any of the Mars orbital stations, they sent a comm message requesting diplomatic contact with representatives of the three most powerful governments of Earth, informing us—in English, Chinese, Russian and three other human languages—that they inhabited the Vega System, a bit over eight parsecs away. They didn't ask for one government and not for every one; just three. As it happened, that was a particularly important number for them.

At first we didn't believe that they'd come from Vega. Alpha Lyrae is a bright Class A star, probably no more than half a billion years old—and that's too damn young for a habitable planet to have formed and life, especially intelligent life, to have evolved. But that was their story and they stuck to it: Vega was where the rashk "emerged from the Three," an ambiguous statement if ever there was one, and that might have meant just about anything. (Later, when humans visited Vega System and found three habitable planets in the same orbital located exactly one-third of its circumference apart, we were pretty much convinced that the worlds had been placed that way, and they'd been seeded there sometime in rashk prehistory. Score one for the smart monkeys.)

After considerable debate in the UN General Assembly, the North American Union, the African Federation, and Greater China were chosen to represent the Earth for the first contact. Several other nations, including the EU, Brazil, India, and others—all of whom felt that they'd been screwed by the UN by being left out of the negotiations—disobeyed a direct resolution of the Assembly and sent their own private messages to the rashk delegates, adding to the confusion.

A hastily-erected enviro bubble on the surface of Deimos served as the meeting place with the rashk delegates. There were no human scientists present: just a single high-ranking diplomat from each of the distrustful human governments. They arrived in separate ships and arrived at about the same time.

The rashk arrived after all three humans. There were three of them, and the representatives of the Earth governments had all they could do not to gape. The aliens were a meter and three-quarters tall, massing close to a hundred fifty kilos each; they had three eyes and six limbs—two legs and two pairs of arms—and were reptilian. They were dressed in what looked like long bathrobes in the most hideous colors imaginable—bright orange, brilliant purple, and a sort of streaky yellow; it turned out that they were hydrating suits to keep their skins from drying out. It didn't speak much about their fashion sense.

"Glad we are," said the orange-robed one, "here with you, speakings to have." He spoke in perfect unaccented English, though the syntax was tortured.

One of the three humans spoke. "We are glad to be here also. I am Charles Mbele of the African Federation. On behalf of my colleagues, Mr. Li Tsao of Greater China and Ms. Caroline Addison of the North American Union—" he gestured to each—"we welcome you to our solar system."

"Peace and goodwill for you have we. S's'i'i Kra'tok am I, with also E'e's's Bna'tal and F'f'n'a Bna'tal. Here to you an offer to make come have we."

It took a moment for the humans to untangle the word order—part of the gentle charm of carrying on conversations with them.

"An offer?" Addison said at last. "What sort of offer?"

"Your solar system toward us is moving, slowly however; the process to speed up come have we, ha ha ha," S's'i'i answered, ending his sentence with three sharp coughs. The other two began to move their pairs of arms in some sort of pattern.

"I'm afraid I don't understand—" Addison began.

Li held up his hand.

"The solar apex," he said. "Your pardon. Our solar system is moving toward a point not far from their home star. But," the Chinese representative smiled—"it is about half a million years away."

"Just so," S's'i'i said. "The technology to travel as do we, need you to acquire."

"*Acquire*?" Mbele said. "You want to give us faster than light technology?"

"Sell," one of the other rashk said. The third one repeated, "sell," and they began moving their arms in a different pattern.

"And the price would be . . . "

"Mineral rights," S's'i'i said. "In your asteroid belt many heavy metals are, also in the satellites of outer planets to be found are they. Also want would we, a permanent base to establish."

"In exchange for faster-than-light technology?"

"A *fair* exchange, think you not?" S's'i'i said. His upper arms moved around each other a few times, followed by his lower arms. His facial expression remained in a toothy grin.

"How would this technology transfer be accomplished?" Mbele said at last, looking at each of his colleagues.

"Ah." S's'i'i reached into one pocket and then another until he found a comp. He dropped it on the table in front of Mbele. "This you would give we."

"And this is . . . "

"Technical specifications. Of engines, plans and summary. With this—" he pointed to the comp. "Build jump-capable ship, can you."

"Jump?"

"Faster-than-light transition. We can this do; with this technology, can you as well."

It was an easy sell for the rashk. No one wanted to be left out, and the rashk were more than happy to sell to all comers—and not just the original three nations. The UN had clear jurisdiction; the Treaty of São Paulo of 2098 divided up all of Sol System's interplanetary property by pro-rated shares among the many nations of the Earth. Any number of countries were more than willing to sell off their mostly undeveloped birthrights for a chance at interstellar travel. Most of them couldn't afford to invest in the former, and would never have the technology to exploit the latter—not that it mattered.

The rashk set up housekeeping in Brazil, apparently the closest place to their native environment that they could find on the surface of the Earth.

Three nations took the technology under UN sanction and ran with it. Greater China began to work on *Star-Rider*, building in the Chinese section of Station Two at the Earth-Moon L-5 point, as far away from others as they could manage; the African Federation set up shop at Station One in Earth orbit, building *Uhuru* and posting regular 3V updates on their progress. The North American Federation began to construct *Clement* in Grimaldi Crater on Luna.

For the Chinese, secrecy was the key: they didn't have any interest in keeping anyone informed about their intentions. The Africans made sure that everyone knew how well they were doing. For us North Americans, the *Clement* effort became a race between science and bureaucracy. I was part of the initial design team; soon we had a ship under construction.

Thanks to the government bureaucracy that grew up around the NAU's project, I spent almost as much time writing requests and providing documentation as I did studying the specs the rashk had sold to us. They'd never admit it, but that might have contributed to someone's inattention.

Then again, it might've just been the syntax.

Eight months after the projects got underway, the Chinese boosted *Star-Rider* into the outer system. For two weeks, everyone assumed that the Chinese had won the race to the stars. The *Star-Rider* jumped; Hawking and the other telescopes recorded its transition, right on time, directly on target.

It should have been two days' jump to Epsilon Indi and two days back. A week after *Star-Rider*'s departure, the Chinese were nervous; two weeks later, all of the nations that had bought the rashk tech were publicly upset.

After three weeks, there was talk of military action.

I was examining a holo of a fluid-dynamics schematic one afternoon when I was interrupted by a comp flying through the air and landing on the desk in front of me. I must have jumped two meters, which amused someone no end.

I looked up to see Allan Martinez, the governmental liasion assigned to the North American Union's FTL project.

"You're not going to get much out of me if I have a massive heart attack," I said, picking up the comp from the desk where it landed.

"Today's newsvid," he said, walking into the room. "Have you seen what people are saying?"

"What people? And what are they saying?"

"Everyone. The Africans, primarily. They call our lizard friends all kinds of names, and call on Brazil to deport them back to the lizard planet."

"Really." I touched the comp, and my schematic dissolved to a newsvid. I turned the mode from audio to text and read through the feed. The Africans were furious and so was our government: the rashk had sold us a bill of goods, the tech was flawed, they'd seized the Chinese ship and had it captive, and so on.

"Let me ask your opinion, Dr. Corning," he said. Martinez always made an effort to call me "Doctor" when he wanted something. "Do you think this stuff—" he waved airily at the printouts scattered on my desk and the half-built models scattered around the office—"will ever really work?"

"What do you mean?"

"I mean, is the newsvid true? Look, the rashk sold us this tech for a princely sum. They sold the same stuff to China and the African Federation. Then they sold it to Brazil, the Europeans, and India. *Then* they sold it to Australia, Vietnam, and Russia.

"We're as far ahead as anybody but the Chinese, those poor bastards. But even if you're able to build the—build *this*," he said, tapping the scale model of *Clement*. "Even if you succeed, do we have any better chance than they did?"

"We're taking more precautions than they did. The race only goes to the swiftest if he doesn't step on a land mine," I answered. *Never pass up a good metaphor*, I thought to myself.

"But your research follows essentially the same channels that theirs did. Isn't *Clement* going to disappear the same way?"

"What makes you think our research is the same?"

"Oh, please, Dr. Corning. We *know*."

"We're being more careful."

"Thank God for that. I'm sure the President will be glad to hear that the Union's money is being spent wisely."

I waved off the vid and flipped the comp back to him. He caught it in midair and tucked it into a pocket in one smooth motion.

"What do you want me to do?"

"Oh, that's *easy*, Dr. Corning. I want you to win the race."

Martinez was right: everyone had been following the same basic research avenues. He was able to provide our team with some last-minute information about *Star-Rider*'s design, and we stopped building *Clement* for two weeks while we studied it.

It was no more than a simple misunderstanding. This sort of thing happens all the time in the scientific field, something that didn't surprise me: scientists are always committing small errors that make them smack themselves in the head at having failed to notice it. Of course, what's taken for granted among scientists will drive politicians crazy. Or will drive them to war, which amounts to the same thing. While everyone on the planet seemed to be screaming about the duplicitous rashk, a sort of dim comprehension came to me.

The rashk thought in *threes*: three eyes, three sets of limbs, three lobes in their brains. They even used the term 'by the Three', which meant God knows what. The specs called for 'balanced' or 'opposed' engine components, and we'd constructed them with *two* parts instead of *three* — and that was the key to the entire business. Somewhere along the line we'd made some assumption that the rashk made differently. It was as if we'd transposed left and right, or used the wrong unit of measurement. A century earlier something like that had cost us a Mars probe, after all.

I'm not sure whether my government would have sanctioned a direct approach to the rashk — once I had an insight, Martinez ordered me to stay put and figure out the problem. The project director expected us to buckle down and make it work, showing up the Chinese (and everyone else) as shoddy. But it was clear to me that a few clarifications from the rashk could fix the whole thing. Without permission from the project director, I took a hopper to Luna City and a shuttle to Earth, then a charter plane from St. Louis to the rashk enclave in Brazil.

I stepped out of the 'copter into the steaming heat of an Amazon afternoon. By the time I'd gone twenty meters across the pad, I was already soaked with sweat.

There were three rashk there to meet me, their pairs of arms moving in regular rhythm just like you see on 3V. I stopped in front of them, not sure whether to bow or try to shake hands; after an awkward moment, one of them said, "Doctor Lee Corning, to our embassy welcome are you," in perfect Northamerican English.

"You know who I am."

"But of course," the rashk answered. "And why you here come have. Accompany us will you, please."

They escorted me into a building. Inside it was cooler, though still damp. Still, it was a relief from the outside air. They'd set up a conference room with three broad-seated rashk chairs and one shaped for humans, so we all knew where to sit.

"I am S's'i'i Kra'tok," the lead rashk said, when we were all as comfortable as we were going to be. "These are my *j'jt*, F'f'n'a Bna'tal and E'e's's Bna'tal. They emerged from the Three together, ha ha ha." The exclamation sounded like three sharp coughs, but I assumed S's'i'i was laughing.

I nodded to each in turn.

"Without the permission of your government here are you," S's'i'i continued. "With us, not happy are they."

"They think you swindled them," I answered. "I'm not here to ask for our money back—"

"Indeed not," S's'i'i interrupted. "Here are you, our help to get, your ship to build."

"Are you willing to help us?"

"Not so quickly," S's'i'i answered. His two companions' arms were waving madly in some sort of pattern, each pair in a slightly different rhythm. They looked at me, then at S's'i'i. "Trade must there be. Give and take, take and give."

"I'm not sure I take your meaning."

"An explanation in order is. Know you, that we you faster-than-light technology sold have, also to the Chinese and the African Federation. Afterward, to other nations did we this technology sell, then afterward to others—"

"You wound up selling it to every country on Earth that has any chance of putting a ship in space. And for the last year we've been wrestling with each other trying to get it done first."

"The race, have you lost."

"The only flaw is that the Chinese, who *won* the race, launched *Star-Rider*—"

"*Xing Shou*, proper Chinese name is," S's'i'i said.

"3V calls it *Star-Rider* in North America," I repeated. "I understand it's an acceptable translation. In any case, it's disappeared without a trace. So everyone wants to bomb this embassy, seize your ship, or commit unspeakable acts on you. Or, at least, get their money back. Not just the Chinese, but the Africans and the NAU—not to mention all the others who bought your tech under the table."

"Understandable is this."

"You must've known this would happen—and that we'd be angry about it."

"A possible logical outcome, certainly was this. Humans quick to anger are, in violence a solution often see." The arms on the other two rashk were waving madly now, as if they were agitated about the whole idea.

"Why? Why did you come in the first place? Without the technology we can't hurt you—we're stuck here in our own solar system, unable to be a threat to anyone."

"Just so."

"Excuse me?"

"A warlike race, are we not," S's'i'i said. He folded each pair of hands across his chest. "But warlike races out there, surely are there. Some day, by the Three, find them will we—and at that time, humans valuable will be for friendship . . . and protection."

"You want us to *fight* for you? You came to Sol System to sell us interstellar capabilities so that you could hide behind our skirts if you found a bogey man out there?"

"Essentially, yes."

"You're kidding."

"Kidding, mean you that I a joke made have? Certainly not." The smile never wavered; it wasn't really capable of wavering. "A very serious matter is this; why a joke at this time to you offer would I?"

"You want us to *fight* for you," I repeated. "You came twenty-five light-years to sell us this technology so that we'd be your friends when you met warlike cultures."

"Certainly, yes."

"Then I have a question for you. Why don't you think we'd just go to Vega and conquer *you*?"

"Too busy, would you be."

"Busy?"

"Fighting amongst yourselves," he said, letting his arms wave slightly.

It made a sort of alien sense.

"Well, it's damn sure," I said, "that no one is going to do anything until we get your help."

"Revision to the contract possible is," S's'i'i said, gesturing at the holo. It scrolled down to near the end.

He highlighted a section with a gesture. "A fee paid can be, professional services to obtain. A part of the extended warranty it is. Regrettably, all of your governments our services declined."

"The . . . extended warranty?"

"'Rashk interference' the Chinese government wanted not. African Federation scientists, proud of their achievement were, and our help did not need.

"Best rejection of our help from North America did come, however. Words of your President: 'Extended warranties are a ripoff.' Understanding is, he did not wish, something for *nothing* to pay. Indeed, believed he—and the Chinese and Africans as well—to build their ships without our help possible be would. So . . . " S's'i'i poked a hand at the mark on the contract: EXTENDED WARRANTY—DECLINED.

"Now. Care to renegotiate would you?"

I returned to Grimaldi with a revised contract, a set of explanatory documents, and F'f'n'a Bna'tal. I was met by a squad of MPs, who informed me of exactly how the Government Secrecy Acts of 1997, 2016, 2043, 2064, and 2088 were going to be used to commit cruel and unusual acts upon me.

The President of the NAU was apparently furious. My project director was visibly furious. Allan Martinez had practically grown a second head. It wasn't every day that a research scientist essentially committed his government to a treaty of alliance and mutual protection. The NAU wasn't responsible for anything else to start, but someday—if the scary monsters ever turned up—we'd be on the hook.

Confined to my lab at Grimaldi, I went back to work on *Clement* with F'f'n'a Bna'tal, who was more than happy to help. While politicians in North America argued about what to do—especially with me—our team finished a working prototype.

Two months after my unscheduled trip to Brazil, and three months after *Star-Rider* disappeared, we launched *Clement*. There was quite an entourage at Station One watching it track via 3V link to the Hawking. The President of the North American Union was there; he slapped me on the back and called me "a gutsy son-of-a-bitch" to my face—I'm fairly sure he had other things to say behind my back—and then walked away to stand with the other dignitaries. I stood with S's'i'i Kra'tok and the two Bna'tal; we talked in quiet tones, but I know it was all captured for posterity.

"For your polity a great day, is it not?" S's'i'i asked me, looking out at the Earth.

"As long as it works. The day *Clement* comes back will be a greater day."

"Work, it of course will," S's'i'i said. "Just as other ships work will: *Star-Rider II, Uhuru, Rio de Janiero, Union, Brahmaputra, Wollongong*—"

"They bought the extended warranty too," I said. Of course they'd all done it—even the Chinese, though it galled them to do so.

"Naturally."

"And you really think we'll wind up fighting for you someday."

"Somewhere . . . " S's'i'i waved his arms expressively; the other two rashk followed, and they all did so for a few moments longer before he continued. "Somewhere aliens will we find who not so friendly as you humans are, ha ha ha. Fighters are we not. Human saying, what is? Some day, back at this look we will, laughing shall we be."

I had to smile then, and the rashk engaged in a series of 'ha ha has'. The North American dignitaries looked over to see the commotion, but managed to look back just in time to see the *Clement* engage its jump engines and disappear, off to see the stars.

HAL CLEMENT AS I SAW HIM

ANTHONY LEWIS

The facts about the life of Harry Clement Stubbs have been published elsewhere. You can look up his birth, education, military service, occupation, and his avocation of writing and painting. This is mostly what I saw of Hal Clement.

I first met Harry in 1957 when I came to M.I.T. and attended the "smoker" of the Science Fiction Society where incoming students could learn about the activities of the club and pony up dues. Hal Clement and Isaac Asimov were there; it was the first time I had ever met writers in the flesh and I was very impressed with how friendly and approachable they both were.

However, my first contact with science fiction and Hal Clement was in 1950 — I was nine years old — when my father handed me a copy of *Needle*. It had been recommended to him by his old radio club buddy, Hugo Gernsback, who thought that Hal Clement was one of the few real science fiction writers.

Of Harry's early life it is only necessary to say that a combination of heredity and environment formed a decent human being of high integrity — a *mensch* is the Yiddish term. Previously, one could call him a true gentleman, but that term has been degraded.

While studying at Harvard, Harry adopted the pseudonym "Hal Clement" because he thought his involvement in science fiction might reflect badly upon his scientific career. He did not know that his advisor, Prof. Donald H. Menzel was a friend of Hugo Gernsback — the publisher of the first science fiction magazine in 1926. Menzel told us this story at the 1969 NESFA Halloween party to the amusement of all the listeners. Menzel went on to write articles for Gernback's *Science Fiction Plus*, and had a cover or two on *Galaxy*.

A story Harry liked to tell about himself: After the war he learned to drive a car—it's still not unusual for people living in Boston to not need automobiles—after he learned to fly. As a result his reflexes were not quite what was needed. Once, when a car stopped in front of him, he stepped on the accelerator and pulled back on the wheel to fly over it. Luckily for us, it was a dual-control car and his instructor stopped it in time, thus saving many excellent stories for posterity.

Harry was very active in Boston fandom—he had been a member of the Stranger Club before World War II—speaking at meetings of the M.I.T. Science Fiction Society, attending their annual picnic at the Blue Hills Reservation in Milton, Massachusetts—where he would climb Big Blue and sing "Men of Harlech" in Welsh. He attended meetings of the Interplanetary Exploration Society—founded at the behest of John W. Campbell. He expressed scepticism about some of the speakers and was asked, "Don't you have an open mind?" He responded, "Only at one end to let information in. If your mind is open at both ends nothing stays in it."

When Boston convention fandom revived in the 1960s he was a founding member of the Boston Science Fiction Society and a member of its unsuccessful bid for the 1967 Worldcon. When BoSFS metamorphosed into the New England Science Fiction Association in 1967, Harry was a charter member. Up until his death, Harry had attended all 41 Boskones in the second series and some of the first series in the 1940s.

To help the finances of the 1969 Worldcon in St. Louis, Harry donated the manuscript of *Star Light* for auction. I had the pleasure of reading the story on the plane to the convention. At this convention Boston was awarded the 1971 Worldcon. He was active in the successful 1971 Worldcon bid and served as Treasurer until Hugo nominations time came. His novel *Star Light* was nominated. At that time the rules stated that members of the committee were not eligible for awards. We pointed this out to him at a meeting and his immediate response was to say he would withdraw the novel. Of course, this was unacceptable to the rest of the committee and we "fired" him as Treasurer. At the con he worked on registration saying that all local fans should help out—to the amazement of many fans and the amusement of many pros.

Harry was Guest of Honor at CactusCon, the 1987 North American Science Fiction Convention, and we at NESFA Press produced a small book, *Intuit*, with the Laird Cunningham stories, including one written especially for this book. Strangely enough, Harry was not a Worldcon Guest of Honor until the 1991 Worldcon in Chicago (Chicon V)—a long overdue recognition. The delay says more about Worldcon committees than about Harry's status.

Around 1972 Harry took up painting—astronomical scenes of course, carefully calculated so that light, shadows, and colors were correct. He took the pseudonym George Richard when he submitted paintings to the SF art shows because he wanted people to buy them because they liked the painting—not because it was painted by Hal Clement. It turned out that they did like them. And the name? It is the names of his two sons—he said John Campbell told him you should always have a good reason for choosing a particular name for a pseudonym.

In the latter part of the 1990s Mark Olson and I of NESFA Press realized that almost nothing of Harry's was in print. At Readercon 1997 we negotiated with Harry for a three-volume set of his works. I felt weird negotiating with the man who wrote the first science fiction story I had ever read, almost 50 years after I had read it.

The first volume was launched at Boskone 36 in 1999 just as Harry was made the latest Grand Master by SFWA. Michael Burstein—SFWA Secretary and NESFA Vice-president—arranged for an early announcement of this honor so it could be disseminated at Boskone, Harry's "home" convention. This volume and volume two had covers by George Richard—Harry's artist alter ego.

The final volume had to be the Mesklin stories—the novels *Mission of Gravity* and *Star Light*, the article "Whirligig World," and the novella "Lecture Demonstration." We wanted a new story to make this volume something special and Harry agreed to write one. Harry finished "Under" and turned it in to us at the end of 1998. We avidly read the story—we were the first to see it. At the 1998 Worldcon in Baltimore, I was having lunch with Stanley Schmidt, editor of *Analog*, and mentioned that we were publishing a new Mesklin story. He asked if it would be submitted to *Analog*. I told him Harry thought it was too "old-fashioned." He replied, "Who's paying him to edit *Analog*?" And so it was the cover story for the 70th anniversary issue in January 2000.

He was the only person to twice receive the E. E. Smith Award for Imaginative Fiction (the "Skylark") presented to him by the New England Science Fiction Association in 1969 and 1997.

Harry was a Trekkie (not a Trekker) and one of the disappointments of his writing career was that he never sold a script to any of the *Star Trek* series.

He was a great supporter of the Red Cross Blood Donor program and gave over 20 gallons.

He was, in the words of Geoffrey Chaucer: "a verray parfit gentil knight" and I am glad to have known him for 46 years. I miss him.

(Let it be noted in passing that Hal was not excluded entirely from Star Trek. The sixth-season episode of Star Trek: Voyager *titled "Blink of an Eye" featured a planet with ferociously fast rotation that, Mesklin-like, massively distorted its sphericity. There was no science about surface gravity gradients, though, and the aliens weren't ground-hugging centipedes but humanoids with odd foreheads. The writers just borrowed one idea, and as Hal himself noted, ideas are free.*

But I still wonder what he thought when he saw that planet.)

Tony Lewis is a pillar of SF fandom: founding member of the New England Science Fiction Association; chair of the World Science Fiction Convention in 1971, and chair or committee member of numberless other cons; author and editor of four volumes on SF produced by NESFA Press.

REFLECTIONS ON HAL CLEMENT

JEFFREY A. CARVER

I first encountered Hal Clement's writings as a teenager in the late 1960s, in the midst of my most passionate period of exploring the strange worlds of that wonderful literature, science fiction. My first exposure to his work was *Close to Critical*, which I found nowhere in a bookstore, but bought by clipping a coupon out of the back of another SF book and mailing it to the publisher with fifty cents plus shipping. A considerable time later, the book arrived (book-order fulfillment in the 1960s not being quite up to today's standards). As I began to read, I knew I was experiencing a very different kind of writing from most of what I had been reading. Here was an author who made laboratory science come alive, who could make an alien world seem both alien and starkly real. (It was, in fact, exactly the kind of SF that my high school chemistry teacher encouraged his students — yes, *encouraged* us — to read.) And a fascinating journey it was.

In those pre-Cambrian days of the 60s, it was not as easy to follow up on a favorite new author as it is now. Imagine: no Amazon, no Barnes and Noble, no Internet shopping for used books, and independent bookstores that were tiny and mostly lined with hardcovers. For paperbacks, it was the drugstore racks; you either found what you were looking for or you didn't. It was some time before I came across more of Hal's work. But when I saw it, I always bought it. Years later I finally got hold of *Mission of Gravity*, his *tour de force* of hard science fiction writing. It was worth every minute of the wait.

Now fast-forward some years . . . .

Struggling to establish my own SF writing career, I began to attend the occasional odd SF convention (something I'd never done before as a reader—never even knew they existed). As a young writer, I tended to be put on panels to discuss world building. More often than not, I found myself seated near a short, quiet, bespectacled gentleman named Harry Stubbs: the same Hal Clement whose work I had met and admired so many years before.

Along with the other panelists, we talked about the process by which we came up with the worlds that served as settings for our stories. I quickly understood that Hal's methods and mine were utterly different. He started with the chemistry and other sciences, and calculated what his worlds were like before he ever dropped people into them. Slide rules and chemical equations were definitely the order of the day. I, on the other hand, started with the characters and their problems, and only after the story got rolling figured out what kind of world—or universe—they were in. It was no contest whose methods best qualified the work as "hard SF." (If there'd been a contest: it was clear enough that we were emphasizing different things in our writing, and our methods suited our madness.) I stood in awe of Hal's ability to truly build a world from the ground up. In fact, I sometimes felt like a bit of a pretender, sharing a panel with him. But he once stunned me as, in his remarks, he turned and described to me what *he* envied in the characterization and cosmic sense of wonder in *my* writing. I'm not sure I heard much else that anyone said that day about world building. If *Hal* liked my work, I guessed I was doing something right.

Once I asked Hal about his flying experiences. I had recently earned my private pilot's license, flying two-seater Cessnas, which I'd found challenging enough. I knew Hal had flown in the military, and I was curious to compare experiences. Well, yes, he explained—he'd been a bomber pilot in Europe in World War II. Hours of boredom interrupted by minutes of sheer terror. I thought of my landings, of which I was so proud, as I listened to his description of long-duration formation flying, multiple heavy aircraft flying with *wings overlapping,* and just six feet of vertical clearance between them. The reason for the tight formation, he explained, was to keep enemy fighters from diving through and breaking up the formation. He said it as though he were describing a chemical equation. And that's pretty much how he always seemed to talk, with a cheerful matter-of-factness that was more or less how he wrote, too.

Though I always enjoyed such encounters, I never really got to know him well. But a few years before he died, Hal and I were invited to do a joint reading before a seminar at M.I.T. By way of introducing myself to the audience, I noted how I'd grown up reading Hal's work, and never dreamed that I would one day be seated beside him, as a peer, addressing an audience. He just smiled, looking faintly embarrassed. I read my piece first, then sat back to enjoy listening to his excerpt from a work in progress. He began reading a scene involving the exploration of Saturn's moon Titan. I was pretty well lost in the mists of Titan when I suddenly heard my name. One of his characters reported coming up on "Lake Carver." I started—visibly, I imagine—and glanced to my left. I saw the barest twinkle in Hal's eye as, without missing a beat, he went right on reading.

I didn't hear much of the rest of that scene, either.

There's a ritual in Jewish religious tradition that I've always thought rather wonderful: the empty dinner chair that's reserved for Elijah the prophet. Wouldn't it be fitting if at world-building panels in the future, we too kept an empty chair? Not for Elijah, but for Hal.

Jeffrey A. Carver thirteen novels include the Chaos Chronicles and Star Rigger Universe series. His most recent novel, Eternity's End, *was a Nebula finalist.*

SLOW LIFE

MICHAEL SWANWICK

"Slow Life" can be read, if you care to, as an advertisement for Hal's novel *Half Life*, which is about a very different expedition to Titan. I came upon *Half Life* immediately after reading a space exploration novel by a much younger writer which was so sour and joyless that I ended up skimming the last third. Then I picked up Hal's book, where all the protagonists are dying and so, knowing they have little time left, determine to spend the rest of their lives engaged in basic research. Why? Because it's more fun than anything else they could possibly be doing!

I read *Half Life* only a year or so before Hal's death and so, in the normal course of things, you'd expect that I'd never have the opportunity to tell him what a delightful book I thought it was, and that the regret for not having done so would follow me around for the rest of my life. But as it chanced I ran across him at a science fiction convention and gushed happily about what he'd done. I also told him that I'd written this story and, acknowledging the debt, named the mother ship the *Clement* and the lander the *Harry Stubbs*. So I have no lingering regrets, no obligations left unexpressed.

Which was another gift from Hal to one of his readers and admirers. You have no idea how typical of him that was.

#

"It was the Second Age of Space. Gagarin, Shepard, Glenn, and Armstrong were all dead. It was *our* turn to make history now."

— *The Memoirs of Lizzie O'Brien*

#

The raindrop began forming ninety kilometers above the surface of Titan. It started with an infinitesimal speck of tholin, adrift in the cold nitrogen atmosphere. Dianoacetylene condensed on the seed nucleus, molecule by molecule, until it was one shard of ice in a cloud of billions.

Now the journey could begin.

It took almost a year for the shard of ice in question to precipitate downward twenty-five kilometers, where the temperature dropped low enough that ethane began to condense on it. But when it did, growth was rapid.

Down it drifted.

At forty kilometers, it was for a time caught up in an ethane cloud. There it continued to grow. Occasionally it collided with another droplet and doubled in size. Until finally it was too large to be held effortlessly aloft by the gentle stratospheric winds.

It fell.

Falling, it swept up methane and quickly grew large enough to achieve a terminal velocity of almost two meters per second.

At twenty-seven kilometers, it passed through a dense layer of methane clouds. It acquired more methane, and continued its downward flight.

As the air thickened, its velocity slowed and it began to lose some of its substance to evaporation. At two and half kilometers, when it emerged from the last patchy clouds, it was losing mass so rapidly it could not normally be expected to reach the ground.

It was, however, falling toward the equatorial highlands, where mountains of ice rose a towering five hundred meters into the atmosphere. At two meters and a lazy new terminal velocity of one meter per second, it was only a breath away from hitting the surface.

Two hands swooped an open plastic collecting bag upward, and snared the raindrop.

"Gotcha!" Lizzie O'Brien cried gleefully.

She zip-locked the bag shut, held it up so her helmet cam could read the bar-code in the corner, and said, "One raindrop." Then she popped it into her collecting box.

Sometimes it's the little things that make you happiest. Somebody would spend a *year* studying this one little raindrop when Lizzie got it home. And it was just Bag 64 in Collecting Case 5. She was going to be on the surface of Titan long enough to scoop up the raw material of a revolution in planetary science. The thought of it filled her with joy.

Lizzie dogged down the lid of the collecting box and began to skip across the granite-hard ice, splashing the puddles and dragging the boot of her atmosphere suit through the rivulets of methane pouring down the mountainside. *"I'm sing-ing in the rain."* She threw out her arms and spun around. *"Just sing-ing in the rain!"*

"Uh . . . O'Brien?" Alan Greene said from the *Clement*. "Are you all right?"

"Dum-dee-dum-dee-dee-dum-dum, I'm . . . some-thing again."

"Oh, leave her alone." Consuelo Hong said with sour good humor. She was down on the plains, where the methane simply boiled into the air, and the ground was covered with thick, gooey tholin. It was, she had told them, like wading ankle-deep in molasses. "Can't you recognize the scientific method when you hear it?"

"If you say so," Alan said dubiously. He was stuck in the *Clement*, overseeing the expedition and minding the website. It was a comfortable gig—*he* wouldn't be sleeping in his suit *or* surviving on recycled water and energy stix—and he didn't think the others knew how much he hated it.

"What's next on the schedule?" Lizzie asked.

"Um . . . Well, there's still the robot turbot to be released. How's that going, Hong?"

"Making good time. I oughta reach the sea in a couple of hours."

"Okay, then it's time O'Brien rejoined you at the lander. O'Brien, start spreading out the balloon and going over the harness checklist."

"Roger that."

"And while you're doing that, I've got today's voice-posts from the Web cued up."

Lizzie groaned, and Consuelo blew a raspberry. By NAFTASA policy, the ground crew participated in all webcasts. Officially, they were delighted to share their experiences with the public. But the VoiceWeb (privately, Lizzie thought of it as the Illiternet) made them accessible to people who lacked even the minimal intellectual skills needed to handle a keyboard.

"Let me remind you that we're on open circuit here, so anything you say will go into my reply. You're certainly welcome to chime in at any time. But each question-and-response is transmitted as one take, so if you flub a line, we'll have to go back to the beginning and start all over again."

"Yeah, yeah," Consuelo grumbled.

"We've done this before," Lizzie reminded him.

"Okay. Here's the first one."

"Uh, hi, this is BladeNinja43. I was wondering just what it is that you guys are hoping to discover out there."

"That's an extremely good question," Alan lied. "And the answer is: We don't know! This is a voyage of discovery, and we're engaged in what's called 'pure science.' Now, time and time again, the purest research has turned out to be extremely profitable. But we're not looking that far ahead. We're just hoping to find something absolutely unexpected."

"My God, you're slick," Lizzie marveled.

"I'm going to edit that from the tape," Alan said cheerily. "Next up."

"This is Mary Schroeder, from the United States. I teach high school English, and I wanted to know for my students, what kind of grades the three of you had when you were their age."

Alan began. "I was an overachiever, I'm afraid. In my sophomore year, first semester, I got a B in Chemistry and panicked. I thought it was the end of the world. But then I dropped a couple of extracurriculars, knuckled down, and brought that grade right up."

"I was good in everything but French Lit," Consuelo said.

"I nearly flunked out!" Lizzie said. "Everything was difficult for me. But then I decided I wanted to be an astronaut, and it all clicked into place. I realized that, hey, it's just hard work. And now, well, here I am."

"That's good. Thanks, guys. Here's the third, from Maria Vasquez."

"Is there life on Titan?"

"Probably not. It's *cold* down there! 94° . . . is the same as -179° Celsius, or -290° Fahrenheit. And yet . . . life is persistent. It's been found in Antarctic ice and in boiling water in submarine volcanic vents. Which is why we'll be paying particular attention to exploring the depths of the ethane-methane sea. If life is anywhere to be found, that's where we'll find it."

"Chemically, the conditions here resemble the anoxic atmosphere on

Earth in which life first arose," Consuelo said. "Further, we believe that such pre-biotic chemistry has been going on here for four and a half billion years. For an organic chemist like me, it's the best toy box in the universe. But that lack of heat is a problem. Chemical reactions that occur quickly back home would take thousands of years here. It's hard to see how life could arise under such a handicap."

"It would have to be slow life," Lizzie said thoughtfully. "Something vegetative. 'Vaster than empires and more slow.' It would take millions of years to reach maturity. A single thought might require centuries . . . ."

"Thank you for that, uh, wild scenario!" Alan said quickly. Their NAFTASA masters frowned on speculation. It was, in their estimation, almost as unprofessional as heroism. "This next question comes from Danny in Toronto."

"Hey, man, I gotta say I really envy you being in that tiny little ship with those two hot babes."

Alan laughed lightly. "Yes, Ms. Hong and Ms. O'Brien are certainly attractive women. But we're kept so busy that, believe it or not, the thought of sex never comes up. And currently, while I tend to the *Clement*, they're both on the surface of Titan at the bottom of an atmosphere sixty percent more dense than Earth's, and encased in armored exploration suits. So even if I did have inappropriate thoughts, there's no way we could . . . "

"Hey, Alan," Lizzie said. "Tell me something."

"Yes?"

"What are you wearing?"

"Uh . . . switching over to private channel."

"Make that a three-way," Consuelo said.

Ballooning, Lizzie decided, was the best way there was of getting around. Moving with the gentle winds, there was no sound at all. And the view was great!

People talked a lot about the "murky orange atmosphere" of Titan, but your eyes adjusted. Turn up the gain on your helmet, and the white mountains of ice were *dazzling*! The methane streams carved cryptic runes into the heights. Then, at the tholin-line, white turned to a rich palette of oranges, reds, and yellows. There was a lot going on down there—more than she'd be able to learn in a hundred visits.

The plains were superficially duller, but they had their charms as well. Sure, the atmosphere was so dense that refracted light made the horizon curve upward to either side. But you got used to it. The black swirls and cryptic red tracery of unknown processes on the land below never grew tiring.

On the horizon, she saw the dark arm of Titan's narrow sea. If that was what it was. Lake Erie was larger, but the spin doctors back home had argued that since Titan was so much smaller than earth, *relatively* it qualified as a sea. Lizzie had her own opinion, but she knew when to keep her mouth shut.

Consuelo was there now. Lizzie switched her visor over to the live feed. Time to catch the show.

"I can't believe I'm finally here," Consuelo said. She let the shrink-wrapped fish slide from her shoulder down to the ground. "Five kilometers doesn't seem like very far when you're coming down from orbit—just enough to leave a margin for error so the lander doesn't come down in the sea. But when you have to *walk* that distance, through tarry, sticky tholin . . . well, it's one heck of a slog."

"Consuelo, can you tell us what it's like there?" Alan asked.

"I'm crossing the beach. Now I'm at the edge of the sea." She knelt, dipped a hand into it. "It's got the consistency of a Slushy. Are you familiar with that drink? Lots of shaved ice sort of half-melted in a cup with flavored syrup. What we've got here is almost certainly a methane-ammonia mix; we'll know for sure after we get a sample to a laboratory. Here's an early indicator, though. It's dissolving the tholin off my glove." She stood.

"Can you describe the beach?"

"Yeah. It's white. Granular. I can kick it with my boot. Ice sand for sure. Do you want me to collect samples first or release the fish?"

"Release the fish," Lizzie said, almost simultaneously with Alan's "Your call."

"Okay, then." Consuelo carefully cleaned both of her suit's gloves in the sea, then seized the shrink-wrap's zip tab and yanked. The plastic parted. Awkwardly, she straddled the fish, lifted it by the two side-handles, and walked it into the dark slush.

"Okay, I'm standing in the sea now. It's up to my ankles. Now it's at my knees. I think it's deep enough here."

She set the fish down. "Now I'm turning it on."

The Mitsubishi turbot wriggled, as if alive. With one fluid motion, it surged forward, plunged, and was gone.

Lizzie switched over to the fishcam.

Black liquid flashed past the turbot's infrared eyes. Straight away from the shore it swam, seeing nothing but flecks of paraffin, ice, and other suspended particulates as they loomed up before it and were swept away in the violence of its wake. A hundred meters out, it bounced a pulse of radar off the sea floor, then dove, seeking the depths.

Rocking gently in her balloon harness, Lizzie yawned.

Snazzy Japanese cybernetics took in a minute sample of the ammonia-water, fed it through a deftly constructed internal laboratory, and excreted the waste products behind it. "We're at twenty meters now," Consuelo said. "Time to collect a second sample."

The turbot was equipped to run hundreds of on-the-spot analyses. But it had only enough space for twenty permanent samples to be carried back home. The first sample had been nibbled from the surface slush. Now it twisted, and gulped down five drams of sea fluid in all its glorious impurity. To Lizzie, this was science on the hoof. Not very dramatic, admittedly, but intensely exciting.

She yawned again.

"O'Brien?" Alan said, "How long has it been since you last slept?"

"Huh? Oh . . . twenty hours? Don't worry about me, I'm fine."

"Go to sleep. That's an order."

"But—"

"Now."

Fortunately, the suit was comfortable enough to sleep in. It had been designed so she could.

First she drew in her arms from the suit's sleeves. Then she brought in her legs, tucked them up under her chin, and wrapped her arms around them. "'Night, guys," she said.

"*Buenas noches, querida,*" Consuelo said, "*que tengas lindos sueños.*"

"Sleep tight, space explorer."

The darkness when she closed her eyes was so absolute it crawled. Black, black, black. Phantom lights moved within the darkness, formed lines, shifted away when she tried to see them. They were as fugitive as fish, luminescent, fainter than faint, there and with a flick of her attention fled.

A school of little thoughts flashed through her mind, silver scaled and gone.

Low, deep, slower than sound, something tolled. The bell from a drowned clock tower patiently stroking midnight. She was beginning to get her bearings. Down *there* was where the ground must be. Flowers grew there unseen. Up above was where the sky would be, if there were a sky. Flowers floated there as well.

Deep within the submerged city, she found herself overcome by an enormous and placid sense of self. A swarm of unfamiliar sensations washed through her mind, and then . . .

"Are you me?" a gentle voice asked.

"No," she said carefully. "I don't think so."

Vast astonishment. "You think you are not me?"

"Yes. I think so, anyway."

"Why?"

There didn't seem to be any proper response to that, so she went back to the beginning of the conversation and ran through it again, trying to bring it to another conclusion. Only to bump against that "Why?" once again.

"I don't know why," she said.

"Why not?"

"I don't know."

She looped through that same dream over and over again all the while that she slept.

When she awoke, it was raining again. This time, it was a drizzle of pure methane from the lower cloud deck at fifteen kilometers. These clouds were (the theory went) methane condensate from the wet air swept up from the sea. They fell on the mountains and washed them clean of tholin. It was the methane that eroded and shaped the ice, carving gullies and caves.

Titan had more kinds of rain than anywhere else in the solar system.

The sea had crept closer while Lizzie slept. It now curled up to the horizon on either side like an enormous dark smile. Almost time now for her to begin her descent. While she checked her harness settings, she flicked on telemetry to see what the others were up to.

The robot turbot was still spiraling its way downward, through the lightless sea, seeking its distant floor. Consuelo was trudging through the tholin again, retracing her five-kilometer trek from the lander *Harry Stubbs*, and Alan was answering another set of webposts.

"Modelos de la evolución de Titanes indican que la luna formó de una nube circumplanetaria rica en amoniaco y metano, la cual al condensarse dio forma a Saturno asi como a otros satélites. Bajo estas condiciones en—"

"Uh . . . guys?"

Alan stopped. "Damn it, O'Brien, now I've got to start all over again."

"Welcome back to the land of the living," Consuelo said. "You should check out the readings we're getting from the robofish. Lots of long-chain polymers, odd fractions . . . tons of interesting stuff."

"Guys?"

This time her tone of voice registered with Alan. "What is it, O'Brien?"

"I think my harness is jammed."

Lizzie had never dreamed disaster could be such drudgery. First there were hours of back-and-forth with the NAFTASA engineers. What's the status of rope 14? Try tugging on rope 8. What do the D-rings look like? It was slow work because of the lag time for messages to be relayed to Earth and back. And Alan insisted on filling the silence with posts from the VoiceWeb. Her plight had gone global in minutes, and every unemployable loser on the planet had to log in with suggestions.

"Thezgemoth337, here. It seems to me that if you had a gun and shot up through the balloon, it would maybe deflate and then you could get down."

"I don't have a gun, shooting a hole in the balloon would cause it not to deflate but to rupture, I'm 800 meters above the surface, there's a sea below me, and I'm in a suit that's not equipped for swimming. Next."

"If you had a really big knife—"

"Cut! Jesus, Greene, is this the best you can find? Have you heard back from the organic chem guys yet?"

"Their preliminary analysis just came in," Alan said. "As best they can guess—and I'm cutting through a lot of clutter here—the rain you went through wasn't pure methane."

"No shit, Sherlock."

"They're assuming that whitish deposit you found on the rings and ropes is your culprit. They can't agree on what it is, but they think it underwent a chemical reaction with the material of your balloon and sealed the rip panel shut."

"I thought this was supposed to be a pretty non-reactive environment."

"It is. But your balloon runs off your suit's waste heat. The air in it is several degrees above the melting-point of ice. That's the equivalent of a blast furnace, here on Titan. Enough energy to run any number of amazing reactions. You haven't stopped tugging on the vent rope?"

"I'm tugging away right now. When one arm gets sore, I switch arms."

"Good girl. I know how tired you must be."

"Take a break from the voice-posts," Consuelo suggested, "and check out the results we're getting from the robofish. It's giving us some really interesting stuff."

So she did. And for a time it distracted her, just as they'd hoped. There was a lot more ethane and propane than their models had predicted, and surprisingly less methane. The mix of fractions was nothing like what she'd expected. She had just enough chemistry to guess at some of the implications of the data being generated, but not enough to put it all together. Still tugging at the ropes in the sequence uploaded by the engineers in Toronto, she scrolled up the chart of hydrocarbons dissolved in the lake.

Solute	Solute mole fraction
Ethyne	4.0×10^{-4}
Propyne	4.4×10^{-5}
1,3-Butadiyne	7.7×10^{-7}
Carbon Dioxide	0.1×10^{-5}
Methanenitrile	5.7×10^{-6}

But after a while, the experience of working hard and getting nowhere, combined with the tedium of floating farther and farther out over the featureless sea, began to drag on her. The columns of figures grew meaningless, then indistinct.

Propanenitrile	6.0×10^{-5}
Propenenitrile	9.9×10^{-6}
Propynenitrile	5.3×10^{-6}

Hardly noticing she was doing so, she fell asleep.

She was in a lightless building, climbing flight after flight of stairs. There were other people with her, also climbing. They jostled against her as she ran up the stairs, flowing upward, passing her, not talking.

It was getting colder.

She had a distant memory of being in the furnace room down below. It was hot there, swelteringly so. Much cooler where she was now. Almost too cool. With every step she took, it got a little cooler still. She found herself slowing down. Now it was definitely too cold. Unpleasantly so. Her leg muscles ached. The air seemed to be thickening around her as well. She could barely move now.

This was, she realized, the natural consequence of moving away from the furnace. The higher up she got, the less heat there was to be had, and the less energy to be turned into motion. It all made perfect sense to her somehow.

Step. Pause.

Step. Longer pause.

Stop.

The people around her had slowed to a stop as well. A breeze colder than ice touched her, and without surprise, she knew that they had reached the top of the stairs and were standing upon the building's roof. It was as dark without as it had been within. She stared upward and saw nothing.

"Horizons. Absolutely baffling," somebody murmured beside her.

"Not once you get used to them," she replied.

"Up and down—are these hierarchic values?"

"They don't have to be."

"Motion. What a delightful concept."

"We like it."

"So you *are* me?"

"No. I mean, I don't think so."

"Why?"

She was struggling to find an answer to this, when somebody gasped. High up in the starless, featureless sky, a light bloomed. The crowd around her rustled with unspoken fear. Brighter, the light grew. Brighter still. She could feel heat radiating from it, slight but definite, like the rumor of a distant sun. Everyone about her was frozen with horror. More terrifying than a light where none was possible be was the presence of heat. It simply could not be. And yet it was

She, along with the others, waited and watched for . . . something. She could not say what. The light shifted slowly in the sky. It was small, intense, ugly.

Then the light *screamed.*

She woke up.

"Wow," she said. "I just had the weirdest dream."

"Did you?" Alan's said casually.

"Yeah. There was this light in the sky. It was like a nuclear bomb or something. I mean, it didn't look anything like a nuclear bomb, but it was terrifying the way a nuclear bomb would be. Everybody was staring at it. We couldn't move. And then . . . " She shook her head. "I lost it. I'm sorry. It was so just so strange. I can't put it into words."

"Never mind that," Consuelo said cheerily. "We're getting some great readings down below the surface. Fractional polymers, long-chain hydro-carbons . . . Fabulous stuff. You really should try to stay awake to catch some of this."

She was fully awake now, and not feeling too happy about it. "I guess that means that nobody's come up with any good ideas yet on how I might get down."

"Uh . . . what do you mean?"

"Because if they had, you wouldn't be so god-damned upbeat, would you?"

"*Some*body woke up on the wrong side of the bed," Alan said. "Please remember that there are certain words we don't use in public."

"I'm sorry," Consuelo said. "I was just trying to . . . "

" . . . distract me. Okay, fine. What the hey. I can play along." Lizzie pulled herself together. "So your findings mean . . . what? Life?"

"I keep telling you guys. It's too early to make that kind of determina-tion. What we've got so far are just some very, very interesting readings."

"Tell her the big news," Alan said.

"Brace yourself. We've got a real ocean! Not this tiny little two-hundred-by-fifty-miles glorified lake we've been calling a sea, but a genuine ocean! Sonar readings show that what we see is just an evapora-tion pan atop a thirty-kilometer-thick cap of ice. The real ocean lies under-neath, two hundred kilometers deep."

"Jesus." Lizzie caught herself. "I mean, gee whiz. Is there any way of getting the robofish down into it?"

"How do you think we got the depth readings? It's headed down there right now. There's a chimney through the ice right at the center of the visible sea. That's what replenishes the surface liquid. And directly under the hole there's—guess what?—volcanic vents!"

"So does that mean—?"

"If you use the L-word again," Consuelo said, "I'll spit."

Lizzie grinned. *That* was the Consuelo Hong she knew. "What about the tidal data? I thought the lack of orbital perturbation ruled out a significant ocean entirely."

"Well, Toronto thinks . . . "

At first, Lizzie was able to follow the reasoning of the planetary geologists back in Toronto. Then it got harder. Then it became a drone. As she drifted off into sleep, she had time enough to be peevishly aware that she really shouldn't be dropping off to sleep all the time like this. She oughtn't to be so tired. She . . .

She found herself in the drowned city again. She still couldn't see anything, but she knew it was a city because she could hear the sound of rioters smashing store windows. Their voices swelled into howling screams and receded into angry mutters, like a violent surf washing through the streets. She began to edge away backwards.

Somebody spoke into her ear.

"Why did you do this to us?"

"I didn't do anything to you."

"You brought us knowledge."

"What knowledge?"

"You said you were not us."

"Well, I'm not."

"You should never have told us that."

"You wanted me to lie?"

Horrified confusion. "Falsehood. What a distressing idea."

The smashing noises were getting louder. Somebody was splintering a door with an axe. Explosions. Breaking glass. She heard wild laughter. Shrieks. "We've got to get out of here."

"Why did you send the messenger?"

"What messenger?"

"The star! The star! The star!"

"Which star?"

"There are two stars?"

"There are billions of stars."

"No more! Please! Stop! No more!"

She was awake.

"*Hello, yes, I appreciate that the young lady is in extreme danger, but I really don't think she should have used the Lord's name in vain.*"

"Greene," Lizzie said, "do we really have to put up with this?"

"Well, considering how many billions of public-sector dollars it took to bring us here . . . yes. Yes, we do. I can even think of a few backup astronauts who would say that a little upbeat web-posting was a pretty small price to pay for the privilege."

"Oh, barf."

"I'm switching to a private channel," Alan said calmly. The background radiation changed subtly. A faint, granular crackling that faded away when she tried to focus on it. In a controlled, angry voice Alan said, "O'Brien, just what the hell is going on with you?"

"Look, I'm sorry, I apologize, I'm a little excited about something. How long was I out? Where's Consuelo? I'm going to say the L-word. And the I-word as well. We have life. Intelligent life!"

"It's been a few hours. Consuelo is sleeping. O'Brien, I hate to say this, but you're not sounding at all rational."

"There's a perfectly logical reason for that. Okay, it's a little strange, and maybe it won't sound perfectly logical to you initially, but . . . look, I've been having sequential dreams. I think they're significant. Let me tell you about them."

And she did so. At length.

When she was done, there was a long silence. Finally, Alan said, "Lizzie, think. Why would something like that communicate to you in your dreams? Does that make any sense?"

"I think it's the only way it can. I think it's how it communicates among itself. It doesn't move—motion is an alien and delightful concept to it—and it wasn't aware that its component parts were capable of individualization. That sounds like some kind of broadcast thought to me. Like some kind of wireless distributed network."

"You know the medical kit in your suit? I want you to open it up. Feel around for the bottle that's braille-coded twenty-seven, okay?"

"Alan, I do *not* need an antipsychotic!"

"I'm not saying you need it. But wouldn't you be happier knowing you had it in you?" This was Alan at his smoothest. Butter wouldn't melt in his mouth. "Don't you think that would help us accept what you're saying?"

"Oh, all right!" She drew in an arm from the suit's arm, felt around for the med kit, and drew out a pill, taking every step by the regs, checking the coding four times before she put it in her mouth and once more (each pill was individually braille-coded as well) before she swallowed it. "Now will you listen to me? I'm quite serious about this." She yawned. "I really do think that . . . " She yawned again. "That . . .

"Oh, piffle."

Once more into the breach, dear friends, she thought, and plunged deep, deep into the sea of darkness. This time, though, she felt she had a handle on it. The city was drowned because it existed at the bottom of a lightless ocean. It was alive, and it fed off of volcanic heat. That was why it considered up and down hierarchic values. Up was colder, slower, less alive. Down was hotter, faster, more filled with thought. The city/entity was a collective life form, like a Portuguese man-of-war or a massively hyperlinked expert network. It communicated within itself by some form of electromagnetism. Call it mental radio. It communicated with her that same way.

"I think I understand you now."

"Don't understand—run!"

Somebody impatiently seized her elbow and hurried her along. Faster she went, and faster. She couldn't see a thing. It was like running down a lightless tunnel a hundred miles underground at midnight. Glass crunched underfoot. The ground was uneven and sometimes she stumbled. Whenever she did, her unseen companion yanked her up again.

"Why are you so slow?"

"I didn't know I was."

"Believe me, you are."

"Why are we running?"

"We are being pursued." They turned suddenly, into a side passage, and were jolting over rubbled ground. Sirens wailed. Things collapsed. Mobs surged.

"Well, you've certainly got the motion thing down pat."

Impatiently. "It's only a metaphor. You don't think this is a *real* city, do you? Why are you so dim? Why are you so difficult to communicate with? Why are you so slow?"

"I didn't know I was."

Vast irony. "Believe me, you are."

"What can I do?"

"Run!"

Whooping and laughter. At first, Lizzie confused it with the sounds of mad destruction in her dream. Then she recognized the voices as belonging to Alan and Consuelo. "How long was I out?" she asked.

"You were out?"

"No more than a minute or two," Alan said. "It's not important. Check out the visual the robofish just gave us."

Consuelo squirted the image to Lizzie.

Lizzie gasped. "Oh! Oh, my."

It was beautiful. Beautiful in the way that the great European cathedrals were, and yet at the same time undeniably organic. The structure was tall and slender, and fluted and buttressed and absolutely ravishing. It had grown about a volcanic vent, with openings near the bottom to let sea water in, and then followed the rising heat upward. Occasional channels led outward and then looped back into the main body again. It loomed higher than seemed possible (but it *was* underwater, of course, and on a low-gravity world at that), a complexly layered congeries of tubes like church-organ pipes, or deep-sea worms lovingly intertwined.

It had the elegance of design that only a living organism can have.

"Okay," Lizzie said. "Consuelo. You've got to admit that—"

"I'll go as far as 'complex pre-biotic chemistry.' Anything more than that is going to have to wait for more definite readings." Cautious as her words were, Consuelo's voice rang with triumph. It said, clearer than words, that she could happily die then and there, a satisfied xenochemist.

Alan, almost equally elated, said, "Watch what happens when we intensify the image."

The structure shifted from grey to a muted rainbow of pastels, rose bleeding into coral, sunrise yellow into winter-ice blue. It was breath-taking.

"Wow." For an instant, even her own death seemed unimportant. Relatively unimportant, anyway.

So thinking, she cycled back again into sleep. And fell down into the darkness, into the noisy clamor of her mind.

It was hellish. The city was gone, replaced by a matrix of noise: hammerings, clatterings, sudden crashes. She started forward and walked into an upright steel pipe. Staggering back, she stumbled into another. An engine started up somewhere nearby, and gigantic gears meshed noisily, grinding something that gave off a metal shriek. The floor shook underfoot. Lizzie decided it was wisest to stay put.

A familiar presence, permeated with despair. "Why did you do this to me?"

"What have I done?"

"I used to be everything."

Something nearby began pounding like a pile-driver. It was giving her a headache. She had to shout to be heard over its din. "You're still something!"

Quietly. "I'm nothing."

"That's . . . not true! You're . . . here! You exist! That's . . . something!"

A world-encompassing sadness. "False comfort. What a pointless thing to offer."

She was conscious again.

Consuelo was saying something. " . . . isn't going to like it."

"The spiritual wellness professionals back home all agree that this is the best possible course of action for her."

"Oh, please!"

Alan had to be the most anal-retentive person Lizzie knew. Consuelo was definitely the most phlegmatic. Things had to be running pretty tense for both of them to be bickering like this. "Um . . . guys?" Lizzie said. "I'm awake."

There was a moment's silence, not unlike those her parents had shared when she was little and she'd wandered into one of their arguments. Then Consuelo said, a little too brightly, "Hey, it's good to have you back," and Alan said, "NAFTASA wants you to speak with someone. Hold on. I've got a recording of her first transmission cued up and ready for you."

A woman's voice came online. *"This is Dr. Alma Rosenblum. Elizabeth, I'd like to talk with you about how you're feeling. I appreciate that the time delay between Earth and Titan is going to make our conversation a little awkward at first. But I'm confident that the two of us can work through it."*

"What kind of crap is this?" Lizzie said angrily. "Who is this woman?"

"NAFTASA thought it would help if you—"

"She's a grief counselor, isn't she?"

"Technically, she's a transition therapist," Alan said.

"Look, I don't buy into any of that touchy-feely Newage"—she deliberately mispronounced the word to rhyme with sewage—"stuff. Anyway, what's the hurry? You guys haven't given up on me, have you?"

"Uh . . . "

"You've been asleep for hours," Consuelo said. "We've done a little weather modeling in your absence. Maybe we should share it with you."

She squirted the info to Lizzie's suit, and Lizzie scrolled it up on her visor. A primitive simulation showed the evaporation lake beneath her with an overlay of liquid temperatures. It was only a few degrees warmer than the air above it, but that was enough to create a massive updraft from the lake's center. An overlay of tiny blue arrows showed the direction of local microcurrents of air coming together to form a spiraling shaft that rose over two kilometers above the surface before breaking and spilling westward.

A new overlay put a small blinking light 800 meters above the lake surface. That represented her. Tiny red arrows showed her projected drift.

According to this, she would go around and around in a circle over the lake for approximately forever. Her ballooning rig wasn't designed to go high enough for the winds to blow her back over the land. Her suit wasn't designed to float. Even if she managed to bring herself down for a gentle landing, once she hit the lake she was going to sink like a stone. She wouldn't drown. But she wouldn't make it to shore either.

Which meant that she was going to die.

Involuntarily, tears welled up in Lizzie's eyes. She tried to blink them away, as angry at the humiliation of crying at a time like this as she was at the stupidity of her death itself. "Damn it, don't let me die like *this*! Not from my own incompetence, for pity's sake!"

"Nobody's said anything about incompetence," Alan began soothingly.

In that instant, the follow-up message from Dr. Alma Rosenblum arrived from Earth. *"Yes, I'm a grief counselor, Elizabeth. You're facing an emotionally significant milestone in your life, and it's important that you understand and embrace it. That's my job. To help you comprehend the significance and necessity and—yes—even the beauty of death."*

"Private channel please!" Lizzie took several deep cleansing breaths to calm herself. Then, more reasonably, she said, "Alan, I'm a *Catholic*, okay? If I'm going to die, I don't want a grief counselor, I want a god-damned priest." Abruptly, she yawned. "Oh, fuck. Not again." She yawned twice more. "A priest, understand? Wake me up when he's online."

Then she again was standing at the bottom of her mind, in the blank expanse of where the drowned city had been. Though she could see nothing, she felt certain that she stood at the center of a vast, featureless plain, one so large she could walk across it forever and never arrive anywhere. She sensed that she was in the aftermath of a great struggle. Or maybe it was just a lull.

A great, tense silence surrounded her.

"Hello?" she said. The word echoed soundlessly, absence upon absence.

At last that gentle voice said, "You seem different."

"I'm going to die," Lizzie said. "Knowing that changes a person." The ground was covered with soft ash, as if from an enormous conflagration. She didn't want to think about what it was that had burned. The smell of it filled her nostrils.

"Death. We understand this concept."

"Do you?"

"We have understood it for a long time."

"Have you?"

"Ever since you brought it to us."

"Me?"

"You brought us the concept of individuality. It is the same thing."

Awareness dawned. "Culture shock! That's what all this is about, isn't it? You didn't know there could be more than one sentient being in existence. You didn't know you lived at the bottom of an ocean on a small world inside a universe with billions of galaxies. I brought you more information than you could swallow in one bite, and now you're choking on it."

Mournfully: "Choking. What a grotesque concept."

"Wake up, Lizzie!"

She woke up. "I think I'm getting somewhere," she said. Then she laughed.

"O'Brien," Alan said carefully. "Why did you just laugh?"

"Because I'm not getting anywhere, am I? I'm becalmed here, going around and around in a very slow circle. And I'm down to my last—" she checked "-twenty hours of oxygen. And nobody's going to rescue me. And I'm going to die. But other than that, I'm making terrific progress."

"O'Brien, you're . . . "

"I'm okay, Alan. A little frazzled. Maybe a bit too emotionally honest. But under the circumstances, I think that's permitted, don't you?"

"Lizzie, we have your priest. His name is Father Laferrier. The Archdiocese of Montreal arranged a hookup for him."

"Montreal? Why Montreal? No, don't explain—more NAFTASA politics, right?"

"Actually, my brother-in-law is a Catholic, and I asked him who was good."

She was silent for a touch. "I'm sorry, Alan. I don't know what got into me."

"You've been under a lot of pressure. Here. I've got him on tape."

"Hello, Ms. O'Brien, I'm Father Laferrier. I've talked with the officials here, and they've promised that you and I can talk privately, and that they won't record what's said. So if you want to make your confession now, I'm ready for you."

Lizzie checked the specs and switched over to a channel that she hoped was really and truly private. Best not to get too specific about the embarrassing stuff, just in case. She could confess her sins by category.

"Forgive me, father, for I have sinned. It has been two months since my last confession. I'm going to die, and maybe I'm not entirely sane, but I think I'm in communication with an alien intelligence. I think it's a terrible sin to pretend I'm not." She paused. "I mean, I don't know if it's a *sin* or not, but I'm sure it's *wrong*." She paused again. "I've been guilty of anger, and pride, and envy, and lust. I brought the knowledge of death to an innocent world. I..." She felt herself drifting off again, and hastily said, "For these and all my sins, I am most heartily sorry, and beg the forgiveness of God and the absolution and..."

"And what?" That gentle voice again. She was in that strange dark mental space once more, asleep but cognizant, rational but accepting any absurdity no matter how great. There were no cities, no towers, no ashes, no plains. Nothing but the negation of negation.

When she didn't answer the question, the voice said, "Does it have to do with your death?"

"Yes."

"I'm dying too."

"What?"

"Half of us are gone already. The rest are shutting down. We thought we were one. You showed us we were not. We thought we were everything. You showed us the universe."

"So you're just going to *die*?"

"Yes."

"Why?"

"Why not?"

Thinking as quickly and surely as she ever had before in her life, Lizzie said, "Let me show you something."

"Why?"

"Why not?"

There was a brief, terse silence. Then: "Very well."

Summoning all her mental acuity, Lizzie thought back to that instant when she had first seen the city/entity on the fishcam. The soaring majesty of it. The slim grace. And then the colors: like dawn upon a glacial ice field: subtle, profound, riveting. She called back her emotions in that instant, and threw in how she'd felt the day she'd seen her baby brother's birth, the raw rasp of cold air in her lungs as she stumbled to the topmost peak of her first mountain, the wonder of the Taj Mahal at sunset, the sense of wild daring when she'd first put her hand down a boy's trousers, the prismatic crescent of atmosphere at the Earth's rim when seen from low orbit . . . Everything she had, she threw into that image.

"This is how you look," she said. "This is what we'd both be losing if you were no more. If you were human, I'd rip off your clothes and do you on the floor right now. I wouldn't care who was watching. I wouldn't give a damn."

The gentle voice said, "Oh."

And then she was back in her suit again. She could smell her own sweat, sharp with fear. She could feel her body, the subtle aches where the harness pulled against her flesh, the way her feet, hanging free, were bloated with blood. Everything was crystalline clear and absolutely real. All that had come before seemed like a bad dream.

"*This is DogsofSETI. What a wonderful discovery you've made—intelligent life in our own Solar System! Why is the government trying to cover this up?*"

"Uh . . ."

"*I'm Joseph Devries. This alien monster must be destroyed immediately. We can't afford the possibility that it's hostile.*"

"*StudPudgie07 here: What's the dirt behind this 'lust' thing? Advanced minds need to know! If O'Brien isn't going to share the details, then why'd she bring it up in the first place?*"

"*Hola, soy Pedro Domínguez. Como abogado, esto me parece ultrajante! Por qué NAFTASA nos oculta esta información?*"

"Alan!" Lizzie shouted. "What the *fuck* is going on?"

"Script-bunnies," Alan said. He sounded simultaneously apologetic and annoyed. "They hacked into your confession and apparently you said something . . . "

"We're sorry, Lizzie," Consuelo said. "We really are. If it's any consolation, the Archdiocese of Montreal is hopping mad. They're talking about taking legal action."

"Legal action? What the hell do I care about . . . ?" She stopped.

Without her willing it, one hand rose above her head and seized the number 10 rope.

Don't do that, she thought.

The other hand went out to the side, tightened against the number 9 rope. She hadn't willed that either. When she tried to draw it back to her, it refused to obey. Then the first hand—her right hand—moved a few inches upward and seized its rope in an iron grip. Her left hand slid a good half-foot up its rope. Inch by inch, hand over hand, she climbed up toward the balloon.

I've gone mad, she thought. Her right hand was gripping the rip panel now, and the other tightly clenched rope 8. Hanging effortlessly from them, she swung her feet upward. She drew her knees against her chest and kicked.

No!

The fabric ruptured and she began to fall.

A voice she could barely make out said, "Don't panic. We're going to bring you down."

All in a panic, she snatched at the 9-rope and the 4-rope. But they were limp in her hand, useless, falling at the same rate she was.

"Be patient."

"I don't want to die, goddamnit!"

"Then don't."

She was falling helplessly. It was a terrifying sensation, an endless plunge into whiteness, slowed somewhat by the tangle of ropes and balloon trailing behind her. She spread out her arms and legs like a starfish, and felt the air resistance slow her yet further. The sea rushed up at her with appalling speed. It seemed like she'd been falling forever. It was over in an instant.

Without volition, Lizzie kicked free of balloon and harness, drew her feet together, pointed her toes, and positioned herself perpendicular to Titan's surface. She smashed through the surface of the sea, sending enormous gouts of liquid splashing upward. It knocked the breath out of her. Red pain exploded within. She thought maybe she'd broken a few ribs.

"You taught us so many things," the gentle voice said. "You gave us so much."

"Help me!" The water was dark around her. The light was fading.

"Multiplicity. Motion. Lies. You showed us a universe infinitely larger than the one we had known."

"Look. Save my life and we'll call it even. Deal?"

"Gratitude. Such an essential concept."

"Thanks. I think."

And then she saw the turbot swimming toward her in a burst of silver bubbles. She held out her arms and the robot fish swam into them. Her fingers closed about the handles which Consuelo had used to wrestle the device into the sea. There was a jerk, so hard that she thought for an instant that her arms would be ripped out of their sockets. Then the robofish was surging forward and upward and it was all she could do to keep her grip.

"Oh, dear God!" Lizzie cried involuntarily.

"We think we can bring you to shore. It will not be easy."

Lizzie held on for dear life. At first she wasn't at all sure she could. But then she pulled herself forward, so that she was almost astride the speeding mechanical fish, and her confidence returned. She could do this. It wasn't any harder than the time she'd had the flu and aced her gymnastics final on parallel bars and horse anyway. It was just a matter of grit and determination. She just had to keep her wits about her. "Listen," she said. "If you're really grateful . . ."

"We are listening."

"We gave you all those new concepts. There must be things you know that we don't."

A brief silence, the equivalent of who knew how much thought. "Some of our concepts might cause you dislocation." A pause. "But in the long run, you will be much better off. The scars will heal. You will rebuild. The chances of your destroying yourselves are well within the limits of acceptability."

"Destroying ourselves?" For a second, Lizzie couldn't breathe. It had taken hours for the city/entity to come to terms with the alien concepts she'd dumped upon it. Human beings thought and lived at a much slower rate than it did. How long would those hours translate into human time? Months? Years? Centuries? It had spoken of scars and rebuilding. That didn't sound good at all.

Then the robofish accelerated, so quickly that Lizzie almost lost her grip. The dark waters were whirling around her, and unseen flecks of frozen material were bouncing from her helmet. She laughed wildly.

Suddenly she felt *great!*

"Bring it on," she said. "I'll take everything you've got."

It was going to be one hell of a ride.

Michael Swanwick, in addition to writing such novels as Bones of the Earth, Jack Faust, *and the Nebula-winning* Stations of the Tide, *produces some of the best short work in our field. His short fiction has garnered a World Fantasy Award, and four Hugos in the last six years. The fourth came for* "Slow Life."

ANOTHER SIDE OF HAL

STANLEY SCHMIDT

As editor of *Analog*, a magazine to which Hal Clement contributed several stories more memorable for their quality than their quantity, I might reasonably be expected to center my reminiscence for this memorial volume on his relationship with that magazine and his role as a preeminent creator of "hard" science fiction. Certainly I could do that, but so much has been published elsewhere about those things that I don't want to add unnecessary duplication. Instead, what first came to my mind when I was told of this project was my personal relationship with Hal, which looms surprisingly large in my life, considering how little direct contact with him I actually had.

It began with *Needle*, one of the first science fiction books I read, somewhere around fifth or sixth grade. I was fascinated by the science from which the story was spun, but what I remember most is the *story*, as story—and The Hunter, one of the most vividly real, sympathetic, and thoroughly alien characters I've ever met.

In the next few decades I read other stories of Hal's, with comparable fascination, but it wasn't until after I took the helm at *Analog* that I actually met him. Even then our encounters were few and usually brief and unplanned: passing in the halls at some convention or other; coincidentally sharing an airport shuttle at an American Association of Physics Teachers meeting in Columbus, Ohio; converging by chance on the same overlook in the Rocky Mountains after the Denver Worldcon; occasionally appearing together on a panel. (It felt decidedly strange to be asked to moderate a panel on worldbuilding with Hal, Poul Anderson, and Phil Dick as panelists!) Since Hal possessed the rare virtue of only writing when he had something to say, and since most of what he did write in recent years was novels, I published little of his work in *Analog*—though I was very pleased to have the opportunity to kick off our 70th anniversary issue with *Under*, a new novella involving his unforgettable world Mesklin. As I recall, it wasn't until after I had bought that, at the 1999 Nebulas in Pittsburgh, that we actually managed to sit down for a meal together.

I think my single most indelible memory of Hal concerns a side of him that is too often ignored, or even explicitly shrugged off. Much has been made of his playing "The Game," trying to make the science behind his stories as accurate as possible and pursue its consequences to their logical limits—with every expectation that readers would retaliate by trying to catch errors or places where he didn't go far enough. All that is true, but it's not the whole story. Many critics go astray by assuming that since he was so dedicated and careful with the science, he didn't care about character or know how to handle it in fiction. That amounts to a logical leap off a cliff, and the conclusion is just plain wrong. The most time I ever spent face-to-face with Hal was at the first Baltimore Worldcon in 1983, when the two of us ran a two-part workshop on worldbuilding. Ostensibly it was mainly about the science of that arcane art, and ostensibly it was for young readers, say, from grades five through twelve. It drew plenty of those, but quite a few adults came the first morning, and even more the second. And what I most remember about the workshop, especially the second part, was that our conversation ranged far beyond the hard sciences. What Hal had more to say about than anything else was characterization, and everything he said was well worth hearing and heeding.

The common fallacy that he didn't know or care much about character, I think, stems partly from the unusual attention he paid to science, and partly from another fallacy too often fostered by certain self-consciously "literary" folk: the notion that good characterization has to be about characters who are psychological disaster areas. Some of us have been fortunate enough to know from our own observation that sane, competent, even *likable* characters can be just as real, and just as interesting, as tormented souls who have gotten their lives tied into anguished knots and have no idea how to unravel them. Hal was a living example of that, and the characters in his stories—many of whom, like Barlennan and The Hunter, I would be delighted to know personally (or whatever word best applies)—extend the concept into a much wider universe.

Stanley Schmidt has been the editor of Analog *magazine since 1978, garnering 27 Hugo nominations for that work. His most recent novel is* Argonaut, *published in 2002.*

REMEMBERING HAL CLEMENT

JULIE E. CZERNEDA

Headlines about oceans on Mars. Chemistry in the daily news. A renewed—and new—sense of wonder about our universe. If there was anyone who had seen it coming, and nudged it along whenever possible, it was Hal Clement.

I'll always remember my first encounter with this marvelous man. My third convention ever. The program listed a presentation on the possibility of life in binary star systems. Unfortunately, I'd failed to take into account the time it would take to become less than lost in the hotel. I found myself tiptoeing through a darkened, and very full, room mere seconds before the presentation was to begin. Muttering a constant stream of apologies for my bags, for my feet, and likely for my mere presence on the planet by that point, I forced my way to the only empty seat I could see, second row from the front. I squeezed in between the folks on either side—apologizing to them too—and pulled out my notebook. My stomach grumbled, being here instead of finding lunch. "Hope it's good," I whispered to the universe.

The man in front of me turned with a smile. "Me too," he said, then stood.

Oops.

That reddish reflection on the screen? That was from my face.

Both our hopes were answered, of course. For the next hour, I sat as absorbed and enchanted as the rest while orbits skewed and suns waltzed, planets roasted and oceans froze. His soft voice wove wonder from them all and added his own. I went through pages and pages in my notebook, writing so fast much was barely legible.

During it all, he took questions from the dark ranging from astute to truly odd, answering each not only with respect and interest, but with such rapt attention it seemed he hoped to learn from us as much as we from him.

Who was this man? Obviously a scientist. Probably an astronomer, with a vivid and willing imagination. Vastly informed and undoubtedly important.

The lights went up only at the end. Only then did I see the copies of *Mission of Gravity* on my neighbors' laps. With an almost audible thunk, my brain connected Hal Clement from the program book with "the" Hal Clement! An important thinker? Oh yes. I was only feet away from one of the greatest SF writers of our time.

Oops.

I blushed again.

It took two more conventions, and several panels where I sat listening to Hal, learning from Hal, and taking notes at a furious rate, before I gained the nerve to talk to him one-to-one. Nerve? It was more revelation than courage. In a panel, he happened to comment how he'd been using science fiction as a teaching tool for decades in his science classes. I was in the midst of finishing a text on exactly that, but, until he spoke, I'd felt myself very alone—in that daring to tread where there might not be a floor at all, kind of way.

Nothing could have been further from the truth. We discovered a common passion, interest being too mild a word, for the value of science fiction to develop scientific literacy and, conversely, to inspire creativity within science itself. Over the following years, Hal encouraged me each time we met to continue with my work in this field. Through him, I grew to know many others equally committed to sharing the richness of our genre with educators. (As well as anyone who'd hold still in a hallway. As I said, we're all believers.)

Oops.

I seem to be talking about myself. This is a tribute to Hal Clement. But I must be truthful. I didn't know Hal outside of conventions and his writing. It took me an embarrassingly long while to figure out that Hal Clement and Harry Stubbs were one and the same person. Even then, it never occurred to me to call out "Harry" in the hallways. To me, this friendly, wise man was Hal. Like so many others, I wasn't part of his life. Instead, I was privileged to be in his company.

Perhaps that's the reason I speak of Hal Clement in terms of myself. Certainly, Hal's support and joy in what we shared, a love of teaching with science fiction, has encouraged my continuing to work in this field. Without doubt, his insistence that good science made good science fiction has influenced my own writing and editing. But most of all, Hal's kind respect for others and his expectation of learning something of value from everyone and everything around him has affected how I approach interacting with others at conventions, that meeting place we shared these many years. I aspire to his grace with people and ideas.

Our last such meeting typifies Hal to me. During the Golden Duck panel at the Worldcon in Toronto, we sat side-by-side, both arriving somewhat breathless. He winked at me, I smiled back. We sorted out water and microphones. He was every bit as warm and charming as always, despite this being the last day of a hectic convention for us all. His comments were to the point and, as usual, he surprised with his wit when least expected. I count it as a singular honor in my own life to have accepted my Golden Duck award from Hal Clement that day. But what I'll treasure most is when he grew a little silly. Having peeked at a copy of my next anthology while someone else spoke, and noticing mercury was featured in one story, Hal began to lean over at the most improbable moments to whisper in my ear about mercury's odder properties and discuss details of the story's plot. I know I broke into giggles at one point, trying to keep straight what I was supposed to be talking about on the panel. Hal, of course, kept this up with a perfectly straight face and implacable curiosity. He was interested. He had to know. Now.

Not that I was surprised. I'd come to realize one thing about Hal. He didn't simply write or teach about a sense of wonder.

Hal Clement lived it.

Julie Czerneda has produced nine novels since her debut in 1997, her latest being Migration. *Her writing has won her two Prix Aurora awards for excellence in Canadian SF. Her editing credits include the* Tales from the Wonder Zone *series for younger SF readers, and* ReVisions, *her latest volume, co-edited with Isaac Szpindel.*

BY ITS COVER

ISAAC SZPINDEL

"By Its Cover" was my first short story sale and it is very much a story about looks being deceiving. Such was my first experience with Harry Stubbs, as he introduced himself. Here was a pleasant older gentleman whose name I didn't recognize, and a fellow "Science In Science Fiction" panelist. He mentioned that he was a teacher and a writer and that he was looking forward to the panel. And, after the panel started, it took less time for Harry to dazzle us all with his gift for applying science creatively than it did for me to realize that Harry Stubbs was Hal Clement.

"By Its Cover" was originally published in the young adult Wonder Zone anthology edited by Julie Czerneda. Since the anthology was intended, in part, to inspire a love of science and instill a sense of wonder in young readers, naturally the authors who influenced me in this same way came to mind. And, just as naturally, various references to authors like Hal Clement appear throughout the story.

Like Hal, "By Its Cover" is a deceptively modest story, and a Carrollian twist on the old "confidence within" cliché. It quietly conveys a message about people bringing out the best, in each other. And this was what Harry did for me and for many others.

When the story was published, I made sure to personally present Harry with a copy. He accepted it with characteristic humility and grace. A year later, with the story an Aurora finalist, and the anthology a Golden Duck winner, Harry presented the award at what was to be his last Worldcon, with the same grace and much satisfaction.

It gives me satisfaction when this story is read and someone invariably asks, who is Harry Stubbs?

#

Harlan Stubbs was invisible. At home, at school, no matter where he went, it was as if people looked right through him. He could be seen, of course. It was just that no one bothered to pay him any attention. Harlan was so completely ignored that it was like a disease or a mutation had damaged the genes that might have made him a special or noticeable person. Miserable in his condition and desperate for a cure, Harlan found himself on his own, in a strange place, and about to do something he would likely regret.

The place was an old stone building that, like Harlan, stood lost and forgotten within a lonely part of town. Its surfaces had crumbled from neglect and its windows had gone blind under thick layers of dust. Still, despite the building's haunting appearance, hope pushed Harlan into the long line of people that inched single-file toward its entrance.

In line, no one spoke. Instead, they passed their time playing the latest downloadable interactives on their portables. Harlan had left his player at home, so to occupy himself he unfolded and read the flyer that his hands had almost worn beyond recognition.

BETTER LIVING THROUGH CHEMISTRY
Dr. Carol Lewis
Personal Biochemical Enhancements
Confidential
Satisfaction Guaranteed

The small print underneath was no longer readable. It was the first flyer Harlan had ever seen and one of the few pieces of paper he had actually touched. It couldn't be real, he thought to himself.

The line shortened into the building. Inside, the air was dry and the light was low and artificial. Harlan noticed a musty odour, like his grandfather's clothes. The building had been a library before downloadable interactives had replaced books and before the Environmental Protection Act had outlawed paper products. All around, the walls were covered with what appeared to be old-fashioned books. Harlan had seen pictures of books on the net, but had never seen or touched a real one. They were quite dull, he imagined, just plain words on paper. He was glad he hadn't been born fifty years earlier.

"Stubbs?" A high voice startled Harlan from his thoughts. "You're next." The voice came from a small woman carrying a large digital notepad. She wore a ragged old lab coat and looked up at Harlan through glasses twice gone out of style. "You related to Harry Stubbs, the author?" she asked.

"I wouldn't know. My parents are divorced and I don't know my father's family that well," answered Harlan.

"I see," she said, disappointed. "Follow me."

The woman hurried into a small elevator. Harlan bent his tall and clumsy form in beside her. He often felt that his body had been intended for someone else. "Are you Dr. Lewis?" he asked.

"Dr. Lewis?" she asked back.

"Yeah, from the flyer." Harlan showed it to her.

She examined it over her glasses and smiled. "Look at that. That's me, all right. You were looking for someone else, maybe?"

Harlan was puzzled by Lewis' strange response. "I don't think so."

"No, well you're quite right to ask," Lewis responded. "We can't believe everything we see now, can we?"

"I guess," answered Harlan, confused.

After what seemed like an uncomfortably long time to Harlan, the doors opened onto another floor much like the previous one. Immense wooden shelves packed with books extended inward from the surrounding circular wall onto a central laboratory area. Fragments of people and movement showed through gaps in the shelves where books had been removed.

"Previous customers," said Lewis, noticing Harlan's attention. "They won't bother us."

Harlan followed Lewis through the aisles and past earlier customers on a winding route to the laboratory area. "Are they reading those?" he asked.

"Books?" Lewis offered. "It's not a bad word, you know."

"No, but they're illegal, aren't they?"

Lewis spun on Harlan. "My flyers aren't printed on real paper made from trees," she said. "And even if real paper is illegal, books aren't. The people who passed those laws did it to protect our trees. They never wanted us to stop reading or making books. People see what they want to see and forget what's important."

Harlan wondered if his questions were offending Lewis. Despite her unusual behaviour, he had nowhere else to go, and no one else to turn to.

"Would you look at that." Lewis continued. "Now here I am losing track of what's important." She smiled at Harlan and offered him a seat by a broken metal desk. Lewis took her own seat opposite him.

"So what kind of enhancement would you like?" she asked. Her fingers danced silently across her notepad.

"Doesn't it say on your pad? I mean, I answered all the questions and transmitted them with my application." Harlan hoped he wasn't wasting his time.

"I have to make sure my information is correct, don't I?" Lewis responded.

"I want people to notice me," came Harlan's frustrated response.

"Interesting. Not terribly original, but interesting. You want people to notice you as soon as they see you? Just like that?"

"Yes," Harlan answered. Maybe Lewis knew what she was doing after all.

Lewis shot past Harlan, stopped at a laboratory table at the end of the room, and waited for Harlan to follow. On the table, an open maze surrounded a rather large sleeping rabbit. The entrance to the maze was shaped like a rabbit's hole. At the exit, a small bowl held a dried-out carrot.

"So, now that we know what you want," said Lewis, looking at the rabbit. "What do you want to do about it?" Harlan wasn't sure if she was talking to him or to the rabbit.

"I thought you might know," suggested Harlan, still puzzled by Lewis's behaviour and odd choice of location.

"Would you look at that," said Lewis, grinning again. "We do have a few options. A few things we can try, but I can only enhance one system at a time."

"System?"

"You'll understand. More than one system at a time, and the strain's too much for the body. Also, there have been occasional surprises."

"Like side effects?" asked Harlan.

"Like this rabbit. He got my muscle mixture. It should have made him even faster than he already was, but watch." She tapped the rabbit lightly on its back. It woke with a start and took off at near blinding speed. After passing two corners, it came to an abrupt stop and collapsed.

"What happened?" asked Harlan.

"Too hard on the body," Lewis explained. "Heart and lungs can't keep up. A few turns in the maze and it's so tired it has to sleep it off."

"Yeah, but what does that have to do with me?"

"If we enhance your body, you could become a sports star. A real some-body. Famous, even."

"You can do that?"

"Not really. Not this way, at least."

"Then how about making me smart," Harlan suggested. "So I can figure out how to get noticed."

Lewis led Harlan to another table where a large Tabby cat lazed on a short stack of books. "This is Chester," she said pointing to the cat. "Chester got my brain booster cocktail. Now, look at her."

"She's just sitting there."

"Exactly. That's what she does now. Sits there all day with that silly grin, thinks and does nothing else. I made her think more, but I couldn't make her any smarter. If I didn't feed her she'd forget to eat and her body would shut down completely." Lewis stared at the cat. The cat stared back.

"What's she thinking?" Harlan felt he had to ask.

"Now that's a good question," said Lewis, regarding Harlan with new respect. "I'll have to remember to ask her." Lewis and the cat continued their stare. Harlan wasn't sure if he should wait for a conversation to take place.

"Doctor?" Harlan finally interrupted. "How about my problem?"

"Oh yes, of course," she said, returning her attention to Harlan. "Let me see, now. Your skin. We could do something really outrageous to your skin." She picked at him like a tailor measuring a suit.

"Does it have to be outrageous?"

"It will get you noticed. Decorating the skin with tattoos and piercing used to be quite the rage, you know."

"Sounds painful."

"Sure, but reversing it, that's even more painful. Also, people get used to it, so it only works for a short time."

"Is there anything less drastic?"

"Skin pigmentation changes. We could turn you any colour, really. Takes time, though, and weakens the skin. Makes it easier for germs to get in and infect the body. And forget about going out in the sun. How about green? Very soothing. Easy on the eyes, you know."

Harlan was desperate, but so far Lewis hadn't offered any reasonable solutions. "Is there anything safer?" he asked.

"In what you're looking for? I'm afraid not."

"Nothing?" Harlan was crushed. Lewis, he thought, was his last chance.

"I do have something, but it's experimental," said Lewis, flashing her eyebrows for comic effect.

"Any side effects?" Harlan was almost too afraid to ask.

"Unpredictable. Mostly, it works or does nothing at all."

"Sounds like it's worth a try," said Harlan.

"Also, I seem to be missing one ingredient," said Lewis.

"What is it?" Harlan knew there had to be a catch, the experiment sounded too good to be true.

"If I knew, it wouldn't be missing."

"I guess it couldn't hurt," said Harlan, trying to sound brave. Realistically, he had no other choice.

"Okay then, let's get started." Lewis disappeared through a wooden door behind one of the tables. Harlan heard some crashing sounds, the squeal of a tap turning and the sound of a container filling. Lewis emerged moments later carrying a dusty test-tube full of a clear liquid. "The instructions are on the label," she said, holding it out to Harlan.

"'Drink me'?" Harlan read the label aloud.

Lewis nodded excitedly. "Fluids get absorbed directly. None of that messy digestion in the mouth and the stomach."

Harlan hesitated, tipped the tube into his open mouth, swallowed, then wiped the dust away from his lips. The liquid tasted exactly like water.

Lewis circled Harlan and inspected him. It looked like she was waiting for something to happen. Suddenly, she pulled him into a hug and pressed her ear tightly against his chest.

"What are you doing?" asked Harlan, shocked by Lewis' unexpected closeness.

Lewis didn't answer, but released her hold.

"Did you do something to my heart?" asked Harlan, thinking that an enhanced heart might improve both his strength and his endurance. He could become an athlete without the rabbit's nasty side effects.

"You could look at it that way," answered Lewis in her usual peculiar manner.

Harlan followed Lewis back to her desk. There, she set her notepad aside and searched through the clutter that covered its surface. Some of the paper she was sifting through, thought Harlan, must have been real.

"Now, as to the issue of your payment," said Lewis, still rummaging through her desk.

"I have some money saved up," offered Harlan.

"Not like that. You're an experimental subject, so I can't charge you. You'll be helping with my research instead," said Lewis continuing her search. "Besides, we are still missing that unknown ingredient and I do have a guarantee." Finally, she slid a yellowed card out from under the mess and offered it to Harlan. It contained some written words and a long code of numbers and letters separated by a decimal point.

"I've never seen anything like this," said Harlan.

"It's an index card." Lewis said. "We do things here the old-fashioned way."

"What things?" asked Harlan suspiciously.

"Good old-fashioned research. Book research," said Lewis with an air of satisfaction.

Harlan was less impressed. "But that'll take me ten times as long and be a hundred times more boring. Isn't there an interactive version of this stuff?"

"Sure, but it's not quite the same. My research requires imagination, and this particular problem, your problem, requires a very special kind of imagination. Those interactives are full of other people's imaginations. Books let you to use your own."

"I don't know if I can. I mean, I've never read one before."

"Good, an open mind. The code on the card will help you find what you're looking for."

Harlan turned the card over in his hands. "It could take me weeks to read just one book." He could tell by the expression on Lewis' face that she had little sympathy for him.

"Would you look at that," said Lewis, glancing at her bare wrist. "I have people waiting. Come back when you've found what you need." She waved Harlan off and disappeared into the shelves.

It didn't take long for Harlan to realize that the code on his index card corresponded to labels on books and to guides on the surrounding shelves. As he searched for the match, he passed by other customers, alone and in pairs. None of them paid any attention to him.

After a few wrong turns, Harlan came to a long row of similar looking books. There, the code led him to the far end where he quickly realized that he had company.

She was about Harlan's age, and like Harlan, she seemed to be searching for something. Her face was thin and delicate and her hair, dark and long. She stood more than a head shorter than Harlan, stretching from the tips of her toes, trying to get a better view at the top shelf. She was uncomfortably close to the area in which Harlan was searching. Sensing either his presence or his discomfort she turned to him and smiled. Harlan felt his face go hot.

"Are you helping with Dr. Lewis' research?" she asked.

Harlan nodded, but couldn't manage to speak.

"Me too. My name's Julie."

"I, I'm Harlan," he stuttered.

"Nice to meet you, Harlan."

"Me too," said Harlan. And in an effort to excuse his nervousness, "I'm not used to books."

"Me neither," said Julie. "They don't look like much on the outside and they're full of words on the inside."

"Yeah, a lot more work than an interactive." Harlan was feeling more at ease. Someone else, at least, felt the same way he did.

Julie kept her eyes on Harlan and smiled. "Do you need any help?"

"No. I think I can manage." Harlan wished he had said the opposite.

"Oh," said Julie, disappointed. "I could use some help."

"I'm not very good at this," said Harlan, fumbling again.

"Actually, you're perfect." Julie pretended not to notice Harlan blushing and pointed to the top shelf. "Mine's up there," she continued. "I went back to tell Dr. Lewis I couldn't reach it, but she just acted like she already knew and said I'd get what I came for, eventually."

"I can do that for you," said Harlan, finally able to express himself properly.

"Great. I'll help you find yours after we get mine. It's up on the top shelf, third from the end." She handed Harlan her card. He looked it over for a moment, then held his own up beside it.

"Is something wrong?" asked Julie.

"I don't know. I think they're the same," said Harlan, handing both cards to Julie. He could feel his heart beating harder.

"What should we do?" asked Julie.

Harlan couldn't answer. His breath was coming too quickly and his heart was beating too heavily for him to speak.

"We could try to read it together. If you want to?" Julie suggested, shyly.

Harlan could only manage a short reply. "I'd like that." He could feel the blood rushing up to his face again, so he turned away from Julie and slid the book off the shelf. It was thick and dusty and it gave off the same musty odour that Harlan had noticed when he had entered the building. After he felt like himself again, he handed the book to Julie.

"Looks long," she said, stopping to blow the dust off its jacket. "I hope you have plenty of time."

"Lots," said Harlan between breaths. Then, after a moment of consideration, "What about the missing ingredient? Do you know what to look for?"

Julie held the book close to her chest. "No, not really. But I'll bet we can find it together."

Something told Harlan that she was right. "I'll bet," he said, repeating Julie's words. "Want to go somewhere? You know, to read?"

Julie nodded her agreement. Harlan noticed, for the first time, that she was blushing as well.

Together, they made their way through the maze of books and shelves to the elevator. Once inside, neither spoke. Harlan lost himself in thoughts of Julie, books and strange experiments.

The elevator descended to a stop and opened its doors on the ground floor. There, Harlan noticed the difference immediately. A change was occurring. The people in line were starting to pull themselves out of their interactives. They were looking up and watching Harlan and Julie leave. Harlan suspected they were staring at the book in Julie's arms, but before long he realized it was something else entirely and then, somehow, it didn't seem to matter.

Isaac Szpindel is also an Aurora winner for his screenwriting on the series Rescue Heroes, *and is currently head writer for the international series* The Boy, *with plenty of other TV and movie work to his credit. His short fiction has also earned him critical acclaim.*

ON HAL CLEMENT

JACK WILLIAMSON

Hal and I were fellow veterans of World War II, though I didn't meet him until the early 1950s. On his graduation from Harvard, with a degree in astronomy, he had joined the Army Air Corps Reserve, receiving his wings in 1944 and flying 35 combat missions as pilot of a B-24 Liberator bomber. Recalled to active duty in 1951, he had served as a squadron executive officer and then as a technical instructor at the special weapons school at the Sandia base here in New Mexico—though all that was still classified at the time and he kept silent about it.

With his wife, Mary Elizabeth, and an infant son, he came by Portales to visit me and Blanche before they left New Mexico. He spent most of the rest of his life teaching high school science at the Milton Academy in Milton, Massachusetts. He was a teacher, I think, first of all. His stories, even, tend to have more science than fiction.

Yet science fiction was a very serious hobby. He had already made his name in the field before we met, with his first story published in *Astounding* while he was still in college. His first novel, *Needle*, an innovative mystery, had been serialized in 1949.

He made a bigger splash with *Mission of Gravity* in 1953. Set on an imagined high-spin planet with gravity at poles 700 times that of Earth and peopled with creatures designed to survive there, it set the pattern for all the "world-building" tales that have since filled so many science fiction shelves. Not content with writing, he became a painter, "George Richard," producing convincing science fiction and astronomical art.

Many times through the years I saw him at conventions, a popular guest and still a devoted fan. He was at Mile High Con, speaking of his work in progress, just a few days before his unexpected death. He will be recalled as one of our trail-breaking pioneers.

Jack Williamson's writing career spans three-quarters of a century, with the Legions of Space, Legions of Time, *and* Humanoids *series some of the highlights. His most recent hardcover novel,* Terraforming Earth, *included the novella "The Ultimate Earth" that won the Hugo and Nebula Awards. He is a past SFWA president, and was named a SFWA Grand Master in 1976.*

MEMORIES OF HAL

MICHAEL A. BURSTEIN

This is the essay I never wanted to have to write, but I imagine that this is a book that all of us feel had to appear far too soon. Hal Clement was such a part of our lives; it's still hard to believe he's gone.

Hal Clement was a gentleman. What more can one say? How can I explain how much he meant to me?

Let me try.

#

I. Meeting Hal and the Skylark Award

I don't remember exactly when I first met Hal, but it must have been at my first fan-run convention, Arisia '92, held at the Boston Park Plaza Hotel. After all, Hal made a point of attending some convention every weekend, and he never missed a local one.

Like many of us, I probably first encountered him as he wandered the halls, staring straight ahead, toting a bag over his shoulder. I can still imagine him now, walking through the halls with a far-away look in his eyes, blending into the background of the frenetic activity that surrounded him.

Hal never presumed. If he knew you, he would give you a nod as he walked past, but he would only stop to chat if you made a point of approaching him. Once I got to know him for real, I made a point of approaching him often. We talked a few times about our similar paths.

Hal and I had both studied Physics at Harvard and had gone on to teach and to write. But, of course, he was older than I was and had done much more in his life. I came to know the man behind the stories, and I started to realize why all of us in science fiction fandom admired and liked him so much.

Every year, the New England Science Fiction Association (NESFA) gives the Skylark Award to a professional in the field who has also made major contributions to fandom. Back in 1969, NESFA awarded the Skylark to Hal Clement. Then, at Boskone 34 in 1997, the members of NESFA decided to do something they had never done before—give the award to the same person for a second time. Inevitably, that recipient was Hal Clement. Hal was taken by surprise, but delighted to receive the award yet again. But that wasn't the end of the story.

In 1998, my wife Nomi and I served as the administrators of the Skylark Award. Traditionally, the previous recipient is asked to present the award to the next recipient, and so we called Hal about a month before Boskone 35 to ask him if he would be willing to present. He said yes, but I couldn't help noticing a certain wariness in his voice.

I found out why at the presentation ceremony. Nomi and I had managed to tell Hal just a few minutes before the name of the 1998 recipient: James White. Until that moment, Hal had thought that NESFA might have been trying to do something sneaky, such as getting him to present a third Skylark Award to himself! Hal is the only professional I can think of who could be counted upon to present an award to himself with modesty, but as noted, the award actually went to James White. Hal presented the award with grace and aplomb, and that would be the last time I was involved with Hal and awards.

Or so I thought at the time . . .

II. Books and Grand Master

On May 1, 1999, the Science Fiction and Fantasy Writers of America (SFWA) presented the 1998 Nebula Awards in Pittsburgh. Hal Clement had been chosen unanimously by the Board and the former presidents to be the new Grand Master. For the longest time, Grand Masters had not been announced until the same night as the Nebula winners. However, in the few years previous to the Pittsburgh Nebula Banquet, SFWA had gotten into the habit of announcing the Grand Master slightly earlier.

Now, it so happened that at the time, I was serving as both the Secretary of Science Fiction and Fantasy Writers of America and Vice-President of the New England Science Fiction Association. And NESFA had just decided to reprint some of Hal's classic stories in a collection called *The Essential Hal Clement, Volume One*. The other two volumes would be forthcoming over the next few years. Given my two positions, a natural thought occurred to me. I consulted the other people in charge at both SFWA and NESFA, and everyone agreed to my plan.

So on the Saturday morning of Boskone 36—February 13, 1999—we held a SFWA regional meeting and announced that Hal Clement had been named the new Grand Master of the Science Fiction and Fantasy Writers of America. This was the earliest that such an honor had ever been announced, but by doing so, SFWA managed to make the announcement at the same time NESFA Press released the book.

Right after the regional meeting ended, I rushed over to the Hucksters Room with a sign stating that NESFA congratulated Hal Clement, the new SFWA Grand Master. As I put the sign up at the NESFA Press table, Tor editor David G. Hartwell was sitting across from us at his *New York Review of Science Fiction* table. Someone walking by saw our sign, turned to Hartwell, and said, "So Hal Clement is the new Grand Master?" Hartwell's response: "I guess so."

Finally, I was the insider, the person in the know. And it was all thanks to Hal Clement.

I will never forget watching Hal that Boskone. His face bore a broad smile throughout the entire convention. By making the announcement a few months early at Hal's home convention, we gave him the chance to bask in the glow among the people in fandom closest to him. The way I put it at a memorial panel for Hal at Boskone 41 (2004), Hal got to enjoy his new honor among his *mishpocha*, which is Yiddish for one's extended family.

And NESFA sold many copies of Hal's new book, which was good for everyone.

But let it not be thought that the actual presentation of the award at the Nebula Banquet was an anti-climax. Hal was feted all weekend in Pittsburgh, and praised to the skies by *Babylon 5* creator J. Michael Straczynski, who presented Hal with the award. Straczynski compared his own work in television with Hal's in prose, pointing out that Hal never needed set designers or actors to create his remarkable landscapes; he just used his technical knowledge and limitless imagination.

Hal received more than just a Lucite block that night. David Truesdale had created a poster with photographs of every previous Grand Master, and Hal was given the very first copy, on a large wooden plaque. I helped Hal back to his table, and a lot of people were amused that I carried the relatively smaller Grand Master award and made Hal carry the large plaque. People told me later that they thought I was coveting Hal's award. While it is true that I wouldn't mind being given such an honor myself, the fact was that such an honor was the last thing on my mind that night. I was kvelling over the role I had played in honoring Hal, and I carried his award for him to ensure that nothing untoward would happen to it on his way back.

Hal got a lot of pleasure out of that award, but it never went to his head. For the next few years, he continued attending conventions in his modest way, doing program items for children when no one else would.

III. Readercon 15 Guest of Honor

In the middle of 2003, I was waiting to hear about my program schedule from Readercon. Hal had been chosen as one of the Guests of Honor for that convention.

Ellen Brody, one of the people running program, contacted me to ask if I would be willing to serve on one special event. For Hal's Guest of Honor presentation, he had requested an interview, and Ellen wanted to know if I would be willing to serve as the interviewer.

My reply to her was something like, "Gack." But I said I was willing to do it if they really thought it was appropriate.

She assured me that they and Hal thought I would do an excellent job. Apparently, Hal had specifically requested me to conduct the interview.

Hal may have had confidence in me; I most certainly did not. So I emailed three BNFs (big name fans): Tony Lewis, Mark Olson, and Bob Devney. I explained the situation and asked them for ideas of questions to ask Hal. Mark knew a lot about Hal's work and gave me some pointers. Bob produced a list of questions and suggested I ask Hal about his singing. And Tony also had some useful advice to share.

"Remember," he said when I saw him before the convention, "people are coming to hear Hal. Not you."

I assured Tony that I was well aware of that.

Readercon weekend arrived, and I met with Hal on Friday afternoon.

We sat on one of the sofas in the hotel hallway, and I went through the list of questions I wanted to ask him about at his interview.

One thing that came up was the perennial story Ben Bova would tell of Hal's appearance at the Heidelberg Worldcon. The way Ben would tell the story, Hal had been asked by a group of German fans if he had ever been to Heidelberg before. Hal supposedly thought for a moment, then said, "I was a little bit south of here once," but chose not to explain that at the time, it was World War II, and he had been bombing them.

The only problem, though—that afternoon, Hal assured me that the story was apocryphal. I promised him that we would use the interview to set the record straight.

Before I said good-bye to Hal, I presented him with my copies of volumes two and three of *The Essential Hal Clement* and asked him to autograph them to me. He did so. Afterwards, I told him that I had almost forgotten to bring the books with me to Readercon, but I figured that it would have been okay. After all, I expected to see Hal again at the next convention.

At 4 PM on Saturday July 12, I conducted what appears to be the final public interview with Hal Clement. Hal was sparkling and witty.

One exchange that was not planned in advance occurred when Hal mentioned that he remembered the very first cover of the very first science fiction magazine he had ever seen.

"Really?" I replied. "That's amazing."

"That's right," Hal responded. "It was *Amazing*."

As a gentleman to the end, Hal wouldn't take the bait when I gave him a chance to defend hard science fiction and attack other forms of SF and fantasy. I mentioned Greg Benford's oft-reported comment that other forms of science fiction were like "playing tennis with the net down," and I asked Hal if he wanted to say something equally controversial.

"No, sir," he said, with a comment to the effect that his only concern was with his own work.

We did get to the Heidelberg story, and dispatched it quickly. Hal never wanted to tell his war stories. When asked why, he said he didn't want to be the kind of bore who told war stories all the time. But if coaxed, he would, and some of those stories were the most fascinating I've ever heard.

Hal told a lot of great stories, but probably the most remembered comment from that interview will be the one about Mesklinite pornography. Mesklinites, the aliens from *Mission of Gravity*, look vaguely like caterpillars, and at a panel once someone asked him what Mesklinite pornography would look like. Hal replied that he had no idea, but after the panel someone approached him with the answer: rubber bands, of course.

Hal may have been serious about his world-building, but he also showed a delightful sense of humor as well.

IV. Final Voyage

For many reasons, the week of Wednesday, October 29, 2003 was a difficult one for me. But the most difficult part of that day came when I saw an email in the afternoon from Mark Olson, reporting that Hal Clement had died that morning.

I didn't want to believe it. I knew that Moshe Feder at Tor had been the editor who worked with him most recently, and I called him to confirm the news, which he sadly did. I also knew that *Analog* editor Stanley Schmidt didn't check his email very frequently, so I called him as well to share the bad news.

A few of us wanted to make sure that Hal got his due, and we contacted the *New York Times* and the *Boston Globe* to make sure they would each run a proper obituary. I got called at work on Thursday by Tom Long, the obituary writer at the Globe, who asked me many questions about Hal. Long wanted to do right by our friend, and he did.

The October 31, 2003 issue of the paper included the obituary "Hal Clement, 81, craftsman of sci fi novels." And to my embarrassment, Long had quoted me prominently in two places. The good part was the two things I said about Hal:

"He had an ability to use real science to create incredible planets, worlds, and landscapes that could legitimately exist in our universe under our physical laws."

"Other writers would read him and say, 'My God, how did he do this?' He was a writer's writer; writers read him to become better."

But the odd part was finding myself cited and referred to in the first place. Hal lived to be 81 years old, and I had only gotten to know him in the last decade or so of his life. I felt illegitimate having such a prominent place in his obituary, given how little I felt I actually knew Hal, and how little Hal had known me.

Then my wife reminded me that Hal had asked me to interview him just a few months earlier, and that he and I had shared a bond. If the universe put me in a position to praise Hal Clement, well then, it was okay for me to do so.

Hal was a mentor to all of us who dream of other worlds.

Michael A. Burstein is a leading young writer in SF, having won the Campbell Award in 1997, and having eight Hugo and two Nebula nominations to his credit. He has been an officer in SFWA and NESFA and, as did Harry Stubbs, he works as a science teacher.

THE DIAMOND SKY

DAVID GERROLD

The hull of *The Martian Queen* was diamond-plated. By design.

A seemingly-endless field of panels reflected the distant starlight with a plated sheen halfway between metal and ice. She looked more like a careless array of solar collectors than the spacecraft she really was.

Captain Adam Neace reviewed the vessel with a critical eye. He wore a VR headset and he rode *Little EVA,* one of the external spider-bots, up and down the long rows of panels, quietly inspecting. He didn't expect to find anything, the spider-bots were more thorough and more relentless than any mere human could ever be, but Adam Neace wasn't a mere human and he was old enough to remember a time when bots were merely extensions of human effort, not independent agents. He liked to look for himself. Despite his own augmented being, he still believed in human intuition; that sometimes the human mind could sense possibilities and connections that a simple intelligence engine might overlook. But mostly Captain Adam Neace rode the bots because he liked being "outside" more than inside.

. . . another successful breeding season at the Auckland Seaquarium. Alex is the largest giant squid living in captivity, nearly six meters in length. In the wild, giant squids can grow to 16 meters or more. The Auckland Seaquarium covers an area of sixteen square kilometers and is the second largest land-based ocean laboratory in the southern hemisphere. The South African and Australian seaquariums also have breeding programs for . . .

The Martian Queen was eleven years old, built to standard design: a kilometer-long keel, speared through the axis of a mandatory habitat-centrifuge. To an external observer, she might have seemed an unwieldy conglomeration of panels, struts, guy wires, pipes, engines, tanks, sensory gear, ancillary thrusters, and life-support modules; but in actuality, she was a carefully balanced machine, a space-going laboratory as well as a precision vacuum factory. Although she was capable of interplanetary leaps, for most of her life, she'd stayed in perpetual eclipse, riding the shadow of Mars; a tricky but not impossible orbit. It was a necessary maneuver to keep the vessels isolated so that the delicate fabrication processes of her factories would not be contaminated by stray solar radiation. Solar storms could be violent even this far out from the hearth.

   . . . evolutionary advances in digital archaeology have made it possible to cross-correlate multiple time-data frames, allowing researchers to track the interaction of real-time trends across multi-dimensional matrices, including economic, political, ecological, and sociological causitives. Cusps of chaotic potential appear as three-dimensional spikes in the strata . . .

"Captain?"

Neace put the bot on auto and flipped up his VR goggles. First Officer Mark Ensley came floating forward into the bridge. "We've got mail. From Admiral Palmer." Ensley pulled himself down into the copilot's seat and belted himself in. Neace touched his display and brought up the message. The first sentence told him everything he needed to know: "Congratulations, Captain Neace." The rest of it was formality: "The Review Board is satisfied that *The Martian Queen* and her crew have met or surpassed all requirements. The Board is pleased to certify *The Martian Queen* as ready for service. You may proceed with the next phase of your mission immediately."

Neace scratched his neck thoughtfully. The message wasn't unexpected, as the ship had been prepared for several days. They were already testing the long-range laser-links off the asteroid-belt repeaters. But bureaucracy had to be served—for two reasons. First, bureaucrats needed to feel important, and second, you always had to have enough paper to cover your ass. Just in case. Even so, the official confirmation felt good.

   . . . announced the successful insertion of the ice-asteroid into a close approach orbit, timed to coincide with the Summer Olympic Games in Dallas-Fort Worth.

Comet Janisian will have a red, white, and blue tail stretching across one-third of the sky and will be visible for nearly three weeks . . .

"I'll have the Venus link up as soon as we move out of shadow," Ensley reported. "And we'll have direct acquisition of Earth-Luna at 0803. Not quite the optimal triangle, but it'll give us a baseline."

"IRMA, secure the bots; begin your checklist, please."

"Working . . . ."

. . . high point of the all-robot revival of Hello Dolly *is the astonishing "Waiter's Gallop" sequence, with over a hundred glimmering metal bodies leaping and dancing in pinpoint synchronization, juggling trays of full glasses and pitchers, all without spilling a single drop of . . .*

For most of her life, *The Martian Queen* had been one of several orbital facilities producing large form diamond-substrates. Working in the universe's largest clean room—the universe itself—her external factory bots vacuum-layered pure crystalline carbon onto panels several meters across to create the largest *and flattest* diamonds possible. The resultant sheets were the ideal substrate for optical and electrical chips, for display panels of all sizes, for precision collectors and reflectors, and for a thousand other industries that needed atomically flat surfaces—for example, mirror arrays for radio, optical, and X-ray telescopes.

As each panel was completed, it was measured and graded. Any panel that failed the "flat as ancient Kansas" test could not be certified. Although there existed a considerable market for these lower grade diamond sheets, shipping them wasn't cost-effective for a ship in Martian orbit; local suppliers could provide the panels cheaper; but this was understood long before *The Martian Queen*'s keel had been drawn. It had been planned from the beginning that Captain Neace would install the castoff pieces around critical components of the vessel as ablation shields against strikes by micro-meteorites.

. . . ethics of animal implants remain unresolved. Meanwhile, Sparky has added another thirty words to his vocabulary. As you can see, Sparky enjoys meeting new people, and he speaks his thoughts enthusiastically, as our onsite reporter discovered. <Sparky:> "Maya smell good. Maya mate, yes?" . . .

But the fabrication and sale of A-grade panels was only a sideline for the *Queen*—a very profitable sideline, but a sideline nonetheless. Her very best surfaces were reserved for a much more ambitious task. Not all the panes she produced were pure diamond, and not all were flat. Many were doped with layers of other materials to provide specific physical properties, many were subtly curved to fit into a precise design. *The Martian Queen's* sole job was the construction of several thousand diamond mirrors, the most optically precise reflectors ever made, all components of the largest distributed array ever constructed.

Her certification had never been in doubt, for the most part, she was constructed with "off-the-shelf" technology, but now that she was officially online she could assume her duties as the third and final coordinating station for the Dispersed Array Space Telescope. Two similar ships rode in the orbits of Earth and Venus. Other vessels were planned for the future, but at least three were necessary to coordinate.

. . . in a limited decision, the court declined to rule on the ethics of Klingon-deprogramming. However, the court did agree that Acht-Facht had not left the Enterprise orbiting hotel voluntarily and that the lawsuit could continue. Representatives of the Klingon Church petitioned to the court to compel The Human Adventure to reveal Facht's whereabouts . . .

DAST was an inevitable idea, an outgrowth of Arecibo and Paranal and Farside. Spaceships carried telescopes—all kinds—optical, radio, microwave, X-ray, gamma-ray, gravitational, deep-resonance, and stress-field. Link up several telescopes, point them all in the same direction, collate their separate images, and you create a virtual telescope as large as the distance between reflectors. The proof of concept was over a century and a half old, dating back to the days when all astronomy was Earth-bound. The four linked lenses at Paranal had eventually produced pictures even more spectacular than the orbiting Hubble eye.

In the early 21st century, this idea had been exported to space. Four identical planetary probes were linked by laser to each other. All four focused their telescopes on the same set of objects and synchronized their separate exposures. Even as a proof of concept, the results were staggering; the detail of their deep space imagery left astronomers hungering for more. The Distributed Array Space Telescope had been an ongoing project ever since. Almost every ship in transit between Earth and Mars linked its onboard telescopes to the Lunar Coordinating Base at Gagarin; long-range lasers transmitted a steady stream of timing and position data; each ship synchronized its exposures to the nano-second, and returned its images along the same laser beams it used for position-referencing. It was not only the largest virtual telescope in existence, it was also the most cost-effective, using existing observational tools already in place. Even the software was off-the-shelf. All it required was a coordinating station.

. . . dead at 137. She was the last living survivor of the . . .

But as humanity pushed outward, to the asteroid belt, to the moons of Jupiter and Saturn—as more and more ships and telescopes came online, synchronization became exponentially difficult. Management became the essential problem. *The Martian Queen* and her two sister ships were intended as a triangle of anchor points, providing precision synchronization data; each one linking to and coordinating all participating ships within her own sphere of influence. The projected increase in resolution was expected to be at least three orders of magnitude.

Each of the *Queens* needed multiple laser-units and reflector panels for every ship in the linkage. Additionally, to provide a baseline for comparison, each of the *Queens* carried one of the three largest telescopes ever dispatched to space; when fully opened, the array would be several hundred meters across. From the outset, each of the *Qheens* had been designed as a space-going factory, each one fabricating all of her own delicate reflectors.

. . . said that the quake, measuring at least 6 points on the Maslow-Richter scale, would be centered in the San Fernando Valley, and would occur in the first week of February. Voluntary evacuations are recommended for the area. FEMA will be sending in over a thousand quake-proofing consultants to advise residents . . .

"We're out of the shadow," Ensley reported. "We've acquired *The Venus Queen*."

"Right," said Neace, studying his own displays. "Let's say hello. Three beams." He pressed record and whispered into his microphone, "Peek-a-boo—" The beams were effectively invisible in the vacuum of space; at one part per godzillion, there wasn't enough dust to illuminate them; but 12.3 light-minutes away, *The Venus Queen*, in the center of the targeting cone, would be able to distinguish three specific pinpoints of color—red, green, and blue. The subtle differences between the beams would allow *The Venus Queen* to calculate Doppler shift, precise distance, and timing for synchronization.

Allow three minutes for Captain Radley Nakamura to receive the message and record an acknowledgment, *The Martian Queen* should receive its reply no more than thirty minutes after sending its initial message; once the first laser-links were in place, the primary synchronization could be completed in a matter of hours; even allowing for slippage, no more than eight hours should be required to establish the first backbone channel for the DAST network. At these distances, however, mostly the job involved waiting.

—which is why the ideal candidate for long-term space missions was an immortal.

. . . largest ever expansion of a sea-going environment, Atlantis will add 20 square kilometers of pontoon-based platforms over the next seven years. Construction will cost 1.7 billion plastic dollars and will increase the sea-nation's surface area by 20%. In off-market trading, share prices went up a half, with further increases expected when the market formally reopens after the weekend holiday . . .

Neace hadn't set out to be immortal, but as he aged, it had become more and more convenient—and necessary—to augment his biological processes with biotechnological aids. By the time of his 80th birthday, he was nearly 80% augmented; and at the present rate of accretion, his centenary would see the completion of the various processes. He was neither impatient nor apprehensive, merely resigned to the inevitability. He wanted a berth on the first interstellar expeditionary fleet. Non-immortals need not apply. At one-quarter light-speed, the journey to Sirius and back would take 66 years.

His primary motivation, however, had involved Captain Nakamura. He'd been fascinated by her from the first, although he hadn't recognized it as infatuation until later. Their romance had been passionate, but all-too-often interrupted by the exigencies of career. A variety of assignments had sent them careering across the solar system, only occasionally allowing them to match orbits. When she had gone immortal, as most starsiders eventually did, he had followed her lead. Ideally, he hoped they would both secure assignments aboard the same ship of the Sirius mission. But even if not, as an immortal, he now had time to wait. One of the lesser advantages of immortality was the ability to downshift; to place oneself into a slower time-speed—relative dormancy—and thus transform long periods of imposed inactivity to shorter subjective experiences.

. . . found the stock certificates almost by accident in a stack of fanzines. Purchased for only twelve dollars a share in 1987, the certificates now represent holdings of more than . . .

"Laser linkage acquired," IRMA reported. "Incoming message." Radley Nakamura's voice whispered a near-flirtatious response: "—I see you!" To an immortal, the twenty-seven minute interval was negligible.

Neace nodded dispassionately. "Initiate calibration." The two ships would ping-pong a complex set of signals and tests, triangulating on each other as they moved through their separate trajectories, and ultimately establishing precision-predictive-positioning data accurate to a tenth of a millimeter, plus or minus an error below the ability of the measuring equipment to detect.

There wasn't much else to report to *The Venus Queen*. Despite the fact that this was the first time in eleven years that the two ships had achieved direct line of sight, they had never really been out of contact, relaying their messages via whatever satellite and ships-in-transit links were currently available. Bouncing messages off relays always added delays, and depending on the number of intermediate steps, it could easily double transmission times. Direct acquisition meant that the time lag between message and response was now appreciably shorter.

. . . announced that she will again change gender, this time to play the role of Seth in the BBO production of A Season of Passion. *The change will take four months, and filming will begin in the spring. Although no casting has been announced for the role of Diana, producers are said to be in negotiation with Ric Carliss, the only other performer to have won awards for both best male performance and best female performance . . .*

"Peek-a-boo" was almost a six-decade-old joke between the two Captains. In his first year at the Academy, Neace had installed a digital camera on the terrace of his student apartment. The unit had a self-synchronizing motorized mount, automated motion-detection-and-capture, holographic lenses, 6-color correction, UHD resolution at 120fps, and a telephoto ratio of 375x. As an exercise in engineering, he'd written software for it to monitor all the visible windows of two facing dormitories, zooming in for close-ups wherever motion was detected. He wasn't the first student to have done this—it was one of several real-world assignments handed out to freshmen. Neace's addition to the software included multi-spectrum collation, extrapolated removal of obscuring artifacts (such as window glare and curtains), digital image enhancement and noise reduction, clothing detection (including lack of), sorting all retrieved data by amount of skin revealed, followed by additional sorting based on conformation of body mass to selected optimal characteristics—including breast size. The video display in Neace's apartment automatically updated to play a repeating slideshow of the most interesting images captured.

Radley Nakamura did not show up in any of these scans, which singular fact was enough to reduce Neace's grade on the project from A+ to merely A. Due to her short hair, her propensity for wearing sweatshirts and sweatpants, the recognition algorithm had erroneously classified Ms. Radley Nakamura as a boy. Already in her junior year, and well familiar with the prevalence of cameras in the buildings opposite, Ms. Radley Nakamura did this deliberately. The instructors, equally familiar with Ms. Radley Nakamura, included her as a test of the recognition abilities of Neace's software project.

. . . replacement of the three wind-turbines damaged in the last Martian sandstorm is expected to take . . .

This being a tiered assignment—with final grade dependent on the student's ability to implement improvements and corrections—Neace focused exclusively on Radley Nakamura's window, determined to fix his gender-recognition algorithm. He began correlating a weighted value system, based on Adam's-apple size, wrist size, complexion, general softness of features, center of gravity, motion characteristics, body-fat ratios, generalized behaviors, and other characteristics with specifically measurable differences between the sexes. Very quickly, he realized that the problem stemmed from Ms. Nakamura's commitment to her career. Having decided that gender identity was an inconvenience, she had gone androgynous, preparatory to becoming immortal. The androgynous part was reversible, of course; but not the immortality augments. Neace had to rewrite his recognition algorithm to allow for androgyny superposed over gender. It wasn't a trivial problem, and he aimed his camera directly at her balcony to gather sufficient observational data to establish a personal baseline for Radley Nakamura to measure against the statistical norms.

Unfortunately, the video software failed to update any motion from Ms. Nakamura's balcony. Reviewing the capture in real-time revealed why. Ms. Nakamura had hung a curtain across her balcony, blocking any further intrusions of her privacy. Even more to the point, she had set up her own camera, pointed directly back at Neace's.

Neace got the point immediately. He hand-lettered a sign and hung it below the lens of his camera. The sign said, "Peek-a-boo."

. . . presented a new plan for shadowing Venus. Based on their preliminary results, researchers now believe that Venusian temperatures could be reduced in less than 150 years . . .

A day later, Ms. Nakamura's camera displayed a matching sign. "I see you."

Neace hung a new sign on his camera. "Dinner?"

She replied. "Diner. 7pm."

Over dinner at the diner, Neace discovered—among other things—another reason why his recognition algorithm had failed. Nakamura was genetic male, female by choice, and as previously determined, temporarily androgynous. Neace wasn't old-fashioned, he'd dated members of several genders with enthusiasm, and varying degrees of success; he was simply annoyed with himself that he hadn't included this possibility. After briefly debating with himself about a possible appeal of his project grade, he decided instead to recode the recognition algorithms and win his points fairly.

. . . encyclical from Pope Maria Theresa reaffirms the church's stance on the sanctity of all sentient life, whether it's carbon-based or silicon . . .

Nakamura found Neace amusing. He was intrigued by her unusual insights, a product of her peripatetic gender identity. Although their mutual schedules allowed for only the occasional hurried meal at the diner, they kept in constant touch by e-mail, and by displaying increasingly cryptic messages on their respective balconies, each one a puzzle. If the recipient couldn't solve the problem, he or she had to pay for the next dinner. Neace ended up paying for most of their meals.

It wasn't that she was smarter or that he lacked puzzle-solving skills; rather, he was methodical and determined where she had grown up outside the lines. He knew why he was fascinated by her; but for a while, he couldn't understand what she liked in him. Eventually she had to tell him. "It's the strength of your determination. Determination without genius got more ships launched than genius without determination." For Neace, it was a moment of sheer *aha!* The two them complemented each other.

Which was why, even 12.7 light minutes apart, they were still able to play "Peek-a-boo, I see you."

. . . representatives from Roma, Cathay, Nubia, and Babylon again failed to reach agreement with the World Health Organization on the issue of vaccination. Health care has always been a sore point for the historical simulacra, with extremist factions decrying modern health measures as anachronistic influences that distort or destroy the accuracy of the recreated cultures . . .

"We've got Earth/Luna," said Ensley. "Just coming up over the horizon. We've got radio tracking."

Neace glanced up at the high resolution display. A highlighted frame expanded to reveal a bluish pinpoint, imperceptibly sliding out from behind the shield of the red planet.

"And we've got incoming—"

"Nice timing on their part," Neace noted.

The hearty voice of Manda Sahir boomed from the speakers, with just a hint of single entendre. "Gotcha! Enough with the peek-a-boo. Let's play pattycake."

"I love you too, Manda," Neace replied, even though it would be 6 minutes before Captain Sahir heard his response.

. . . tourism to Bradbury is projected to increase with the completion of the third phase of the Grand Canal project, with other Martian cities expecting to benefit as well. Burroughs will increase its Thoat-breeding programs, and Wellsopolis will make the Invasion of London-1890 an annual event. (That's

Martian-annual, not Earth-annual.) Bookings will need to be made at least two years in advance . . .

Captain Manda Sahir had always been aggressive, so much so that she'd earned several astonishing nicknames during her career, "scream-and-leap" being the least objectionable. But in truth, her attitude was far more playful than passionate; she wasn't flirtatious, she was just "kidding around with the guys" and she'd calculatedly rebuffed several who misunderstood where the boundaries had been drawn. Neace had been one of the lucky ones, caught between missions. The affair had been affectionate, playful, friendly, and ultimately noncommittal. Nevertheless, Neace now regarded himself as the hypotenuse of the farthest-spanning triangle in human history, although it would have been more geometrically accurate to consider his position acute angle—at least until the movements of the several planets and their orbiting *Queens* altered the shape of the triangle.

. . . spokesman for the Reich predicted a seventh consecutive victory over the Allies in the upcoming replay of World War II. The simulation is expected to attract over a million players, and nearly that many observers. The ReichsKampf also released further information about the Vaterland-1936 enclave, now under construction at . . .

"We've got RGB from *The Lunar Qheen*," said Ensley. "Right on target."

"Did you expect less?" Neace grinned. "Light her up. Initiate calibration, let's see what we've got." Neace waited until the displays flashed green, then half-turned to his first officer. "Congratulations. We're online. Let's take some pictures. Earth, Venus, Jupiter and Saturn. Then I want a long shot of Sedna. After that, the standard celestial repertoire. Horsehead, Crab, Orion Anomaly, the whole package. We'll need the shots for comparison after we've established first collation."

"Working," said Ensley. The program had been written months before. All he had to do was call it up and check off the appropriate targets. The computer would do the rest. Indeed, the program was as much a test of the synchronizing software as it was of the telescope itself. They'd already had a dozen test runs while still in the shadow of Mars. There was no significant importance to this shoot, except that for the first time, it was an *official* test.

. . . super-clustering over thirty million subscribers, with a projected real-time decryption matrix . . .

IRMA beeped softly. Incoming messages arriving. The first of thousands that would arrive over the coming weeks, as various ships in transit sought to establish their own linkages. Aside from their individual participation in the Dispersed Array Space Telescope, there was a much more immediate objective — accurate mapping of the solar neighborhood, accurate positioning within that map, predictive analysis of gravitational rumpling and mascon perturbation of smaller space objects.

Ensley briefly reviewed the ship's e-mail. Most of the requests for connection would be auto-replied over the next few days, but no additional connections would be made until the *Queens* established their own baseline. The big problem here would be correlating massive amounts of data in real-time. Once the DAST was online, that problem would expand exponentially. It wasn't that the ship didn't have the processing power — it did — the problem was throughput: the allocation of bandwidth resources.

But several of the messages did require human attention and Ensley began working methodically through them. It was the commentaries in the science journals he was most concerned about. Occasionally, someone or other would so totally misunderstand the workings of the Dispersed Array Space Telescope that it required an immediate response, before a whole mythology of ignorance was inadvertently allowed to take root — like that most notorious of all scientific misunderstandings, dating back to the early 20th Century, that a rocket couldn't work in a vacuum because there was no air to push against.

. . . breaking the record for the longest sustained (non-fatal) orgasm ever recorded, Yates credited all three of her partners . . .

Some of the questions raised about DAST included, "How can it be a telescope if it's mostly space and very few mirrors?" and "How do you focus a virtual reflector 400 million kilometers across?"

The more literate objections dealt with parallax and resolving power. "Won't parallax issues make collation of the separate images problematic, especially for objects close to or within the solar system?" "Isn't the ultimate resolving power limited by the resolving power of the individual reflectors?" "Aren't existing space arrays sufficient? Doesn't this take us way beyond the point of diminishing returns?"

There were answers to all of these. Ensley had already authored several articles and a short book addressing the various issues in language as accessible to the lay reader as possible. But even he acknowledged that in some regards, astronomy had gone way beyond the proverbial "rocket science." The simple process of scanning the diamond sky now required technology that even many astronomers did not fully understand. As one wag had put it, the gap between theory and engineering was now estimated to be several light hours and expanding exponentially.

. . . but that argument still doesn't address the legal issue; if an adult rejuvenates to an adolescent or even a pre-pubescent body, is he or she still an adult capable of informed consent? When individuals choose to become infantiles, dependent upon others, how can they still claim adult privileges and responsibilities? Should sexual encounters with infantiles and rejuveniles be considered acts between consenting adults with body-mods — or are we seeing a new form of statutory rape? We have to ask if those who seek out and engage in such relationships are expressing a pedophilic intention. Does this create an environment that ultimately endangers all sub-adult beings . . .

When the first high-resolution pictures of Earth and Luna finally came up, both Neace and Ensley breathed a sigh of relief. Neither man had realized they were holding their breath. The resolving power of *The Martian Queen*'s array was at the high end of optimum, almost approaching the theoretical limits. It was better than expected, more than was hoped for.

. . . documentary on the completion of Mons Rushmore, including interviews with the descendants of . . .

The next few shifts kept both men busier than usual and left little time for flirtations, long-distance or otherwise. The pictures of Jupiter and Saturn were excellent, and the project shifted easily into its next phase.

All three *Queens* synchronized on schedule and their first collated image was of far-distant, frozen Sedna. Sol's tenth planet, first discovered in 2004, wandered in an elliptical orbit as close as 76 AU's, as far as

1000 AU's, taking over 10,500 years to complete a single orbit. Sedna was moving away from Sol now, and would continue to do so for several millennia, looping out again toward its home in the Kuiper belt. These were not the first or even the best pictures of Sedna; several robot probes had already mapped the planetoid's bright red surface; but the pictures of Sedna were still important. They would be used to gauge the resolving power of the DAST coordinating stations.

During the same period, each of the *Queens* began receiving pings from ships-in-transit, robot probes, orbital stations, and all three Lunar observatories. Once the Sedna test was completed, the *Queens* began assembling an intricate web of laser connections; the assignments were made on the basis of bandwidth and telescope-size. Although, other planetary networks existed, none of them required the same nano-second-precise synchronization. That most of the separate pieces of the network existed light-minutes apart complicated the job enormously. Each and every node had to predict the Doppler shift of every node it was connected to.

. . . defense department has awarded the contract for the 4-meter S-14 mobile infantry powered armor to the Lockheed Skunk Works. The Secretary also announced the purchase of an additional 500 R-60 Patton Attack Bots, to be produced by McDonnell-Boeing . . .

This distant from Earth/Luna, Neace and Ensley were somewhat insulated from the flash crowd of distant interest—that proportion of the twelve billion human beings on the home world that actually wondered about the marvels hidden in the night sky. Had they known that their fifteen minutes of fame had also created a moment of system-wide breathless anticipation, it might have unnerved them; they considered their work important because it was *their* work; they hadn't considered that the human race as a whole might share some of the same fascination.

So the reaction to the Orion Anomaly caught them mostly by surprise. The first pictures of the Horsehead and Crab Nebulas and other familiar visions were remarkable for their depth of detail and resolution, but unless you were viewing them on a wall-size display capable of Extreme Definition, they did not appear significantly sharper than the previous observations of various space-based observatories.

The Orion Anomaly, however, was something else entirely. Behind the Orion Nebula lay a star system that had always photographed fuzzy and uncertain. Even the smaller proof-of-concept dispersed array space telescope projects of the past had failed to resolve the object or objects. Computer enhancement produced unsatisfactory results because the computer had no idea what it was enhancing. Whatever it was, it was as large as the solar system, possibly larger. Too large to be an exploding or fragmented star—and not enough mass anyway. A whirligig of orbiting bodies? A cosmic whirlwind? There were more theories than facts; but whatever the theory, the evidence refused to abide. The Orion Anomaly remained one of the more tantalizing mysteries of the sky.

. . . despite the lopsided gender ratios, the Chinese birth rates remain strong as increasing numbers of males choose to carry their own embryos to term; because a majority of the male-borne fetuses are also male, this will exacerbate the problem for the next generation of Chinese husbands. Until China and other Asian states learn to recognize that female children are as valuable as males, the imbalances will continue . . .

By the time the DAST was ready to focus on the Orion Anomaly, several thousand ships, probes, and orbiting stations had linked up to the three *Queens*. Because of the wide dispersal of the participating components, collation of the images took several hours. But the resolution of the image was high enough to finally reveal some of the details of the Anomaly. The Extreme Definition display revealed it as a scattering of thousands of small fairly-bright objects in irregular orbit around a mid-line star. Not comets. Something else—something that still defied explanation. The mystery wasn't solved, it was only deepened.

Unfortunately, further observations were interrupted by a flurry of solar storms which disturbed the linkages between the various ships. The slight but continuing perturbations of orbit confused the predictive synchronization of the coordinating stations, effectively destroying the synchronization necessary to accurate surveillance. During the interregnum, the DAST components would still continue mapping the local distances between planets and asteroids and ships-in-transit. Most of that monitoring did not require predictive calibration. It was routine work and the bots would handle it automatically.

. . . mixed reactions in the community of body-mods. Most people still view modding a cosmetic enhancement or fashion statement, but more serious modders disregard casual modding as little more than fad-chasing. Tigerman adds, "Modding isn't about the look, it's about the experience. That's why the sensory augments are so important. All the new tastes, smells, colors, sensations . . . "

Neace spent much of his down-time meditatively jogging. The ship's centrifuge turned slowly and the uppermost levels provided a mere one-third gee, which allowed for a languid, almost thoughtful stride; the jogger spent most of his time airborne, barely tapping the floor to stay aloft. For many runners, the experience was close to flying. In fact, the jogger had to lean so far into his stride that he appeared almost prone, like an oversized road-runner, but bouncing from point to point instead of racing.

The long, slow strides provided a time-stretched aerobic workout and Neace could submerge himself into the rhythm as comfortably as if he were floating in an isolation tank. He could run for hours at a stretch, keeping himself physically balanced at a level of exertion simply unachievable at Earth-normal gravity. The result was a Zen-like state of endurance and health that most human beings never realized. It was during such workouts that Neace often had his most remarkable insights — many other starsiders had also reported their own experiences of centrifugal nirvana or "jogging eurekas."

Neace had already calculated that the crew of the first starship to Sirius would spend at least one-third of their time jogging, possibly more. They would be able to brag that they had sprinted to Sirius and back. Nowhere would the unbreakable relationship between time and space be more evident than aboard a long-range starship. Even the shorter hops among Sol's family of planets could take weeks or even occasionally months. It was no accident that a large number of exceptionally thoughtful books and articles had been written in transit. Authorship remained the best offense against boredom.

. . . most serious breach since Stan-18's tell-all book, It Only Hurts When You Laugh. *A spokesman for the Laurel-Hardy company said that the situation was a personal and private matter between the clone-families, and would not interfere with the upcoming production of "Laurel and Hardy on Mars" . . .*

This day, however, Neace's thoughts came inevitably back to Radley Nakamura and Manda Sahir. Among starsiders, most relationships were not only long-term, they were also long-range. Perhaps part of it was a physical byproduct of immortality, and part of it was an emotional adaptation to the accretion of age—the underlying assumption that with immortality, now "we have all of time and all of space." But Neace felt that explanation was too easy, and therefore insufficient. Researchers had long since proved that human beings were chaotic events, a cross-section of processes and intentions, pressures and needs, expressing from moment to moment as an illusion of consciousness, only occasionally achieving exercises of actual sentience. But the illusions of consciousness were still useful, because it was on the shoulders of such illusions that the moments of sentience stood.

No, Neace's own theory about the languid pace of starside affairs was that it was an essential adaptation to the expanded time-sense of orbital existence. It was a recognition that every human being is on an individual trajectory, sometimes parallel, more often not. You have no choice but to live inside the moment as it occurs, or as Jarles "Free Fall" Ferris once put it, "Breathe here now."

There wasn't anywhere to go with the thought. It didn't inspire a course of action. And that, too, was part of the adaptation—that thoughts could be complete in and of themselves, without requiring immediate expression or eventual deed. It was simply part of the larger construction of the ground of being on which true identity would later stand.

. . . although this solar probe lasted 8 minutes longer than any previous close-approach satellite, the photosphere still hasn't given up all of its mysteries. Next year's Magenta series, however, will be the first test of hyperstatic shielding and should allow the probe to penetrate . . .

Neace was successful because he was meticulous; a skill he had discovered in school and honed to near-perfection throughout his career. He didn't just plot a course, he plotted consequences. But while the mechanistic approach worked well for creating opportunities for passion, it did not create passion itself. Neace had come to that understanding somewhere between "Peek-a-boo" and "Gotcha."

Thereafter, he had planned his affairs so as to put himself into matching orbits with women who were aggressive enough to take the initiative in sexual relationships. In that sense, they completed him, providing the triggers for passion that he himself had never quite mastered. This particular insight was not new to Neace, he revisited it frequently while meditatively jogging. He was neither satisfied nor dissatisfied with the realization. He had accepted it as part of his internal construction.

But this day, the moment of insight that came to him as he purposed methodically through the air—that identity is the construction of self. And that everything he had done up to this point in his life, every problem he had taken on, every challenge he had accepted, had ultimately been about nothing more than his own satisfaction of achievement. He was *self*-centered.

Adding Radley and Manda to his personal equation hadn't ever been about constructing a triangular relationship—it had been solely about completing the structure of his own identity. For a moment, Neace felt guilty.

. . . four more cases of hyper-chocolate poisoning, bringing the total number to 73, with 9 known fatalities. All-Mart Industries has ordered all hyper-chocolate products removed from store shelves until further review . . .

But the moment passed, the sense of guilt eased. What *other* kinds of relationships were possible in space? And didn't Radley and Manda equally use him as adjuncts to their own constructions of being? Of course, if he approached it from that perspective, he considered, then he was committing the error of methodical analysis again—and he'd already had this conversation with both women; that some human interactions were beyond both method and analysis, particularly those of the heart.

And then he got it.

. . . each of the new plastic coins will contain V-70 ultrawave circuitry. While the long-term goal is to create a more accurate cross-sectioning of economic flows, consumers will experience immediate benefits. Each coin will also function as an independent node in the wireless web, providing 2000% packet redundancy at GBS rates and expanding available mobile bandwidth to . . .

Intellectually, he'd had the answer for the better part of a century—that the condition of love, beyond the mechanics of trust and intimacy, existed only where the other person's well-being was essential to your own. He'd known that as an equation. He'd never quite realized it as an *experience*. Until now. For no reason at all.

Except perhaps that for a moment, a single overarching moment, a breathless pause, while his body continued to pace methodically, languidly, gracefully through the centrifuge—for that single moment, he actually felt *lonely*.

He missed Radley. He missed Manda. The graceful curve of Radley's neck, the breadth of her shoulders and the muscled strength of her legs—the voluminous sensuality of Manda's embrace, the delicious pressure of their bodies together. He'd once wondered if it was possible to love two women at the same time—then surrendered to the inevitability of the truth.

And now, in this moment, with no apparent trigger except the silence in his own head, he *understood*.

He continued jogging, savoring the transformative knowledge. The sweat beaded on his body. He had a joyous grin on his face. He had an erection.

. . . *critical threshold of processing for constructed sentience on a super-cluster. Below that threshold, holes in the processing matrices reduce confidence to the organic level, which is unacceptable for accuracy in* . . .

Later, he knew he'd have to share the insight with both of his lovers. He wasn't quite certain how he would phrase it—and on some level, he understood that this message would be best delivered in person, with skill, delicacy, and of course all the passion he could generate.

But he also knew that this bit of self-knowledge wasn't about what existed in himself as much as it was a recognition of what *didn't* exist within. It was the realization of the need to rebuild a sense of identity that was beyond his own control—an identity that existed as a partnership, as a fusion.

He wondered if that were even possible in a starside environment. Then moved immediately from there to the acceptance of the challenge. It was now something else to be invented.

Laughing, he sent both women the same message. "I get it. I've been a jerk. That's why you should marry me. Because I finally get it."

. . . *expected to issue its report on the financial costs of the solar flare by the end of the week. Reassembly of the DAST array has already resumed, with optimal calibration expected in the next few hours. Included among the targets scheduled for closer examination, the Orion Anomaly has had astronomers arguing . . .*

Later—everything aboard a ship is always *later*—on the bridge, waiting for their separate replies, now more than an hour overdue, Captain Adam Neace sifted impatiently through all the separate images that had accumulated since his last review. The targeting scopes stayed focused on the other *Queens* but the latest pictures showed both ships looking different now, so he directed one of the larger arrays to capture clearer images.

A few moments later, the enhanced views came up on his display and he began to laugh. Arrayed in lights along the side of *The Venus Queen* was a simple message: "Peek-A-Boo." *The Lunar Queen* displayed, "Gotcha."

Neace opened a channel and said, "I see your sign, Radley."

Half an hour later, the message came back. "Yes, we'll marry you, Adam. But the sign isn't for you—it's for them."

Them?

Who?

Them—!

And in that moment, Adam Neace became the second human being in the solar system to understand the Orion Anomaly.

David Gerrold has sterling credentials across the SF board. His Star Trek *episode, "The Trouble With Tribbles," is a perennial favorite. His novelette, "The Martian Child," pulled the Hugo-Nebula double play. His novels include such standouts as* When Harlie Was One, The Man Who Folded Himself, *and the recent* Bouncing off the Moon *trilogy, the first of which won a Golden Duck award for young adult fiction: the Hal Clement Award.*

The original short story he presents here is, by his reckoning, the deepest he has ever voyaged into hard science fiction. For a tribute to Hal Clement, he would do no less.

AN APPRECIATION

JOE HALDEMAN

I first read *Mission of Gravity* as a preteen amateur astronomer, long before I ever thought about being a writer, and its pure scientific imaginativeness held me absolutely enthralled. It still works, nearly fifty years later. It has affected my writing more than dozens of more "legitimate" books actually do, the Hemingways and Flauberts and their sciencefictional equivalents we drag out when people ask about influences.

His science fiction was the pure stuff, distilled from pulp magazines on the one hand and the thrill of laboratory and telescope on the other. He was full of wonder about science, and lived to share his love. As large an effect as he had on us writers, you have to wonder how many more lives he must have dramatically changed as a teacher.

Harry—he was never Hal to me after we actually met—was the most self-deprecating writer I've ever known, with absolutely no false modesty. He startled me once, walking toward his guest-of-honor speech at a Philadelphia convention, by saying "You know, I don't think I've ever written a believable character." I'd just reread *Needle,* and knew that he had indeed. But he wouldn't hear my protestation; he might as well have said "the atomic weight of oxygen is sixteen."

He was always dropping unexpected bombshells, sometimes literal ones, as when he looked at a rash on his arm and remarked that he'd been one of the soldiers who'd witnessed the first atomic explosion, and every now and then something from it would bother him. When we sat down to do a panel at the Worldcon in Holland, he noted he'd been here forty-some years before, but hadn't set foot on the ground—he was fifty feet over it, in a B-24.

He couldn't have been unaware that he was an avatar. For a half century, if you thought "hard science fiction," his name only would immediately come to mind. He wore the distinction lightly and with good humor. Those of us fortunate enough to count him as a friend will always remember the way he'd react to praise—the rueful smile and the furrowed brow as he desperately sorted through his thoughts for something to change the subject. A rare man, greatly missed.

Joe Haldeman is a winner of five Hugo and four Nebula awards, including taking both for his novels The Forever War *and* Forever Peace *and his novella "The Hemingway Hoax." His latest novel,* Camouflage, *was serialized in* Analog *and has since come out in hardcover. He is a past president of SFWA.*

KNOWING HAL

PAUL LEVINSON

Tina and I and our daughter just returned from the memorial service for Hal Clement in Milton, MA. It was a fine service. Lots of New England writers and fans were there. We were sitting behind Allen Steele and Tom Easton, and next to Tony Lewis. I recalled the first time I had seen Hal's name, on a library shelf in the fall of 1959. *Mission of Gravity* was instantly one of my favorite books. A trip to the library was never in vain, if one of Hal's stories that I had not yet read was in waiting . . .

Decades later, in the 1990s when I started writing science fiction, I realized that Hal had the same effect on me at cons: no matter how bad a con otherwise was, if Hal was there, being there was worthwhile. There was a reassurance that all was okay, at least in the science fiction section of the universe, if Hal Clement was walking in or out of a dealer's room, whistling.

Rob Sawyer, my predecessor as SFWA President, called me one evening in the Fall of 1998 (I was Vice President then). He asked me what I thought of giving the Grand Master Award to Hal. Former Presidents and the rest of the Board had to be polled, but Rob was keen on the idea, and wanted to know what I thought. I told him it was a terrific idea. I was just the first of many with the same reaction . . . I presided over the Nebula Banquet in Pittsburgh the following Spring, and what a thrill it was to see Hal up there on the stage, graciously accepting the honor he so eminently deserved. Dave Truesdale, editor of the *SFWA Bulletin* then, said he wanted to go all out with a display in the *Bulletin* for Hal. He came up with a superb picture of all the Grand Masters, with Hal, as the newest one, in the center. Dave presented a poster of the picture to Hal. I still have a copy on my wall.

Another of my favorite recollections of Hal is also from a Pittsburgh convention, Confluence, where Hal was Guest of Honor a few years ago. Phil Klass was giving a reading. The crowd enthusiastically applauded when it was over, and slowly left the room. I was talking with someone in the back, and when I looked at the front of the room, only one person was left, other than Phil. It was Hal, animatedly making some point to Phil, gesturing, with Phil responding with equal zeal. What a moment. Two titans of science fiction, whom I had been reading for half a century, talking as if they were kids. The eternal golden age of science fiction.

But my fondest recollection of Hal comes from a Boskone. This was held in the hotel in Framingham. I brought along my daughter, then about 11 years old. I was downstairs on the first floor, and she was in our room, on the eighth floor, when fire alarms sounded. The elevators were frozen. I rushed up eight flights of stairs, to our room, but it was empty. We were not yet quite in the age of cellphones, and we had no way of reaching each other. I ran back down the stairs, and looked around on the ground floor, frantically. An announcement said the alarm was due to a malfunction—there was no fire—but I still needed to find my daughter . . . At last I saw her, in a corner, happily chatting with Hal. I thanked him for reassuring her, and he was on his way (probably whistling).

I asked her if she had been scared. "I didn't know where you were," she said, "and I was looking for you, and I was worried. Hal came over to me and said 'Are you looking for your father?' I said yes. He said he wasn't sure where you were, but not to worry, because 'knowing your father, he's probably somewhere talking to someone about his books . . . '" And they both laughed, and Hal stayed with her until I arrived.

Well, knowing Hal, he's probably somewhere talking to someone about everything that's interesting in science and science fiction. And we'll be talking about Hal, and his gentle soul and sharp intellect, for a long, long time.

These words were written only days after Hal's death. Paul Levinson is the author of four SF novels, most recently The Pixel Eye. *He is also a prolific non-fiction writer on communications and technology, with* Cellphone *his most recent work. He was SFWA President from 1998 to 2001, which had an impact on Hal's career that you will see in a few pages . . .*

PART THREE
HAL'S WORDS

As much as one can learn about a man from what others say about him, it remains best to go straight to the source. We no longer have that opportunity in the flesh with Hal Clement, but he was a man of words, words that endure. If it is not the immortality that writers often believe their work will give them, it is a lasting imprint of his thoughts, and a window into the mind of a man now gone from us.

This portion of the book gives you Hal Clement in his own words—with a couple of intermediaries. It provides one of his last pieces of short fiction, and an extensive interview that brings out memories as far back as his teenage years. But it begins with his receipt of a great honor from SFWA (of which our last writer, Paul Levinson, was president at the time), and the words he had on that occasion.

REMARKS ACCOMPANYING THE PRESENTATION OF THE SFWA GRAND MASTER AWARD

J. MICHAEL STRACZYNSKI AND HAL CLEMENT

Hal Clement received the Grand Master Award from the Science Fiction and Fantasy Writers of America on May 1st, 1999, at the Nebula Awards banquet in Pittsburgh, Pennsylvania. The SFWA Grand Master Award is given in recognition of a lifetime of excellence in writing, and is arguably the greatest honor the field has to offer. J. Michael Straczynski, receiving SFWA's Bradbury Award that night in honor of his series Babylon 5, *had the honor of making the presentation. This is what he, and Hal, had to say. (With one tangential joke about Kosher chicken excised. Mr. Burstein, you owe me.)*

J. Michael Straczynski: Giving this award to Hal Clement is a bit like a lay priest being called upon to say High Mass in Rome on Easter Sunday before the Pope. It is an intimidating experience.

When I asked them why I had been chosen to give this award to Hal Clement, I was told, quote, "Because you and Hal are both world-builders." I don't think so.

I write on a sheet of paper, "EXTERIOR—CENTAURI PRIME," then an army of designers, carpenters, art designers, art directors, make-up people, effects guys get together and build this thing. We've got the JPL involved: they crunch numbers and get the math right. Hal Clement does all this on his own . . . which pisses me off massively. He doesn't have experts or carpenters or consultants: he does the math himself. When I sat down to write this I looked at his year of birth, 1922, and the current year, and deduced his age as follows: {JMS lifts up his fingers} two from nine is seven; other two from nine is seven—seventy-seven years old. Hal

Clement doesn't count on his fingers. He doesn't have to.

We both build worlds? I don't think so.

Science fiction at its best delivers stories that create a sense of wonder that we felt as children reading science fiction for the first time. Science fiction at its best also does not flinch from the science part of that equation. It doesn't settle for rounding off the numbers, fudging the data, or saying "No one's going to notice." This is not news to those people in this room, some of the best and brightest in the science fiction genre . . .

We all know it's fairly easy to do one or the other of those two, but damned hard to do both. Hal Clement can dance that dance. He understood at an early age that you create a sense of wonder by being factually correct. When you look at a Chesley Bonestell painting, it's as exciting as though you were standing in that crater, looking up at Saturn or the Earth: that's exactly how it would look. That's the exciting part of it. Hal's work has inspired many of the writers in this room to build their own worlds, to get the science right. So it's only proper he should get this award tonight.

Since his first story was published in 1942—{lifts fingers}—two from nine is seven; four from nine is five—fifty-seven years ago, Hal has always been marching in the parade of scientific accuracy and storytelling, and has been carrying a banner and beating a drum.

Mr. Clement, here is your new baton.

{Hal Clement steps up and receives the Grand Master Award}

Hal Clement: Well, I'd be embarrassed to express any false modesty. I don't think I have any real modesty left to express. As I've confessed a couple of times in the last few years, I'm at least as conceited as our late friend Isaac Asimov. I just have been less outspoken about it. I *like* to show off. I have, sadly a few more years picked up to gather trivia to show off with—{to JMS} by the way, I won't be seventy-seven until the end of this month. And I use them. I'll try to use them, anyway.

There is an ad which has been appearing regularly on tape, at least in the Massachusetts area, frequently, in which a gentleman is coming up the stairs with a briefcase and asking, "Have you ever wondered why there are so many lawyers in the world?" I thought the answer was obvious. I couldn't see why he was asking the question. And I'm dead serious, by the way. If anyone laughs, it'll be an accident.

The fact is, there are far more objects and concepts in the Universe than there are noise patterns. It is therefore unavoidable that a single word is going to have to be used for a great many things, and will therefore be ambiguous. To cut down the ambiguity, you have to put words together that make sentences—this is not usually sufficient—and eventually you wind up writing trilogies. This is, of course, if you want to *avoid* ambiguity. I realize we don't always want to—it's one of the essential legs of humor, which probably has as many legs as a Mesklinite—but the ambiguity is there, almost all the time, with one exception.

There is one concept in which one fairly short sound pattern leaves very little ambiguity. Several languages—here's the showing off—have done it with a few [syllables]: *Efharisto* if you're Greek; *Shenorhagal em* if you're Armenian; *Diolch* if you're Welsh; *Asanteni* if you speak Swahili; *Arigato* if you're Japanese; *Mahalo* if you're Hawaiian.

English and English-based languages seem to have done better. They squeeze it down. In the American version of English, we're down to one syllable, and the Australians have even shortened the syllable. I'm using it now, not trying to name anybody, really, but it starts with Mary and our kids and goes outward in all four dimensions.

Thanks.

AN INTERVIEW WITH HAL CLEMENT

DARRELL SCHWEITZER

(Conducted at Eeriecon, Niagara Falls NY, April 2001.)

Q: Let's start with a bit of background and how you started writing.

Clement: I started trying to write in the 1930's. I had a Canadian cousin. I used to spend all the summers on the farm with him and his family. We got interested in science fiction and reached that age where we were beginning to learn a little bit. Sometimes there were errors in the stories we read, rather egregious ones. We both felt, well, really, we were teenagers, and we knew enough not to make errors of this sort, and we began trying this. I was 17. He was a little bit younger. We both wrote a story, in pencil. Nothing beyond that ever happened. That was the last year that I saw him, actually. We left the farm on September 1st, 1939, the day the Panzers [went] into Poland, and he was killed in the Canadian army a few years later in Italy. So that was it.

I tried again in the summer I was 18. That was also done in pencil. My mother typed it. She went on strike thereafter. Never again. I would have to get my own typewriter, or at least use hers.

I sent the story in to John Campbell, and got one of the famous Campbell multi-page rejections, of the encouraging sort. So I tried again the next summer and he took the darned thing. This coming October will be the 60th anniversary of my first sale. Don't ask me what day the letter came. But that was "Proof." It was published in the June 1942 *Astounding*—and it was *Astounding* then—and that was it. It and the story written a few

176

months later, and also published in August of 1942 converted my parents. I don't know that either of them ever became a science fiction fan, but the $245 those stories collected made quite a dent in Harvard's $400-a-year tuition. I know this dates me . . .

Q: It does, but it also means that if you adjust for inflation, you were being paid *extremely well*.

Clement: I never complained about the pay, and I always regarded it as a hobby anyway. I never seriously considered trying to make a living off it. I was a school teacher, and papers had to be corrected first.

Q: When you were first starting to write, who did you look to as examples of how to write good SF? Or did you merely look at the pulp magazines of the middle 1930's and decide you could do better?

Clement: There were several. Probably my most extreme childhood hero was and still is Jack Williamson. I don't know if he can be called a childhood hero anymore, because even I am not exactly in childhood. Jack Williamson, Doc Smith, Sprague de Camp. Who else was working then? I hate to shock anyone, but Neil R. Jones, who doesn't wear well when I read him as an adult. But the others I can still happily re-read.

Q: Did you make a conscious effort to study these writers and how they did it?

Clement: No. As far as the actual art or science, whichever it is, of writing is concerned, I think that the main thanks go to my parents. They were very, very firm on proper use of the English language. They both were quite annoyed after my sister and I started school and our English usage deteriorated. Not enormously, but we got awfully slangy. I have never had much trouble in making myself clear. I occasionally get caught in an ambiguity, but generally speaking, people can understand me.

Q: But somewhere outside of grammar class you have to learn things like point-of-view and how to pace a story, how to make a dramatic scene, and so on.

Clement: I never really learned those. Either they have come unconsciously, or possibly I don't have them yet. (Laughter from audience.)

Q: Oh, I think you do. This gets to the point of what is the secret to the patented Hal Clement story. You have a distinct method of writing a story that is quite different from anyone else's.

Clement: The idea almost invariably comes from a bit of scientific news. My favorite source is *Astronomy* magazine. The slide talk I will be giving tomorrow goes through some of that. The item was in the May

2000 issue of *Astronomy* in their news column. The basic idea was seeing what the stellar system being reported was actually like, trying to find out as much as I could about it from friends who are on the Internet, doing some calculating: what planets might there be here at all? Would they be hot, cold, a short year, a long year? You name it. At this point I have a modest-sized collection of possible planets in the system. I haven't started to write a story about it yet because there is another one on the front burner. This is the general way. The idea comes from science. I have never been able to outline a story and stay with the outline, however. By the time I am twenty or thirty thousand words into the script, I am so far from any outline I ever started with or had in my head that it might as well never have been produced.

Q: What I mean is that you've been described as starting a story "from the gravity up." Most writers start with a scene or an idea or an image, or maybe a line or two, but you seem to begin a story with mathematics and data. How do you get from an interesting astronomical object to a story with people in it?

Clement: It is mostly calculation at first. As I build the planet or planetary system as the case may be, I think of the things that might happen in it because of the odd nature of its environment. Every time a possible event occurs to me, it goes down on a 3-by-5 card. Eventually the stack of cards tends to be quite high. I don't have a table like this twelve-footer before us in the house, so I use the living room floor. But I start going through the cards. They're never in any particular order. Even in the beginning they're only in the order that the thoughts occurred to me. "Right, here's something. This could happen." I put the card in the middle of the floor. This may fit into it, but it had to happen first, so the card goes a little over to the left. And, "Oh here's a bit with an ending line." So, way over to the right. And so on. Eventually all the cards are in a reasonable chronological line on the floor and there's the story. It's much easier than this "plotting" stuff the English teachers used to tell me about.

Q: Did you learn any of this from John Campbell? He surely influenced a lot of his writers on how they approach ideas and what they do with them.

Clement: I got ideas from him, quite frankly. Generally he either didn't explain them to me or I didn't grasp the explanations of just what I should do with the darn things. The idea was there. This made certain events possible. While I didn't develop the 3-by-5 card technique that early, it amounted to the same thing. I had a flock of things that could happen, and I began writing.

Q: So, where did the idea for *Mission of Gravity* come from and how did that develop?

Clement: *Mission of Gravity* was one of my own. John did not suggest it. It had been cooking very slowly on a back burner for several years, actually. I first remember saying something about it to a college crowd I was talking to, and that must have been in the late 1930's or early 1940's.

We read stories about very heavy gravity planets and very light gravity planets, and spaceship adventures where there was no weight at all—but don't let me hear anyone say there's no gravity—and I had never really thought, until somewhere in the '30s, I guess, about a planet which had notably different gravity in different parts. The Earth does. Any rotating planet does. But your weight at the North Pole of the Earth is not noticeably and significantly different than at the Equator. Measurably, yes.

But I just tried to make the whole thing extreme. I'm a very conservative type, actually. I don't like things like gravity-screens because I haven't the faintest idea of how they could work. Strictly speaking, of course, I am inconsistent and hypocritical, because I haven't the faintest idea how a faster-than-light drive would work either. But I faced the fact quite early in my writing that there was no place in the Solar System except Earth and not very much of that, in which the hero could rescue his heroine in shirtsleeves.

I had to move out of the Solar System quite early on, and I never did come up with a really convincing method of faster-than-light travel. If I did I suppose I'd try to patent it. There we are. I prefer other systems because I can make up my own planets, and, boy, can you do funny things to the environment without too drastic changes in the planet. It can be a perfectly *plausible* planet, and boy, the weird things that can happen.

Q: Don't you feel that you can also do that with our own Solar System, particularly as it keeps getting revised?

Clement: Oh, yes, and I have written things set in this solar system. But I have not had heroes rescuing heroines without wearing environment armor of some sort. And I don't usually bother to have heroes rescuing heroines. Nowadays you can't get away with it. The heroines, if anything, are supposed to be doing the rescuing.

Q: But in *Mission of Gravity* they're trying to retrieve a valuable object.

Clement: Yes. The motivation has always been my own. I like science. I majored in science. I think that most of our problems, if they're going to get solved at all, are going to be solved by science, and I just like stories that work that way. Also, you don't, usually, in a story of this sort worry about the villains being obviously French or obviously Asiatic or obviously Black or obviously female and getting nasty letters. The indifferent universe makes for a perfectly adequate villain.

Q: Then again, you have a very different story in *Needle*, which is one that didn't start from building a planet.

Clement: This is quite true. I had it happen right here on Earth. I think that originated from my nasty tendency, whenever I hear someone say "Of course," or imply, "Of course," I start wondering what would happen or what could happen if that particular "Of course" weren't true.

The "of course" in this case came from an article by the late Sprague de Camp, called "Design for Life." It ran as a two-parter in *Astounding* somewhere in the 1940's. He came up with a whole flock of reasons why an intelligent being should be pretty much humanoid, such as having its major sense organs as close as possible to the major nerve center to make quick reflexes possible; the advantage of being up to stand upright, look over the grass, and duck down if you had to. He had a lot of points there. He had restrictions on size. It shouldn't be much less than about forty pounds because if it were it wouldn't have a complex enough structure to have real human intelligence. It shouldn't probably be bigger than, say, a Kodiak bear, for comparable reasons of co-ordination.

I'm afraid I was trying to make a liar of him when I invented my virus-sized cells which made up the Hunter.

Q: That is one of the great strengths of science fiction, that you can always take what someone else takes for granted and stand it on end.

Clement: That's the idea, yes. Every time I am giving a talk at a convention, I try to remember in the course of events to tell everyone who is listing that if they get any story ideas from anything I've said, the ideas are theirs. They'd better go write them. I couldn't copyright a basic idea even if I wanted to, although I gather it has been tried. I don't want to!

Q: Also, if we gave an idea out to everyone in this room and they all wrote them, the stories would all be different.

Clement: That's a safe bet, yes. So I have never worried about that aspect of it.

Q: I think this comes back to what I'd call the Hal Clement method. If anybody else did take one of your ideas and write it, they would not produce a Hal Clement story. You have a recognizable method.

Clement: Yes, and I suspect that the author would be recognizable from whatever he or she did, at least to people who knew him or her well.

Q: For example, the other night I picked one of your stories at random, and read a story called "Dust Rag." It's a story about who explorers who get into trouble on the Moon because, due to the difference in the electrical charges between their spacesuits and their faceplates, magnetic dust adheres to the faceplates, blinding them. So they have to figure out how to change the charge so the dust will fall off. I can't think of anyone who would write a story quite like that. My sense of the archetypal Hal Clement story is that it tells us that science happens all the time, not just in the laboratory.

Clement: Science, as an industry, if you want to think of it that way, is an attempt to find out what the rules are. It is based, obviously, on the assumption that there are rules. And the more of them you can bring in, the more fun it is, especially if they're ones that everyone knows about, but never thinks about using for problem-solving.

Q: The only actual assumptions behind all this that is taken on faith are that the universe is knowable and the senses report useful information.

Clement: Yes, I believe that as firmly as I can believe anything. I am not absolutely *sure* that we are not living in a whimsical universe run by one or more beings not subject to law as we understand it, but the notion offers no real opportunity to think, as far as I am concerned. It is much better, and more comfortable incidentally, to believe that there are laws.

Q: So I guess you wouldn't ever actually write a fantasy.

(Laughter from audience.)

Clement: I'm not sure about that. When I was a teenager, I was very stuffy about that sort of thing. I wanted science fiction to be as hard as it could get, and I couldn't bring myself to read a fantasy. I have softened over the years, very considerably. I have read Terry Pratchett's *Feet of Clay*, I think, twenty-three times, and got fun out of it each time. I am a Discworld junkie. But whether I could write a fantasy is an entirely different matter. I was asked to once. Somebody was proposing a vampire anthology, and I had read *Dracula*, so I figured I knew all that had to be known about vampires. (Laughs.) Well, Stoker did make most of it up.

So I wrote the story, and when it was done it was hard science fiction. My vampire was a retired Roman army surgeon of about the time of Galen, who had the misfortune to sire four haemophiliac sons, of whom one was still alive at the time of the story. He got his unpopular reputation with the neighbors by his attempts to solve the problem of blood transfusions a couple thousand years before we knew enough to have any chance of doing so.

Q: But I suppose you could take a premise which you know is not true and develop it with the same rigor you would use in your science fiction. For, example, the one I'd like to see you do would be a story set in a universe in which astrology works, then worked out to its logical conclusion with your usual rigor. The result would be very entertaining and very strange.

Clement: Yes, if I retained my sanity during the operation. (Laughter from audience.) I am willing to consider it, but it is certainly not on the front burner at the moment. The story that's being done is as real as I can imagine, even if it's a rather weird place.

Q: Can you talk about this story you're writing?

Clement: I don't mind. The world involved is okay, anyway. It's a water-world. I know, people have made movies about water-worlds . . . (laughter from audience) but none of those that I have seen or read about consist of a planet whose radius is about fifteen percent greater than Earth's, whose density is low enough so that that surface gravity is about one-third that of the Earth, and the reason is that the ocean — and I do mean ocean — is about 2800 kilometers deep. Now when you start figuring out what would happen there . . . well, what would the total lack of mountains do to the climate? What would the total lack of disturbing factors in ocean currents do to the distribution of heat? Even your mistakes you can sometimes turn to use. I was going to have a few floating islands of pumice. The point where the ocean does meet — there's no real crust there — the mantle is intensely volcanic. In fact, the tentative title for the book is *Noise*. Why shouldn't I have pumice? Well, a rough, and I do mean rough, calculation indicates that the pressure at the bottom of this ocean is about 80,000 atmosphere, and if lava does pop into the water, I refuse to believe that under that pressure we're going to get any steam bubbles to turn the lava into pumice.

Q: I should think that the pumice would never get a chance to float to the surface anyway.

Clement: If you could boil some little holes in the pumice and fill them with slightly vaporous water . . . which you can't do. The things are just going to be scrunched back down by the pressure.

Q: No islands . . . . Let's take some questions from the audience.

(Silence.)

Clement: I've snowed them already.

(Laughter from audience.)

Question from audience: The focus of a lot of your stories seems to be the astronomical elements. Why don't you focus on the people as a primary factor?

Clement: I am afraid I focus mostly [on] astronomical and chemical facts. For one thing, I am not a good character writer. I have been watching the human species more or less in detail for over three-quarters of a century and I just don't understand the beings. They don't make particularly much sense. About all the motives I can figure out and sympathize or empathize with are curiosity, self-preservation, and the various appetites that go with the needs for self-preservation and reproduction. I don't do very much with the reproduction motive, I suspect, because I was brought up with a rather Victorian household, but the excuse I use is that I consider sex to be an extremely private matter. If anyone here wants me to write that sort of thing, I'm sorry.

Q: You could do alien sex.

Clement: That's been suggested. When I wrote *Mission of Gravity*, I never gave a thought to how the Mesklinites reproduce. I implied that they were quite long-lived, but that was the closest to anything that might be cultural background for them. Later on, of course, at conventions people asked me questions of that general nature. And I thought about it a little, but never went into it at all deeply. Once or twice I mentioned the existence of marine worms on this planet [Earth], whose technique is to crawl along the bottom of the ocean until they can find some rather firmly anchored spot, hang onto it with their rear legs, keep on crawling with their front ones, and pull themselves in two. It happens, so, okay, but when this came up at an I-Con a few years ago, I suggested that it might be fun to figure out what these beings regard as pornography. (Much laughter from audience.) After the talk, a couple of ladies who had been in the back row came down front and asked me, "How about rubber bands?" (Laughter from audience.)

Q: How about those magic acts where they saw a lady in two?

Clement: All right. This implies that they have enough technology to have saws, made of something or other.

Q: Your aliens are memorable, though. You've even remarked yourself that the reason they seem alien is that they behave logically.

Clement: That's the conscious difference. If I really want something to seem not quite human, I make it behave reasonably.

Q: What would a crazy Mesklinite be like?

Clement: This would depend on at what latitude you found him, I suspect.

From audience: Or how much latitude you gave him.

Clement: Well, I was measuring latitude in terms of gravities.

Question from audience: Could you give new writers some guidelines for creating what you think are realistic or believable aliens?

Clement: I would only demand that they obey reasonable engineering laws. A lot of people now keep saying that you absolutely need water for life. I don't feel that's true. I agree that you need a solvent. You need a liquid. Gaseous life is going to be very difficult because the molecules needed to do all the things that life does, selection and rejection of materials taken in, moving around, and all that sort of stuff, would take complex molecules, and molecules that complex you're not going to find in a gas, because if you try to heat up anything that complex into the gas state, which is theoretically possible, molecules of that sort are going to break up and they're not going to be the same molecules anymore. You can get all the complexity you want in the crystalline form, but what does it *do*? I have never been able been able to dream up a convincing beach boy who couldn't show off his biceps to his girlfriend until he had been massaged with a blowtorch into a dull red heat. As far as I am concerned, it is solution chemistry that you need, but I am not narrow-minded enough to insist that it be water.

Question from audience: Where did you get the name Mesklin from? It sounds so much like mescaline.

Clement: I don't think that when I dreamed up the name that mescaline and similar substances had reached the popularity they achieved later on. It was just a short, pronounceable word, and that was it. I had no special love for that word, but it was a handy one to use. It didn't seem to mean anything.

Q: What areas of recent scientific development do you find most promising for use in more science fiction?

Clement: Very largely the nano-tech, the pseudo-biology, you might say, the various fields which seem to be coming together so that we may have the ability to manufacture things which have many of the properties of life. I've been calling it pseudo-life. I think the first story in which I used the idea was in *Astounding* or *Analog* in September 1966, "The Mechanic." It's been reprinted in the second volume of the NESFA collections. I've gone to the point where I've used hackers in that particular field making trouble for other people with their own micro-life. You can buy molecular seeds at this stage of the game, and just as regular hackers can buy chips and do unplanned things with them. A story of that sort did get published a few years ago in what is now *Absolute Magnitude*.

Q: Thank you very much. We're run out of time.

Darrell Schweitzer seems to have a hand in everything, as a novelist, anthologist, poet, essayist, reviewer, co-editor of Weird Tales *magazine, and a few other things I'm sure I'm missing. We tap his talent as an interviewer here, in an exchange that runs a fascinating gamut. It even lets you know what Mesklinites might be doing with those rubber bands Michael Burstein mentioned a while back.*

If the last words of that interview piqued your curiosity, you have a chance to gratify it immediately. Reprinted here is the very story Hal talked about, appearing for the first time since its debut in the Spring 1998 issue of Absolute Magnitude. *The story has no far-flung worlds or extraterrestrial creatures, but it does have one of our own varieties of life acting in quite alien manners, and the content is vintage Hal Clement.*

OH, NATURAL

HAL CLEMENT

Jaques D'Orrey wriggled a little farther forward and wiped the sweat out of his eyes. The Maine sunlight was merely warm, the sea breeze a hundred fifty meters up was almost cool, but the nearly skin-tight camo suit was hot; its capillaries were not quite up to handling his thermal output.

Nearly five meters below, extending from the base of the rock where he lay, spread some two thousand square meters of ground. It was studded with small boulders, nearly covered by patches of grass and shrub and almost surrounded by woods. A rabbit could have hidden almost anywhere in the area, but nothing of human size, even D'Orrey's, could have done so unsuited.

Camouflage aside, he was occupying the best place in the vicinity to see without being seen; vegetation also topped the rock. He was peering carefully through the leaves of a convenient blueberry bush so that even the suit was just now superfluous. However, he never thought of removing or even opening it; it was habit, and the scene below held all his attention.

A dozen meters from the foot of the rock a field mouse was sitting up and looking around, evidently suspicious. It had a right to be. Only a few paces from it to D'Orrey's left, apparently hidden from the small mammal but not from above, lay a timber rattler somewhat over a meter long. It was not coiled for action or announcing its presence audibly, but extended at nearly full length, making the size judgement easy. Its enlarged midsection suggested that it had eaten too recently to be in a hunting mood, though that point might be too abstract for the rodent.

The intelligence of snakes is also minimal, but not zero. Its silence now did not surprise D'Orrey; what had caught his attention from above was the familiar rattling a moment before. He had heard it clearly and with pleasure. He had been hoping for it. Presumably the mouse had heard also. *Something* had certainly caught the little creature's attention.

"See 'em?" D'Orrey muttered at just above a whisper. He knew the approximate locations of his helpers, having posted them himself, but wasted no time trying to see them directly from where he now lay. They, too, were suited.

"The snake, yes. The mouse is pretty small, but filters help." The incoming voice was little louder in his bud phones than his own had been; Vicki, too was being careful. Snakes are deaf, but most mammals are not.

"How about you, Pete?"

"Sure. No trouble."

"Does either of you see any other animal?"

"Not from here," came the woman's voice.

"No. What is there? What are we supposed to see?" The boy was young enough to be bothered by any suggestion that he might be missing something, and spoke loudly enough to betray the feeling.

"Watch. It's much better hidden. It's what I was hoping for. If the other day means anything, you'll both see it soon."

"The snake's moving," cut in Vicki. Jaques D'Orrey nodded, quite pointlessly.

The rattler had indeed started to weave toward the man's right and slightly away from him. The motion made no difference in his ability to see it from above, but did take it into the mouse's line of sight. The rodent spotted either the snake itself or the movement at once. It crouched down, drawing together as though to leap away; then, since the menace was not approaching, it froze again and kept watching while the rattler sine-waved onward three or four times its own length, still without drawing any nearer.

"What goes?" Peter asked, more quietly than before. "It must know it's there!" Neither adult bothered to criticize the dangling pronouns; the meaning was clear enough, the boy would have defended himself, and this was no time for arguments.

"Right. You'll see. Wait," D'Orrey muttered just loudly enough for his suit's throat mike to pick up.

"When?" The response was louder again and slightly indignant.

"Ask the snake. Watch." The biologist's impatience was as plain as the hacker's, though the former was ten years older.

The rattler might almost have meant to answer directly. Its line of travel changed. It turned a little to its own right, keeping its distance from the potential prey nearly constant and also holding the animal's full attention. D'Orrey, with the whole stage visible below him, could see what was coming and was satisfied. He might not believe the impending events himself; he'd certainly doubted them earlier, but at least this time there would be other observers with other instruments. Later he could even hope for records, if equipment were still uncompromised.

"Three or four more meters," he whispered.

"To what?" It was still Peter, of course.

"You'll see. It's happening again. Watch 'em both." He was not baiting the eighteen-year-old deliberately; he had hired the fellow more for his demonstrated skills than at his mother's—D'Orrey's sister's—insistence. He simply wanted the others to be at peak alertness, with no more preconceived notions than had been needed to persuade them to come at all.

The snake poured itself onward, following an arc with the mouse at the center until it was heading almost back toward the rock. The still nearly motionless mammal was almost below the man, the rattler now four or five meters to his right. Even D'Orrey, able to see what the others had not yet spotted, grew a trifle tense, though he was far more concerned for his demonstration than for the welfare of the doomed animal. He was not a vegetarian himself, and would have admitted without hesitation that morally he ranked with the snakes.

Events climaxed abruptly. The moving reptile turned toward the victim and increased its speed, now rattling loudly. The rodent responded predictably, turning away from the approaching death and leaping toward D'Orrey's left. The second jump brought it down within centimeters of the second snake, which had been lying motionless, unnoticeable to the prey or the two more distant human beings, coiled and ready. It did not rattle; it merely struck. The mouse saw it in mid-jump, tried too late to change direction, squealed as it felt the fangs, and landed on its side a meter from the already recoiled serpent. It made one more awkward attempt to leap, wriggled briefly, and lay still.

"I don't believe this!" came Vicki's murmur.

"Neither did I. Watch!" replied the man. Nothing was heard from Peter.

Both rattlers were now beside the body.

"They can't *divide* it. They have to swallow things whole. Snake teeth don't cut, and they'd never get enough traction to tear it apart even if they were strong enough. They'll fight, surely!" whispered the woman.

"Does that fit with what just happened—*team hunting*?"

"No. Of course not. Did they find someone's dropped knife, maybe? And how would they—"

"You're getting wild," D'Orrey cut in patiently.

"I certainly am. Watching *snakes* cooperate would drive anyone over the edge. It's not natural—"

"That's what we want to make sure of."

"Are you sure you didn't sneak a false-witness into these glasses?"

"That's closer to sanity but no, I didn't. How could I? You take care of your equipment, don't you? *I* haven't had a chance to get at 'em—though that could be just because I haven't been looking for one. Don't take my word for it—get 'em checked when we get back, or have Pete do it now. I'm looking for help in a research job, not just confirmation for a Ripley. I had *my* glasses done after I saw this first, and told the hacker w—pardon, told my respected colleague—I'd seen something I couldn't believe. I didn't tell him just what, of course. He said that the smallest false-witness he could design himself which could handle such a job—do the wave patterns, carry the record, allow for changing view line in both planes, be programmed to run only against an appropriate background or in a preplanned inertially located spot, and coordinate in both barrels of a pair of binoculars at once would be at least peanut size, and that there was nothing anywhere near that big except the regular machinery in the glasses. All *that* was working as it should; nothing had been sneaked out to make room for a false-witness."

"Who was the hacker?" asked the boy, speaking for the first time in several minutes.

"A colleague, Jerry Chu. Associate Professor at Orono. Why? You know him, I suppose?"

"Sure, who doesn't?" It was not obvious whether Peter regarded the name as that of a co-hobbyist or a rival.

"Trust him? Is he good as I've always thought? Do you like him?"

"Oh, he's good." There was a pause. "Maybe too good." Another pause, then D'Orrey was surprised by a rush of candor. "He made a fool out of me a while ago."

"So you don't trust him."

"Well—I guess I *trust* him. Maybe I was asking for it. But I don't *like* him. He's just a spare-time hacker, anyway; he's in the bio department, of all things, at Orono."

"And what's wrong with biologists? Your uncle is one, after all. Are we too cooperative with the rest of science, or just not—"

"Is it all right if I get closer? I can't see how the snakes are settling who gets the dinner."

"Something wrong with your glasses?" D'Orrey had not really expected an answer.

"I'd like to use my own plain, unsupported eyes. I know no one's sneaked anything under my eyelids, and if there's going to be a snake fight I want to believe what I see."

"There isn't, but come on over. Just remember these two may not be the only rattlers in the neighborhood."

"I'm not worried."

"That's why we are. Keep your untampered-with eyes open, and get on over there if you must." Vicki allowed some annoyance to creep into her tone, and raised her sending volume enough to make it obvious.

D'Orrey was right; there was no fight. The action was still unbelievable, but happened just as he had seen it before. The rattlers were now together beside the victim, but the larger, the one which had done the herding, watched with apparent indifference as the actual killer proceeded to work its jaws around the corpse and engulf it in ordinary snake fashion. When it had finished, the two wriggled off together to D'Orrey's left, the smaller leading, and finally disappeared even from his binoculars among the bushes. He waited five minutes longer before speaking.

"That's it for now, I expect," he said in ordinary tones. "I'm closer to the trail. I know it doesn't seem natural, Vick; that's why I want to make sure whether it's technical. Shall we meet right here?" He stood up as he spoke and switched his suit off.

"All right. At least, all right if I can get out of this tree without tearing anything. I paid for this suit myself," came the woman's voice.

"Are you sure it's all over? Shouldn't we follow them?" asked Peter.

"I don't say it's over at all. I hope it isn't. I want to set up close observation on those critters. I want to know whether this was natural and new, or some hacker is amusing himself, or what. We're not ready to do it now, though; we have no food and not much water up here. There's a lot of planning to do before we can start a real study. Knowing that it really happens, and right around here, was all I hoped for now. We can talk it over on the way back; I'd rather not do it through the suit coms. I'm coming down." He turned his camouflage back on, since animal behaviorists prefer to be seen by potential subjects as little as possible, and began to make his way carefully down the sloping side of the rock, retracing his original path up. He had more confidence in his suit's durability than Vicki seemed to, but took no major chances with sharp stones or thorns.

He was several minutes reaching ground level and getting around to the front of the boulder. Both his companions were approaching, though he had to look carefully in the direction he knew she must be to detect the woman at all; her suit, too, was on. The boy's was not, and he was walking around and among the bushes as though he felt no concern for his cam unit or anything else.

"There could be more rattlers around," D'Orrey pointed out again as calmly as he could. Peter took this as implied criticism, quite correctly, but his response was more impertinent than abashed.

"I know. And I know there's snake-bite equipment in the first aid kit, but I'd just as soon they knew I was coming. They can see I'm too big to swallow. Even y—" he broke off; both adults felt they knew why, and were rather pleased. In the week they had been together, and in spite of who was paying the bills, Peter Ben Becker had shown a tendency to make rather perky remarks to and about his uncle, commonly about their seventeen centimeter height difference, which the boy regarded as being in his own favor. D'Orrey had felt that objecting was beneath adult dignity, and was reluctant to have trouble with his older sister. He was pretty sure, however, that Vicki had said something once or twice when he himself was out of hearing.

If the kid were really trying to curb his wit, all to the good. If he were beginning to realize that there were more valuable personal qualities than height, even better.

The man just barely stopped himself from switching off his own suit again. The point about letting rattlers know they were coming had been very well taken, but it seemed poor policy to be guided too obviously by the youngster's advice. In a few seconds he forgot the matter. Vicki's garment also remained active.

No more was said until they met at the kill site. Woman and boy examined the area for details they hadn't been able to see from their trees, but neither found anything which helped answer the obvious questions. The man had seen all he needed. All that really caught his attention was the difference in convenience of watching what the others were doing.

Vicki Kalani's suit was much like his own, though of different make. Its eyes, like his, were the size of split walnuts studded with hundreds of minute lenses, but she had only two, one on the outer side of each shoulder. D'Orrey's numbered three, one on top of his head, one between his shoulder blades, and one at his breast bone. Both pattern processors were where the belt buckles would have been had either garment been belted — prolate hemispheres of coppery polymer about eight centimeters by four, though the man's was mounted with the long axis vertical. Dr. Kalani's also fit better, less because her eight centimeter superiority in height made her easier to fit than because her suit's more sophisticated processor handled warp and woof tension as well as light paths.

All fibers, both fabric components and control and sensor connectors, were far too small to see with the unaided eye. With the suits turned off, as Peter's was, the basic material was almost transparent. The eye-hurting pattern of the tight shorts which were his only inner garment, a random alteration of patches displaying leopard spots, tiger stripes, and geometric exercises in fluorescent colors, could be seen too clearly for comfort.

Vicki's face was also visible as she released her mask; she had knelt to examine the ground more closely, and brought out her pill vial. Her features were rather broad and round for D'Orrey's personal tastes but much easier to look at than his nephew's shorts.

"Nothing the tracks tell me," she announced after several minutes of careful examination. "Any project details?"

"Some. We'll thrash it over on the way down," D'Orrey replied. "Or do you want to stay longer, Pete? Can you think of anything else we ought to do now?"

"I guess not. I'd like to see where they went, but you're right about not staying much longer without supplies. I know better what equipment we should bring up, now. We ought to have brought more food with us this time."

"If I'd been sure we'd see anything, we would have. Now we can feel pretty sure of finding them in this area, we can set up for a longer stay — maybe even move the camp."

"Are you sure these snakes are the same ones you saw before?" Vicki asked suddenly. She had stowed the pills again without opening the container.

"Not at all. They could be, but I can't recognize individual rattlers by sight. But if they are, they seem to work this area fairly regularly, and if they aren't, there could be a whole tribe of them around. Either way this should be a good place to work; there's a lot of clover and berries, and presumably a lot of mice and rabbits."

Peter nodded, and the three started down the trail which opened into the clearing a few meters from the lookout rock. They quickly found themselves in more comfortable shade, but discussing plans was harder than D'Orrey had assumed. The way was usually too narrow to let them travel side by side, steep enough to demand full attention to footing much of the time, and the woman's sneezing was now up to full antihistamine-free level. She used her pills only when this would interfere with work. Nothing was really settled in the half hour they took to get almost back to sea level.

Here the mixed pine and second-growth hardwood opened out once more, and they could see the lake.

Here it was also a good deal hotter, and the midafternoon sun was nearly straight ahead of them. The sea breeze from behind and to their left was blocked almost entirely by hills. As they approached the road—little more than a track, but usable by vehicles—which led out toward the tip of the peninsula, Peter scored another point.

"Suits off," he said quietly, deactivating his own. This time neither adult compromised with common sense; even though nothing wheeled could be seen or heard, crossing a road in an operating camouflage suit was what the boy would have called pure crack. D'Orrey switched his unit off without comment; Vicki thanked Peter. None reactivated the garments when they reached the other side.

The camp was still half a kilometer away, beside a brook which emptied further on into the lake. The way was quite open now, and they could talk more freely. Little had really been settled, however, when Peter stopped and gestured for the others to do the same. His other hand went to his waist. His suit, unlike the others, had a belt which carried several items besides the camouflage logic unit; as a matter of courtesy, neither of the adults had asked what these were. Hackers liked to keep their tricks to themselves when not in showoff mood.

He seemed to be listening, but had not asked for silence so was presumably not using an ordinary eavesdropper. He had not removed anything from the belt, but was touching first one point and then another on it, waiting two or three seconds before each new shift of the finger. It was fully a minute before he relaxed and turned to his companions.

"No one's been in the camp, and nothing—no animal—into the tents or the food."

"As far as you can tell," appended his uncle.

"Of course. If I'm wrong, someone's curious enough about what we're doing to cover it very carefully."

"Well, if the snakes are a hacker's trick, maybe someone is. If it's legitimate research or, perish the thought, a natural change in snake behavior, no one should be." D'Orrey thought a moment, then risked a guess. "I take it you left sound and maybe other sensors and recorders in and around the camp, and have been playing them back."

"That's the idea.

"The same general sort of stuff you said you'd use for me to track animals up on the Stage?"

"Right."

"Good. How long will it take you to set them up back there?"

"Not long." Peter grinned smugly. "You were here when I set these after we arrived, but never saw me."

"Great. I didn't think of it when we first talked this over, but can you keep our glasses and other gear checked for false-witness tampering?"

Peter frowned thoughtfully for a moment. "I could, but it'd be better for you to stay with Jerry, wouldn't it?"

"Why?"

"Because I'm part of this team. Shouldn't the checker be independent? You should keep your personal observing gear—glasses, cameras, recorders—out of my reach, and you should quarantine mine for checking if I ever report anything you don't see or hear."

"Unless you record it, I suppose that's true. But you *can* record, obviously."

"Sure, if you want to trust my records—"

Vicki cut in. "Of course we do. Any record can be faked; everyone knew that even before UFO days, but there's no point assuming it has been until there's trouble repeating an observation. Otherwise no one gets anywhere. You said it just now: you're part of the team, as reliable a part as we are. Science is certainly a *search* for truth, mixed with a reasonable effort not to decide too easily that you've already found it, but you're worrying far too much about the faker-defense aspect."

The boy glanced at D'Orrey, who nodded. "Even if I had any reason to suspect you, which I don't, she's right. I know about the never-ending war among hackers, anti-hackers, and other hackers, but nothing ever gets done if we spend all the time worrying about rivals and liars. This is where prevention is *not* better than cure; it gets in the way of the work. We assume no one wants to live with the only cure there is for liars unless he's forced to. So stop worrying, be ready to record anything any of us decides is worth keeping, and pardon the lecture. You cook this evening; deal out some of that chili you did before if there still is any. It's good."

"Thanks. I like flattery, but you still cook tomorrow." His uncle made no answer, but shed his camouflage suit and stretched happily.

The meal was quickly prepared in an extremely old-fashioned kettle over a jellied-alcohol fire — burning wood was still taboo in the park — and almost as quickly eaten. D'Orrey took three helpings without looking at the boy, whose only comment was a repetition. "You still cook tomorrow."

"And I wash up tonight," added Vicki, getting to her feet. "Don't dawdle too long over that last helping, Jaques." The man made no answer; his mouth was full.

Vicki and Peter, the latter rather pointedly, took advantage the next morning of D'Orrey's culinary duties to remain late in their tents, but the sun was not very high when the three left camp together with the built in back-packs of their suits loaded with food, water, and carefully selected equipment. They hoped to stay away until the study was done, so the tents and unused equipment were collapsed, cased, powered down as appropriate and stowed in a single travel pack concealed in a tree. Bears and smaller mammals could be a nuisance, but Peter felt that human interference was much more likely. The adults were pretty sure he was carrying equipment which would warn him if the bundle were disturbed. They didn't ask, but both noticed that he had paid little attention while Vicki carefully adjusted the camouflage wrap on the container.

It was still cool when they started back up the hill. The sea breeze had not yet developed, and would have had little effect at the camp anyway. It would help later, but they wanted to get up to Stage, as Vicki had named the work area, before the sun became too oppressive. Once across the still deserted road, all activated their suits.

They wanted to get there early, but even Peter was too experienced to wear himself out at the start. He was willing—again rather pointedly—to allow D'Orrey to set the pace once the slope began to steepen. Vicki tactfully brought up the rear.

This proved to be, not exactly a mistake, but unfortunate.

They had climbed nearly a hundred meters, the woman's natural morning sneeze pattern was well established, and they were at a point where the trail was not only narrow and steep but offered very poor footing in loose crumbled granite, dry dusty loam, and even drier pine needles. All were careful; they had passed this way twice before. Even the fact that it was much trickier descending failed to make anyone careless; Vicki was simply unlucky, perhaps because she *was* behind and encountering freshly loosened surface.

She ejaculated some words which would have been considered more appropriate for a male—one of low culture—not too many years earlier, as her weight came on her left foot and the substrate slipped from under it. Her hands were both free and her reflexes good as she grabbed for branches, but the only one she caught proved unworthy of trust. Her other foot, rising for a forward step, came down abruptly on an equally unreliable surface well short of the spot she had intended; it slipped too. This brought her chest, stomach, knees and face into violent contact with the trail.

The others heard, but had no time to do anything. She stopped herself after a couple of meters of sliding, at a spot where the slope flattened a little, and struggled back to her feet. She had said nothing after the first moment and still remained silent, checking damage.

The suits were designed for outdoor use, and hers had been actually pierced in only a few places. Her skin had not done so well. She had a deep slash over her right eye, and her knees and palms were dirt-plastered crimson messes. Damage to her suit was at least as eye-catching. Several control fibers had been severed, mostly in places not matching visible bodily injury, and fairly large areas of its body and legs no longer responded to the logic unit. About half her headpiece above the level of the cut revealed the mahogany red-brown of the hair inside, and a roughly triangular area from right shoulder downward to her waist and inward to the small of her back showed the fabric of the sweat suit she was wearing under the camouflage unit.

"Can you walk?" asked D'Orrey. "There's a place a few meters up where we can get close enough together for first aid."

"Nothing seems broken," she replied. "No, don't try to get beside me and help. There isn't room. One of you might get below, so I won't have to worry about slipping again, if you like."

Peter silently came down the trail, passing very carefully the spot where she had slipped, and made his way with equal care around her. The climb was resumed more slowly.

Jaques had been right about the level spot. There was even a boulder large enough for a seat, and after making sure that it was solidly embedded Vicki settled herself on its fairly smooth top.

"At least I *can* sit," she remarked.

"Don't be flippant. Those knees are a mess."

"And my hands. You'll—both of you—have to use the kit. And am I bleeding into my right eye? *Something* has certainly happened to my head."

"It sure has. We'd better work from the top down. Pete, you use the tester; find if there's a skull fracture under that cut. I'll take care of the blood."

The first aid kit was open now, and the older man pulled out a squeeze tube, snapped off its tip, and began to spread a layer of opaque brown gel over the gash. Peter had silently taken out a golf-ball-sized capsule, opened it in walnut fashion, touched the convex sides briefly to each other and pulled them apart. They were now connected by a filament extending from the apex of one hemisphere to the other. He placed the flat side of one over Vicki's left eye at the point corresponding to the cut over the right, waited for D'Orrey to finish his anointing plus a few seconds for the gel to crust, and placed the other over the wound itself. A monitor screen in the lid of the kit came to life, and all three read it with interest.

"Put some goo on this side, too," the boy said after a moment, lifting the sensor to permit the operation. D'Orrey obeyed, and Peter replaced the instrument. The seniors expressed satisfaction, the man with a nod, Vicki grunting approvingly. Moving her head was uncomfortable.

"They match well enough. I guess I didn't crack the egg. I got quite a wallop, though."

"Do you feel dizzy or sick?" asked Peter.

"Not really. I can use a P-pill, I guess; even if I don't really have concussion or shock, it won't hurt."

"At least you're not like Mom."

"Should I be relieved or worried? How *did* you mean that?"

"She'd have you lying down while she brewed some sort of herb poultice to plaster on you, and some other sort of tea to pour into you. She doesn't believe in antibiotics, and less in nano or pseudolife repair gadgets. Let nature heal, she says."

"Hmph. Mostly I agree with her. But why aren't antibiotics natural? They originally came from molds, didn't they?"

"Don't argue with me. I'm just a hacker, as far from nature as anyone can get, she complains."

"At least she knows it's natural for kids to disagree with their parents," cut in D'Orrey. "Let's not wait for nature with these hands and knees. They must hurt."

The symmetry test for fractures was harder with the kneecaps, since both areas were damaged about equally, but after much moving around of the sensors and a certain amount of argument all three decided that neither patella had been damaged. The chemicals and nano repair devices suspended in the gel could be expected to deal with infection, pain and, within an hour or so, to finish healing.

Even so, walking wasn't easy for a while. They went on, partly because all wanted to get to work and partly because it was better for the damaged knees to be in normal use during repair. More information was available to the nanohealers. Travel was much slower, of course, and now Peter brought up the rear while Vicki set the pace.

She was happy to rest and pull out her pill vial after they reached the study site, while Peter criss-crossed the Stage to plant his instrument layout. This time he kept his camouflage on and travelled very slowly and watchfully; he was quite willing to let any snakes know he was coming, but if he scared the small mammals away it might delay operations. Even so, the process was much more obvious to his companions than it had been at camp. Two or three creatures did bound or scurry out of his path, but none of the group saw anything resembling a mass exodus, and kept their hopes up. Vicki had taken her first pill; D'Orrey hoped it would not prove incompatible with the first aid equipment already at work, but made no comment. She was old enough to have her own judgement—several years older than he.

The rock he had used the day before seemed the best observing site, and it was agreed that all three should stay there. Using trees would have allowed broader coverage of the Stage, but it seemed better to have all three watchers monitor the same area so that memories as well as objective records could be compared. False-witness units were easy to sneak into monoculars, but many times harder with binoculars because of matching, correlation, and cross-connection problems, and *almost* impossible with multiple sets of instruments being used by different people from almost, but not quite, the same point—especially if the observers occasionally moved a trifle with respect to each other. This was not a matter of worry in the sense that D'Orrey had been preaching, but had long been lab routine like clean glassware.

The older two had binoculars and video rings; Peter didn't reveal much about his own equipment, which he had presumably designed and grown himself, but the others assumed he would not only be recording vision and sound but other factors. Use of radiation equipment which might stimulate, activate, track, or control animals and observing gear through minute receivers and transmitters was standard research procedure, and an obvious possibility even to the non-hackers. Neither D'Orrey nor Vicki would have wanted to implant anything in a rattlesnake, but there were many who would consider it an interesting challenge. The hacker mindset had expanded naturally from data processing to nanotechnology, pseudobiology, and gene engineering, which after all differed little from each other.

His elders did not, therefore, try to watch Peter at all closely as he went around the area presumably planting sensors and transmitters, and the boy showed no urge to brag about, or even demonstrate, what he had. He spent about a quarter of an hour moving around the Stage. Apparently he met no snakes, or at least aroused none, and eventually he rejoined the others at the top of the rock.

He was now carrying openly a palm-sized monitor unit. Its screen showed a very active display, but this was not pictorial; symbols neither of the others could understand flickered endlessly on its surface. Peter made no effort to keep them from looking, but wore a half-amused, half-contemptuous smile when they tried. Vicki thought briefly of asking whether he would tell them anything, but decided not to give him the amusement of refusing. D'Orrey faced the same temptation but decided not to give him the amusement of explaining. The man had no objection in principle to showing off—he enjoyed it himself—but considered that Peter's feeling of superiority because of his height needed no encouragement. He confined himself to a different question.

"Is there anything we can do but wait and hope we're lucky again?"

"Nothing I can do, if you mean about persuading the snakes to come back. There's lots of rabbits and smaller animals, but if only the two rattlers we saw yesterday are involved, they may not want to hunt yet. How long would it take to digest a mouse as big as they caught yesterday?"

D'Orrey didn't know, but guessed, "Maybe three or four days. I'm hoping there are more snakes in on this. I'm budgeting for a wait, though; I don't expect yesterday's luck again so soon."

His pessimism proved justified, but the cause was not serpentine satiation. The trio spend over two hours on the rock while the sun rose higher and higher and grew less and less supportable, and nothing animal but a couple of mice came into view. Vicki, oldest of the group by several years and far the most patient by nature, simply waited, thinking silently most of the time but sometimes making a remark. Her suit was healing itself slowly but apparently without errors. Her personal injuries, because of or in spite of artificial intervention, were progressing far more rapidly. She took her pill faithfully every hour to keep from scaring subjects away.

D'Orrey, whose own suit was having its usual thermal trouble, spoke more often, though he wouldn't descend to futile complaint. Peter divided his attention between his monitor and the Stage, sweeping the latter frequently with a pair of binoculars which he didn't offer to share with the others. His uncle thought of asking for a look, but didn't want to hear something like, "Aren't yours just as good?"

He suspected that they weren't, that Peter had incorporated devices of his own in his optics, but couldn't imagine what advantage these might confer—or rather, he could imagine many things, from infra-red and ultra-violet vision extension to time-lapse interferometers permitting better than ordinary resolution, but couldn't guess which might be most likely. It would depend heavily on the kid's specific skills; human limits forced even hackers to specialize.

Vicki's healing completed itself, and after allowing with some distaste a dozen ladybug-sized mechanisms from the kit to crawl over the sites of her injuries scavenging spent chemicals and healing devices, she returned them to the case and resumed her own monitoring of the Stage.

The real interruption came late in the morning. The sun had been ducking behind clouds off and on as fair-weather cumulus began to build; all, even Peter, had taken this as welcome relief. Now a much darker shadow swept over the rock. The wind, which had been rising slowly as the sea breeze developed and had even been of some comfort, grew gusty, and large raindrops spattered on the rock and the watchers. For a moment they hoped for just a brief shower; then the drops grew smaller, steadier and more frequent.

Peter, after one nonverbal annoyed utterance, clambered quickly down the irregular slope where they had mounted the rock and began dashing here and there about the clearing. He had turned his suit off; apparently he now wanted any rattlers to take responsibility for avoiding him regardless of scientific protocol. He was back in four or five minutes with a slightly embarrassed expression on his face.

"I never thought of rain with some of this stuff. I've always used it indoors."

"Insulation trouble?" Vicki sounded sympathetic, and even Jaques could remember too many of his own lapses to be critical.

"Not so much that. Just . . . " the youngster fell silent, and his uncle was annoyed. Something informative *could* have come out then. If it weren't merely electrical insulation, what trouble could rain cause a micromachine? He felt the surge of irritation which goes with finding a gap in one's knowledge, seeing no way to fill it, and being unable because of conscience to pass it off as supernatural and therefore unknowable. He obviously wouldn't be told; Peter was changing the subject quite forcibly. "Vick, your suit still has sections not working. Shouldn't it be healed by now?"

"I suppose so. I haven't been timing, though, and don't know just how much damage was done. Also, this never happened to me before, and I don't remember what the manual said I should expect for healing times."

"Maybe I should check it—the suit, I mean."

"Can you? Have you equipment?"

"I can cobble some together in an hour or so."

"Here?"

"Well, no. I'll need my kit back at camp. I could take your suit back and you could use mine if you wanted to keep observing. It won't really fit you—it isn't self-shaping like yours—but its camouflage unit can handle wrinkles."

"But if you aren't here and anything interesting happens, will there be any record? Is your layout entirely automatic? I thought you'd have to be on hand to operate at least some of it."

Peter looked uncomfortable once more.

"Well—I've had to turn a lot of it off, just now. Is there much chance of snakes hunting while it's raining, anyway?"

"Rabbits and mice stay out in it. I expect the rattlers' lives go on as usual, too," answered D'Orrrey. "What it boils down to is that the Becker equipment can't observe in the rain, and if this shower lasts more than an hour or two we may as well go back to camp and read Nanofacts for Beginners."

Peter flushed again. There was no way of taking the remark as anything but criticism, though the man had managed to avoid saying " . . . equipment we were counting on . . . "

Vicki, soft-hearted in spite of her own disappointment, cut in. "Pete wouldn't have to read. How long would it take to redesign your stuff to work even in the rain?"

"I don't know. I haven't spent much time outdoors. A lot goes on I didn't think about . . . "

"And it isn't just a matter of improving insulation, you say," D'Orrey added, he hoped not too pointedly.

"Not by a lot. I'll work on it, though. You want me to take your suit, Vick? Or will you be coming back too?" Neither adult could guess whether the youngster wanted to be alone or not.

They debated the question on its own merits for several seconds. Then Vicki sneezed again and reached doubtfully for her pill vial.

"Not just anti-symptom stuff, I hope?" Peter's self assurance suddenly blossomed again.

"I thought you had a low opinion of natural cures," D'Orrey cut in before the woman could answer.

"I do, but that's not the point. Interfering with natural responses to an infection just because they're a nuisance isn't very smart. You should at least decide first whether the responses are helping fight the infection."

"What would *you* do?" asked the woman, rather sarcastically.

"I'd spend a week blowing my nose, until someone—"

"So you do have some trust in nature. That's just what I do, except where sneezing will interfere with the job."

Peter scarcely noticed her interruption. "—cooks up an antibody for just the right virus. I'll have to try that—I haven't done any really fancy chemistry yet, though I grow most of my own gear. I wonder if pseudolife would do the job, or if I'd have to get into high class biochem?" He seemed about to drift completely into abstract thought, but D'Orrey brought the discussion firmly back to practical levels.

"We'd all better go back, I guess, and at least rethink what we should have up here with us. Vicki's nerves and membranes can offer their proper responses to irritation" —another sneeze suggested that they were doing this—"and your gear needs rethinking, you admit. Her suit may need treatment, and even if the snakes come hunting again we can't make the measurements and readings we wanted."

"Maybe *you'd* better stay, though," suggested the woman. "If anything does happen, just knowing something about the frequency of hunts and the possible number of snakes involved could be useful."

The man nodded slowly. "All right. I'll stay 'til sundown, or enough before that to let me get back before dark. You two go on down and do what needs to be done with sniffles, suits, and sensors. Watch your footing—no insult intended."

"Don't worry!" Vicki responded with feeling. Peter had already disappeared down the climbway. She followed, showing no sign of stiffness or other effect of her injuries. D'Orrey's attention shifted back to the Stage as Peter appeared and worked over the area once more. Apparently he had merely turned his equipment off before; now he was collecting it. Vicki was not with him, and Jaques didn't even wonder whether she were waiting at the head of the trail or had started down at once. The boy presently vanished as well—really vanished, by departure, not by activating his suit. D'Orrey stretched himself out behind the screen of bushes, assumed as relaxed a position as possible, and watched the deserted Stage through the still falling rain.

Rabbits, mice, and squirrels might indeed be willing to feed during a shower, but none of them seemed around at the moment. The sun, glimpsed occasionally through brief breaks in the rain clouds, slowly reached the meridian. It sank seemingly even more slowly. The temperature had fallen considerably, which was a relief; the camouflage suit was better at keeping its wearer warm than cool. And at least he had food and more water this time.

No rabbits. No squirrels. No mice. Not even a toad.

No snakes. A few decades ago this would have been no surprise on Mt. Desert, but what some people called Greenhouse Effect and others had named the Warm Ripple, depending on political preference and statistical background, had gradually extended the northern range of the timber rattler by over three hundred kilometers and was still at it. How the creatures had made their way over the causeway from the mainland to Acadia was a matter of speculation, but no one was very surprised. There were far fewer human travelers these days, mostly because of fuel shortage and cost, and even a bear would not have been very startling.

But none of this explained rattlesnakes cooperating in a hunt. Miracles, to D'Orrey, meant high technology or unusual combinations of natural law, not the supernatural. High tech meant people, not spirits. The hacker attitude had spread quite naturally from data handling to nano and bio technology. Shaping micromachines and pseudolife "organisms" using commercially available enzymes and crystal-patterned molecular assembly guides, commonly and—when spoken aloud—confusingly called "ribosomes" from the trade name of an early model, was no more unusual now than the designing of viruses and more benign software around commercially available solid-state data processing chips had been a few decades before. Even casual—much too casual from D'Orrey's viewpoint—gene engineering, though sometimes illegal, was a common field of amateur activity. Knowledge is nearly indestructible, since it does not obey conservation laws. The cooperative snakes might represent someone's personal game, a serious piece of research to be published in due course, mere mischief or, just conceivably, a new natural phenomenon. D'Orrey, as an animal behavior student, needed to know which. New combinations of natural law were eternal; so were the human urges for understanding, power, independence, and amusement—eternal as knowledge itself. They were also as hard to control, as evolution, religious reformations, drug abuse, nuclear proliferation, and the sport of hacking all showed clearly.

The sun was low when D'Orrey started down the trail. He watched the footing carefully, and had no trouble recognizing where Vicki had slipped on the way up; but there was no sign of any similar accident going down until he was almost at the bottom of the steep section. Then he nearly provided the evidence himself as a loose stone went out from underfoot. His reflexes stood up to the test. His other foot moved quickly and stopped the fall; for a moment he felt the prickle of released adrenaline, then a mixture of two kinds of relief—that he had not actually fallen, and that neither of the others had seen the near-incident. He could have treated any minor injuries himself, since neither of them would know when he had started down and no delay would have been obvious; but suits healed themselves much more slowly, and the boy would certainly have noticed anything wrong even with the garment turned off.

Vicki was visible and audible as he neared the camp; the boy was neither. She was still sneezing, and occasionally coughing and blowing her nose. She was not wearing her camouflage unit, but a warm water-repellent coverall. Her suit was draped inside out over a nearby bush, and D'Orrey decided that his nephew was really showing off. Natural, of course, but this time promising a really useful put-down.

He turned off his suit as he approached the camp—he had forgotten to do so while crossing the road—and gave a cheerful whistle. Vicki saw him at once, waved, and noting the raised eyebrows as he drew nearer, nodded toward Peter's tent.

"He's been busy ever since we got here, as far as I can tell. I don't know what progress he's made. I haven't heard any bad language."

"Vick, you know me better than that!" an indignant retort came from the tent, whose soundproofing was evidently off. "I've figured out what to do, and started most of it. The things just have to grow now."

"Then we can go back in the morning, rain or no rain?" Jaques asked.

"I think so. You never can tell just how long debugging will take, of course."

"Of course," the others agreed together. "Coming out soon?" the woman added.

"Might as well. It's on its own now. Just a minute." The tent entrance rolled itself up, and Peter crawled out and stood up. He was wearing the same shorts as before, designed to support pockets as well as dazzle eyes, plus the shoes whose soles had grown much thicker after a few minutes' use around the stony camp site. A nanohack could make himself very comfortable if inclined that way. His nephew was still, D'Orrey felt, conscious of his own physique, but this suspicion might merely represent an undersized uncle's jealousy rather than objective analysis. It *would* be nice to be a few centimeters taller . . .

He could have been, of course, but he had much better things to do with his money. Let the kid gloat if he wanted.

"Anything happen?" Peter asked.

"Nope." D'Orrey shook his head negatively. "Nothing bigger than grasshoppers."

"How much time do we budget for just waiting?" the boy asked. Both pairs of male eyes turned to Vicki, the patient one.

"A week at least," she replied promptly, and firmly. "If that bothers anyone, maybe you could design some snake detectors for us so we could go where they are instead of waiting for them to come to us. I know it's no use tramping around just looking for them; their prey would hear us and take off first, and they'd either go after dinner or at least away from us."

"But don't rattlers usually just wait for the dinner to get near enough?" objected Peter.

"Yes; but is it what they *usually* do that brought us here?"

"No. You're still cooking tonight, Uncle Jaques."

The rain continued, sometimes very heavily, for much of the night, but the sky visible through the branches seemed cloudless again by sunrise. Peter and D'Orrey of course took advantage of Vicki's cooking turn to stay in their tents a little later, but before the sun was very high the three were again climbing to the Stage. They were laden pretty much as on the previous day, but Peter seemed to have learned something; attached to his belt was an object about the size, shape, and from the way he had handled it, the weight, of an ordinary brick. The others suspected he was bringing his entire stock of nano equipment this time.

Vicki's suit now seemed completely healed. D'Orrey had not asked whether his nephew had done anything to it, assuming that the way it was hanging the night before implied the answer. The question seemed unimportant just now; the catechol embarrassment would come later. They reached the rock, this time without incident, unloaded food and water as before and draped reflecting film over them. Then Peter once more set out his apparatus, leaving his "brick" on the rock.

D'Orrey eyed it thoughtfully, but decided not even to test its weight. He was pretty sure that touching it without the owner's knowledge would not be possible, and however harmless the act and natural the curiosity he didn't want to be defending himself.

The kid was close enough to running the group already. His embarrassed ignorance of outdoor environments, even with its resultant delay of the project, had been quite lucky, D'Orrey felt; but it couldn't be expected to keep him down long.

His reflections were interrupted by a yell from the Stage, coming through the suit communicators but also audible directly. For a moment neither of them could see the boy; then he sprang into brief visibility as his suit cut off, vanished again for a second or two, and reappeared once more. Neither watcher could guess whether the garment was being flicked on and off in indecision or was malfunctioning. Still less could they guess at a cause for either possibility until Peter provided it, coherent now but still highly excited.

"Rattlers! Dozens of 'em! They're heading toward you. What'll I do?"

"If they're heading this way, why do anything? Or are you in their way?"

"No, I'm behind them and they don't seem to care about me. But I can't get back to you or the rock. They're in the way!"

"Go around them. You should be able to run fast enough. Or don't you want to get in front? Just make up your mind how badly you want to be up here with us instead of on the ground with them." D'Orrey tried not to sound impatient or superior.

There were several seconds of silence. Peter remained visible, and appeared to be surveying the ground with some care. When he finally spoke again he seemed calmer. "I guess I can see more down here. Do you see 'em yet?"

Both adults looked carefully before Vicki answered "No" as calmly as she could. "How far are they from you? And just how many are there really?"

"'bout seven or eight meters from the farthest I can see. A dozen or so. I think there were more, and they'd be closer to you now. They're really travelling."

"And how many really are there?"

"Well—I can count eight, now. There were more, though. All heading for the rock. Don't you have a flock of mice, or squirrels, or rabbits, or something they might be chasing?"

"Not that I can see," replied the woman. "And would they be chasing? In a pack?"

"Who knows, now?"

"Are there any more behind you, or on either side?" D'Orrey cut in. "Could you tell whether they were all coming from the same place?"

There was a pause before Peter answered, still more calmly this time. He seemed to be getting back his control, and actually to have looked before answering.

"I don't see any more. These were all between me and the rock when I first saw them."

"Can you check in both directions—sideways, that is—and get some idea whether this is just a small bunch or whether more are coming from somewhere?"

"All right." The suit vanished once more, to D'Orrey's satisfaction; Peter must really be thinking again as an observer. He even began reporting his position every few seconds, realizing that the others would have trouble spotting him.

"Ten meters to your left of where I was. No more snakes . . . Twenty meters. Still none. Thirty . . . I'm getting near the trees. Still none. I'm heading back the other way . . . back where I first saw them . . . now to your right . . . ten meters . . . none . . . twenty—Hey! Another bunch from the trees—I'm going back." There was silence for several seconds. "There are fourteen or fifteen in this bunch, mixed up together so they're hard to count. They're heading your way, too. They can't be chasing mice."

"Or you?" queried Vicki.

"No, neither group cared about me. It's something near you, or at least the rock."

"How closely do you feel like following them?" asked D'Orrey.

"I'm keeping them in sight. I'm about five meters behind a couple of stragglers in the new bunch. D'you want my suit off so you can track us?"

"No need. We both have strobes if we need 'em, and as long as you're moving can see you fairly well anyway. If you keep your suit on, you won't have to worry about any more behind you."

"Why not? I'd be less worried if they could see me!"

"Are you sure? We don't know yet what has them excited. If you feel like being experimental bait, of course, we could start finding out."

The boy did not answer for a moment. Then, "Why not? There's plenty of trees. I'll catch up with this batch."

Vicki stirred and almost uttered a protest, then looked at Jaques and merely frowned. Both waited silently and attentively, watching with narrowed eyes the barely visible figure sixty meters away. Not even the first group of snakes he had reported could be seen yet from the rock.

Peter's indistinct outline was approaching them, but not quite directly; apparently he was trying to come up on the right of the group—or should it be called a gaggle, a wisp, or a pride, D'Orrey wondered briefly and irrelevantly. Surely the language had a collective term for snakes; it wouldn't be surprising if it had several for different kinds, though of course serpents had never been game animals in medieval Europe. As far as he knew.

"I'm only a meter to one side of the group, about halfway between front and rear. They're not paying any attention to me so far. I'm going to cut my suit—don't worry, Vick, I'm good and ready to run."

The tall figure sprang into visibility, heading toward the watchers at nearly a run; if he were still matching speed with the rattlers, both adults thought, the snakes were certainly enthusiastic about *something*.

"They still don't care about me. I'm going to get right among them—"

"Don't be crazy!" called Vicki.

"Don't worry. I'm set to jump, far and fast. What was that poem? Snakes to the right of me, snakes to the left of me, snakes before me—they still don't care. I'm going to stop for a minute and check readings."

They watched as he took the monitor from his belt and held it near his face. They then saw that his claim to be ready to jump was fully justified.

He jumped, farther and faster than D'Orrey had thought possible even for someone with Peter's build.

"Hey! They stopped and—reporting later. I'm leaving." The departure could also be watched easily; he did not reactivate his suit. He made four tremendous leaps, the monitor still in his hand, taking him over a dozen meters from his starting point; then he paused and looked back.

"They're interested in *me* now. They're all coming at me. I hope whoever pulled this trick hasn't taught them to climb trees." He resumed his flight.

"Lots of snakes can," D'Orrey remarked, mostly to hide his own mounting anxiety. "Pick a tree with—"

"If that includes rattlers I don't want to know it. Wait a minute." The boy stopped again, once more looking back at his pursuers. Then a chuckle came over the communicators.

"I thought it was too much of a coincidence. They've lost interest in me again. I turned my monitor off. They're milling around sort of confused—now they're starting back your way."

"And your first group is in sight here," added Vicki. "Snakes, but no mice or any other prey."

"Did they get distracted when I had my monitor on?"

"I didn't notice, I'm afraid."

"All right. Let me get farther from this bunch—no, I'll wait here and let them get farther from me, and I'll turn it on again. I'll tell you when to watch for results. All right?"

The woman, and even the uncle, were less worried now; a straightforward and only mildly risky experiment was under way. They waited in relative calm until the second pack—that was the best word, D'Orrey decided—of rattlers had come close enough to count.

"All right, if you think you're far enough—or close enough!" Vicki called.

"Right. Monitor on—now!" The pair on the rock watched the reptilian assembly below for long seconds, but no change in behavior was evident. The creatures had come to the base of the declivity, and some of them seemed interested in trying to climb the relatively smooth stone. This was not worrisome; even the human beings had not been able to ascend this face, though mice or squirrels no doubt could have. D'Orrey felt a twinge of uneasiness as some of the snakes wriggled off to both sides; if they surrounded the boulder, there was at least one place where they could certainly get up.

"They doing anything?" came Peter's voice.

"Not exactly," replied his uncle. "If they were responding to your monitor before, it must be too far away now."

"Okay. This lot is coming back. Easy to check the distance effect, but I'll cut off again and wait 'til they all reach you."

Neither Jaques nor Vicki had to look up to know what Peter was doing; there was only one obvious way to make the test. It made more sense for them to keep observing the rattlers.

These showed no change in behavior for some time, even after the second lot arrived. When they did, D'Orrey felt little relief. The reptiles directly under him were starting to behave aimlessly, as though uncertain of which way they wanted to go, but those farthest to the sides still seemed to keep their interest in the rock itself, and were gradually surrounding it, moving out of sight to each side. He did look outward, then.

Peter was scarcely a dozen meters away, still easily visible.

"You're distracting the ones closest to you, I think," his uncle reported as calmly as he could. "You'd better stop where you are—no, move to one side. Can you see them well enough, or should we warn you if they start your way?"

"I can see 'em. We've settled something, anyway."

"What?" asked the woman.

"They've been implanted with something. They're homing, though I'll need the kit up there to spot the actual radiation. My monitor broadcasts too, of course, but they seem to have a stronger yen for the kit itself. If it had been one of the suit processors, of course, this would all have happened the day before yesterday."

"Why didn't they come to the camp? You were working there for long enough," D'Orrey pointed out.

"I suppose no rattlers, or at least no implanted ones, were close enough. We'll have to try parts of the kit, one by one, to find out just what's the light that's drawing them. I'll shut this off, and come on up."

"Be careful on your way," Vicki spoke up. "The things seem to be working around the rock on both sides. There was only one place we could climb, but maybe you'd better approach that a bit cautiously."

"Sure thing, Ma." What seemed to be progress was apparently restoring Peter's ego. He vanished once more in camouflage, but the others could still make him out vaguely as he started around the boulder to their right. D'Orrey picked up the nano kit and placed it as far to the left as was practical; maybe this would draw the rattlers away from the climbing spot. Turning off its contents would presumably be better, but that would have to be left to its owner.

"Watch it!" Peter's voice came again. "A couple of them are working their way up. I'm not sure I can—"

"Don't try!" snapped his uncle, leaping toward the climbway. There was no sharp drop-off. Smooth top gave way with increasing steepness to an irregular slope much more overgrown than the flat part. The growth hid the top of the narrow path until he had descended nearly half way. No snakes were visible even when he got there, and after a moment he went a little farther and ensconced himself a short distance to one side of the route where the snakes might be expected to pass. The interesting question was whether the lure of the kit would cause them to continue up the rather vague trail or allow them to explore. Toward him. It would depend, he feared, on their intelligence level. He hoped this was no higher than he believed. If they passed him without noticing . . .

The first one, an eighty-centimeter youngster, did. He waited until it was a little farther up than his own position, set his jaw, and snatched at its tail. He caught it just ahead of the rattles and whipped it outward and upward away from the rock, only then wondering whether it would land anywhere near Peter.

A second rattler was now in sight, but he took time to call a warning.

"Pete, I'm tossing them back down, but can't tell where they'll land. Watch for snakefalls."

"Fine. Half a dozen are at the foot of the climb, and more are coming. How do *I* get up?"

No one had an answer for the moment. D'Orrey flipped the second snake back to the ground, and half a minute later processed a third. None of the creatures had so far noticed *him*; their I.Q.s seemed acceptably low, or the implanted homing urge very strong, but he wondered what would happen when his first subject got back. Snakes do have memories of a sort.

"Maybe you could let all the ones on this side get up on top, so I could follow—"

"And get here to find them all wrapped around your high-tech brick?" Vicki finished.

"But if we tossed 'em off the rock from there, it'd take them a long time to get around and back up, and I'd have time to find out which unit was attracting them."

"If you really want to handle rattlesnakes when they've gotten where they want to go and probably have attention to spare, say the word and I'll let 'em up," snapped D'Orrey.

"Well—let me think a minute." The pause was brief. "Tell you what. I'll go back around to the front, and you can keep tossing 'em down here, Uncle Jaques."

"Thanks."

"Then when you can see me, Vicki, and I tell you I'm ready, you can throw me the kit. I'll catch it and start running, turning things off as I go. When they stop chasing me, I'll know which was the right unit and I can keep it off, and the rattlers can go about their business, and I can come back up with you and we can work things out from there. How about that?"

"How long will this all take? I don't want to keep grabbing tails of poisonous snakes all morning. I may improve with practice, but the statistics are against me."

"Right." The boy *might* have been concerned. "It'll be quickest if we start right now. All right, Vick? Heft the kit and try to guess how far you can throw it. I'll get as close as you tell me, unless—" he didn't finish the sentence, but neither listener needed the rest. Vicki picked up the kit, judged it to weight something over two kilograms, and made a number of simulated throws while waiting for Peter to appear. She was careful about this, fortunately; she stood well back from the edge of the rock, and when the smooth surface did slip from her hand on the third try, it did not fall over the edge. She didn't mention the incident aloud. She had decided that a one-hand underarm toss would be most effective by the time Peter appeared below.

He approached the still numerous snakes to within three meters, his suit off, and looked up anxiously.

"Think you can get it out to me here? I'd rather catch it than have it hit a rock, but I don't think I want to get much closer in."

"Should I give a practice try up here once or twice?"

"Not unless Uncle Jaques is through snake-tossing and can get up there to catch it. Maybe—" He left the sentence unfinished, and both hearers guessed that he had been about to suggest that they change places so that D'Orrey could do the throwing, and then remembered the man's lesser size and strength.

"All right," she said. "I'm not guaranteeing to get it all the way out there, so be ready to come in for the catch. All ready?"

"Ready."

Vicki gripped the smooth, stony material as firmly as she could in her right hand, swung the arm backward as far as she could and forward as hard as she could. She meant to hold on a little longer than she actually managed, and the block started out at a slight downward rather than a slightly upward angle. Peter saw, and leaped inward without regard for the snakes so as to catch it before it reached the ground.

He was not quite successful. It slipped through his hands and thudded to the surface, fortunately not directly on any of the numerous rocks. This luck was mixed, however; it buried itself partly in the softer ground, and Peter needed an extra second or two to get his fingers under it. He got it away a hand's-breadth from the head of a very interested rattler, took an extra split second to make sure he had a firm grip, and began running. The snakes, after a second or two of apparent uncertainty, followed. The monitor was off; if there had been any doubt about the center of their attraction, it was gone.

Peter gave himself a good lead before opening the kit. Giving it part of his attention slowed him down, but he had planned his procedure already. Without regard to possible effects on the test devices he had planted around the area, he opened half a dozen switches as quickly as he could. He ran a few more paces, and slowed to look back. The snakes were still coming. He touched another half-dozen, put more distance behind him, and looked back again.

There were nearly eighty units to cut off, and he was not surprised to find that the appropriate ones were in the last group. That was Life. It was also sloppy thinking, but he didn't realize this just yet. He watched, ready to resume his flight, as his pursuers finally lost their interest and began to spread out. One or two were coming almost toward him, but that could be mere statistics; they showed no real interest, though he was fully visible. He began to walk slowly back toward the rock, and incidentally toward the nearest snakes.

"That's done it," he reported. "Good old Murphy—it was one of the last bunch. I can do without this last stuff I've cut off for a while at least. I'll get the rest back in operation right away; I've cut off nearly all the equipment I've set out."

"Are you sure it was Murphy?" asked his uncle.

"What else? It had to be something, and why else would—oh my gosh! They're coming back! What?—Why?—"

"First things first. Can you beat them back here?" D'Orrey seemed unsurprised.

"I'll try. Some of them must be nearly straight ahead of me, though."

"You're a good jumper." Vicki too seemed to be taking the matter calmly.

"Yes, but—yeah, I can get over this couple. I hope the climb is clear. But—but why?"

"You mean why did you assume that only one gadget was attracting them?" asked D'Orrey as tonelessly as he could manage. Peter gave no answer, perhaps because he was concentrating on travel. His uncle was too kind to repeat the question; the point must already be clear.

The youngster came across the Stage at a speed both adults envied, and disappeared to their right. A moment later there was a yelp.

"There are still some back here!"

"Are they blocking the climbway?"

"Well, no. They don't seem interested in anything special. I guess I can dodge them. But why didn't they come back around front with the others?"

"At a guess, when Vick threw down your kit, the radiation had a lot more rock to shine through and not enough of it made the grade to affect their implants. You could check by flipping a switch or two."

"Just a minute 'til I'm a little higher—you're right, I guess. Here they come. One of you will have to take on the snake-tossing duty for a few minutes while I find all the sources. It takes a little while after each cut before I'm sure they're *not* interested any more. I wonder how many—"

"You said something about six variables being enough, the other day."

"It would be for the sort of behavior they were showing. But that doesn't mean they'd home on all the control frequencies somebody chose—that wouldn't make sense—or that there wouldn't be anything I'm putting out that wouldn't attract them even if it wasn't part of this character's control set."

"Bad sentence structure but good thinking—or at least, better. I'll watch the path. Do your testing." D'Orrey worked his way down to where the rock steepened, and met his nephew there. No snakes were following; presumably all significant switches were off.

"We could wait until they've all gone out of range," he suggested.

"How long would that be, if they're moving at random?" Peter asked, already supercilious again. "And why wait, anyway? The sooner I know what we can use, the sooner I can shift to innocent wave patterns. All we'll have to wait for is the mice coming back. That'll be long enough, I bet; they must be scared off the hill with all these snakes."

"We should have brought that can of chocolate syrup," Vicki suggested. "That would at least bring mice—or maybe a bear."

"Or bugs," pointed out D'Orrey. "Actually, haven't we done most of what I wanted your help for? We know, basically, why the snakes were behaving so weirdly. As science, this is a fizzle. Nature hasn't done anything surprising—just some hacker, and who can be surprised at *them*?"

"Don't be insulting, Uncle Jaques. Even hackers have reasons for what we do—sometimes good ones."

"Sure. You want to prove you can do it, never mind side effects. Someone's probably shot the ecology of this island to pieces just for his" —he shot a glance at Vicki—"or her own amusement, like a kid making tracks with a dune buggy. I sometimes wish—"

"Hold it, friend," the woman cut in. "Whoever did this certainly knows just how many snakes were used. He knows or is finding out how much they eat, and how often. He's altered *one* variable, essentially; just their hunting techniques. He's in a position to make a more *quantitative* study of one piece of this local ecology than anyone, to my knowledge, ever has before. Why are you calling him a hacker? He's behaving like a scientist; one who may be amusing himself, as we all do, but one who at least knows what he's doing and why. He's even conducting this field work on an island. And I hope you weren't about to wish nanotech had never been developed."

D'Orrey was silent, and Peter nobly refrained from smirking. After a moment, Vicki went on less emphatically. "I'm just providing the obligatory alternative hypothesis, of course; we're supposed to be doing research—testing an idea, not just finding support for one. I was thinking *hacker* too, but I don't want to get trapped into taking that for granted."

D'Orrey nodded; he, too, would have spent a long time seeking alternative explanations rather than risk being called a watchmakerite, even one assuming a human watchmaker.

"Right. Pete, get what details you can about the homing signals. We should have checked at Orono to see if anyone *is* doing a research project up here. When"—he carefully did not say "if"—"you have them, we'll call there."

The youngster nodded, and settled down with his kit. "You keep an eye out for anything coming up," he instructed. His uncle nodded, and positioned himself where he could see anything working up the climbway, and for some time the only words were terse reports.

"One rattler, but seems casual."

"Another, not headed this way."

"First one interested—heading up."

"Lost its enthusiasm. I'll scare it."

Over an hour passed before Peter said, "I think that's everything. There seem to be ten patterns which make them home this way. For all I can tell not more than one or two of them may actually be meant to make them do anything—maybe none of them; this all may be just a side effect of whatever was planned. We'll have to see another hunt, and try to find what's radiated or what I can do to change that pattern before we can even start to be sure. For all I really know, what I've just been doing may have shut off the intended program and spoiled our own project *and* the other guy's. You'd better *hope* it's a hacker, or Orono will be on your neck for not checking with them first." He started to stand up with his kit. "HEY!!"

There was evidently more than one way up the rock, as far as snakes were concerned. D'Orrey's attention had been on the path they had used, and Peter's on his instruments; Vicki was still on top watching the Stage. None of them had noticed the two-meter specimen approaching from slightly above the level of the experimenters and, as it happened, from behind both. The rattler was still intent on something ahead of it. Peter saw the motion from the corner of his eye as he was rising, and had immediate insight on what the signal must be.

He was also lifting his kit, and as it reached a point about half a meter off the ground—beyond what D'Orrey would have considered striking range—the creature struck.

Its target might have been the kit, but the kit was in Peter's hands, protected only by the gloves of his cam suit.

The serpent dropped away and recoiled itself. The boy lashed out with a kick which sent it flying off the rock before it could strike again.

"Uncle Jack! It got me!"

"Drop your kit. Vicki, first aid! Pete, sit and relax. Never mind your box. If it's still attracting anything we'll solve that later. Let's see your hand!"

The boy obeyed, and both saw instantly what had happened. The fleshy outer edge of his right hand bore the significant double puncture, and without waiting for instructions he tried to place it in his mouth. The location of the wound made this difficult, but not impossible, and he began to suck.

After a few seconds he stopped and spat, and both could see that he was getting an encouraging amount of blood. He was about to repeat the process when Vicki arrived with the first aid kit.

No time was wasted; all knew what to do. She took a matchbox-sized container from the main carton and handed two copper-colored objects the size of split peas to D'Orrey. Peter was resting the arm and hand, palm up, on his right knee. The man carefully placed one of the hemispheres on each of the punctures and touched a tiny button on the matchbox.

Vicki had extracted another device, cylindrical in shape, also copper colored except for a narrow red stripe along the curved surface from face to face, and about three centimeters in length and diameter. She lifted Peter's arm so the elbow was straight and placed the curve of the cylinder inside the joint with the stripe across the large vein which showed there. The boy flinched slightly as she energized the unit and two needles worked their way into the blood vessel; emergency medical equipment did not always have anaesthetic refinements.

"That should handle it," D'Orrey said as he relaxed visibly. "Most of what's at the puncture won't get away from it, and any toxin getting as far downstream as the big vein will be handled by the washer. Not natural—at least, not as natural as the snake or the poison ivy Peter had your suit draped over last night—but it works."

Vicki sneezed, but made no move to take another pill, and no response to either part of the "natural" remark. The man resumed, addressing Peter. "I suppose you have enough material to let me call Orono about this project? You hadn't quite said so when our subject interrupted." He wasn't quite as indifferent, or even quite as confident in the first aid equipment, as he sounded, but wanted to get his nephew's mind elsewhere.

"The interruption was more info. If you'll get my kit, I'll see."

"*If* I can get it. Our friend may be back by now."

"Dropping it should have turned everything off."

"It didn't when I dropped it to you before," Vicki pointed out.

Peter's mouth opened, and he looked blankly at her for a moment.

"You're right! It didn't!" His gaze wandered into the distance, and he started to move his right arm. She stopped him firmly; he obeyed her hand pressure, without bringing his attention back from wherever it had gone.

"Uncle Jaques. Check the kit. If no snakes are near, bring it to me." D'Orrey obeyed without comment; maybe the kid *should* be in charge right now.

"I don't see any," he reported. "Here it is."

Peter seized the block with his left hand as Vicki tightened her hold unnecessarily on his right. He set the kit on his left knee, took the monitor from his belt, and watched its screen for some seconds.

"It didn't turn off this time, either," he said at last. "Something's interfered with my controls. How long before I can use both hands?"

The woman looked at the first-aid screen. "Five or six more minutes should have you pumped out." Peter waited out the time with what his uncle considered surprising patience, learning only later what the real emotion was.

Vicki removed the blood filter pump and the venom denaturant units at last, and he flexed arm and fingers for another half minute.

Then he went to work on his nano kit. He seemed to be examining every separate module and trying every switch, though it was not always obvious to the watchers just what was going on; the control system itself was as hard to see and obscure in detail as the mechanisms it directed. The first aid kit was state of the art as of a couple of years earlier and reasonably familiar to any adult; this, like any hacker's work, was an individual—*private*—development.

Peter spent several minutes at the task, and his uncle got a distinct impression toward the end that he was working very slowly, almost as though he suspected a truth he didn't really want to believe.

Finally he detached completely the plate which until then had hinged out from the brick and carried another monitor screen on its inner face, something neither had seen before.

An imperceptible gesture brought the screen to life. Exactly in its center was a blank area about a centimeter across with a set of tiny red symbols inside it. Peter seemed about to throw the whole assembly to the ground, but he controlled himself, put it down gently, stood up, and walked toward the top of the rock. He stood there silently for two or three minutes, while D'Orrey and Vicki looked at each other blankly. Eventually, the man's imagination clicked back into gear.

He carefully refrained from saying anything like, "Made a fool of you again, did he?" At the same time, he had to know—

"D'you suppose it was Jerry?" he asked.

The answer came before the boy could speak. It sounded in the left ear of each of the trio, in the form of a husky whisper not recognizable as anyone's voice—small size puts physical limits on the detail of any wave pattern produced by a speaker.

"It was. Sorry, Mr. Becker. I had to, and it wasn't all your fault. I apologize to you for bugging your kit, and to all of you for violating your personal privacy with these ear canal speakers. They'll be removed as soon as I've finished talking to you. *Doctor* D'Orrey, just why didn't you check with the department? I have better things to do with my time than ward even the well-meaning curious off my experiments. And I thank you, Dr. Kalani, for your analysis even though I suspect you didn't really believe it. It was essentially correct."

"But you knew what I was doing when I asked you to check my instruments!" exclaimed D'Orrey.

"I did not. You said you'd seen something queer and wanted to check its legitimacy, but you gave me no details. I judged you were hoping to make a discovery, which I can well understand, and wanted no rivals beating you to publication, which I can also understand, so I asked for no more. We're as bad as the hackers, Jaques; we don't trust each other enough. Maybe you can profit by this, Mr. Becker, and don't wind up a complete lone wolf. I fear we two scientists may be too old to change.

"Three," corrected Vicki Kalani. "I guess it's natural. Pete, of course you can do something about the catechols in poison ivy. I haven't started to itch yet, but if . . . " her statement trailed off and Peter Ben Becker looked uncomfortable again.

"Better try the first aid kit," he muttered.

"Better still," suggested his uncle, "try learning to recognize poison ivy. You are planning some outdoor research, aren't you? And Vick—how about taking one of my cooking turns? I cleaned your suit last night while you were both asleep."

MARY'S WORDS

Mary Stubbs, Harry's wife for fifty-one years, had a perspective on him that no one else, save perhaps their three children, had. She briefly shares that view with us here, with opening and closing notes by Hal's Pal Ramona Louise Wheeler.

Hal Clement's modesty was part of his public legend. Mary's words show that it was part of his private life as well.

Mary Stubbs: "When I met Harry I didn't know he was a science fiction writer. After we got married, I was introduced to the world of science fiction. I hadn't paid attention to it before. They say opposites attract, so I guess that's what happened.

"My children are not interested in science fiction, and Harry did not push. When Harry was a teen-ager, his father looked down on science fiction, but when he started writing science fiction in college and started getting checks, his father thought it was OK. Harry did not mind if I didn't go to the conventions. He thought that was OK."

Hal often acknowledged that it was love at first sight, and his loyalty to Mary remained constant from that moment to his last. He once told us that he had experienced the atomic bomb test at the same base where he met Mary, but she was the one who changed his world.

EPILOGUE: GOODBYE, AND HELLO

SHANE TOURTELLOTTE

Not long after I accepted the editorship of this book, I went to a regular Monday evening meeting of my Scrabble club. I was early as usual, and so was the director, Scott Kitchen. Scott is an SF reader and occasional convention-goer, so I knew he would appreciate my modest good fortune. I told him I might be missing a couple of meetings in the next few months, because I was editing a memorial volume for the late Hal Clement.

"Hal Clement's dead?"

I hadn't thought that Scott wouldn't know: maybe that comes of most of the fans I know being much more than casual. Yes, I had to tell him, he passed away last October.

"Oh," he sighed. After a few seconds of poignant silence, he brightened and added, "He made the best fudge."

It turned out he had met Hal once, probably in a con suite, and gotten proof of this first-hand. And maybe he got seconds, too.

This makes a great anecdote: a look at the man from an unexpected source, at an unusual angle. Yet as the weeks passed, it accreted weight with me, as a symbol of my doubts about my place in this anthology.

I never had a taste of Hal Clement's fudge—literally or metaphorically. Meaning, I had never had the kind of personal, intimate interchange with him that makes such a one-sentence eulogy as Scott's possible. So how could I be the right person to edit this remembrance to him? What gave me the right?

The easy answer would be that Hal's Pals gave me the right. They conceived this project, and choosing me reflected their collective wisdom on how to bring it to fruition. The friends I have among them had adopted me as a surrogate member—and maybe that threw off their perspective. For if Hal Clement was, as Lance Dixon called him, a sun, I was not a planet but a moon, circling Hal's Pals, connected to Hal only at a remove.

I did have my intersections of trajectory with Clement's Star. Almost always, though, it was as a spectator. I would sit politely in a hotel room with Hal and his Pals at the tail end of a convention, interacting with them, but less so with him. I would sit across the table at that very Korean restaurant where Hal regaled Allen Steele with tales of skimming the treetops of Holland in his B-24. I would sit to one side at an Albacon ice cream social as he and Carl Frederick sang a duet of a Welsh ballad.

That was Albacon in 2003. The last Albacon Hal Clement would attend. The last time I would ever see him.

And I just sat there. I scarcely dared do more.

I can conjure plenty of explanations and excuses. That I didn't want to impose on his time by striking up a conversation when he had better things to do. That, smart as I like to think I am, I felt intimidated by his deep, practical intelligence and didn't think I could keep pace. That it is youth's privilege, if it is sensible, to be quiet and listen to experience. That I don't know a word of Welsh—except how to say "Thanks."

They all add up to the same thing: I had my chance to be more than a mere acquaintance and admirer of Hal Clement, and I did not grasp it, even as I saw others do so. In early 2002, I brought a friend of mine, Paul Golba, to his first SF convention. On getaway day, I left him in the hotel lobby with our luggage while I had a couple of last-minute conversations with colleagues on matters I've long since forgotten. When I got back, I found Paul had been able to pass the time quite well—talking with this kindly elderly gentleman whom he had seen on one of the science panels.

I knew most of the salient facts and had heard many of the anecdotes about Hal Clement by then—but it's possible that Paul had as deep a personal interaction with the man in ten minutes as I had in the five years I knew him. How galling an indictment of my timidity that is.

I recall how hurt I was the day I learned Hal had died, and how surprised I was at how badly it affected me. It was as though I had lost a personal friend. The truth was worse. I had lost a man I could have, should have been able to call a friend, but never did.

I don't pretend that Hal was impoverished by what he missed. I can't pretend that I was not.

Then a curious thing happened. Over the course of a few months, I got to know Hal Clement anew, and better. Through the tributes of people across the spectrum of science fiction, my knowledge and appreciation of the man broadened and deepened. All the things I already knew about him coalesced from myriad data points into a whole.

I could pretend that this constitutes the happy ending, with my inner demon, if not exorcised, at least given a tranquilizer and a place to sleep. I'm not quite that self-centered. I'm not the point of this book—but through my own perceptions, I can finally see what the real point is.

It is all the people who never met Hal Clement, or who did not know him as well as they wished. It is all the SF fans who knew Hal Clement only by his novels and stories, or by hearing him speak on panels or in lectures, or by seeing him stroll down the hallway at a convention, whistling some old, familiar air.

Getting acquainted with Hal Clement, the writer, is probably easier now than it has ever been. Plenty of his novels and stories remain in print, standing alone or in NESFA Press's collections. With multitudes of dealers' tables at SF conventions, with the proliferation of online booksellers, it would take only moderate diligence and industry to collect every novel he wrote, from *Needle* to *Noise*.

Getting to know Harry Clement Stubbs, the man, grew much harder in October of 2003. We are left with remembrances of the man from his family, his friends, his professional colleagues, and his many students, in and out of school. That's a substantial body, but a diffuse one, hard to tap at one's leisure. We cannot go to a bookstore or to eBay and order one of his solo Welsh ballads, or his kind but firm lectures on thinking things through when we write.

But this book can now provide something a little like that. It preserves many of those remarkably diverse reminiscences, captures some of the respect he engendered, and showcases some of the stories he inspired in those who knew him. It may not be quite as easy to find and buy as *Mission of Gravity*, but it is just as solid and tangible, and with luck will be available for a while to come.

It takes away nothing from those reading this book who knew Hal Clement as fully as they could wish, to say that this book is less a keep-sake meant for them than an opportunity for those who knew him little, or even not at all, to discover (with no apologies to the Bard) what a prince Hal was.

I guess I was the apt choice for editor after all.

So if you have a friend who's got a few of his old 50's paperbacks, a young relative who's just discovered him for the first time, or just hear someone ask "Who is Hal Clement?" do them a favor and steer them toward this book. Selling another one of these will help a pair of worthy charities, but having someone read it will give that person a chance to know Hal Clement better—and that's a worthy cause, too.

www.ingramcontent.com/pod-product-compliance
Lightning Source LLC
Chambersburg PA
CBHW032046240626
47154CB00003B/1102

* 9 780809 550739 *